disha
Nurturing Ambitions

# Quick Revision

## MINDMAPS/ Notes *for*

# CBSE Class 10

(Science, Mathematics,
Social Science, Hindi B,
English Language & Literature)

- **Corporate Office :** 45, 2nd Floor, Maharishi Dayanand Marg, Corner Market,
  Malviya Nagar, New Delhi-110017
  Tel. : 011-49842349 / 49842350

# DISHA PUBLICATION

## ALL RIGHTS RESERVED



**For further information about the books from DISHA,**
Log on to **www.dishapublication.com** or email to **info@dishapublication.com**

# INDEX

## Chapterwise Mind Maps Mathematics (M-1-32)



## Chapterwise Mind Maps Science (S-1-34)

# Chapterwise Mind Maps English (E-1-32)



# Chapterwise Mind Maps Hindi (H-1-18)



# Chapterwise Mind Maps Social Science (SS-1-46)

# CHAPTERWISE

# MIND MAPS

# MATHEMATICS

# Mind

## Euclid's Division Algorithm

Euclid's division algorithm is a technique to compute the Highest Common Factor (HCF) of two given positive integers.

To get HCF of two positive integers $c$ and $d$, $c > d$ following steps are to be followed:

(i) Apply Euclid's division lemma to $c$ and $d$ to get whole numbers $q$ and $r$ such that
$$c = dq + r,\ 0 \le r < d.$$

(ii) If $r = 0$, then $d$ is HCF of $c$ and $d$. If $r \ne 0$, apply division lemma to $d$ and $r$.

(iii) Continue the process till the remainder is zero. The divisor at this stage will be the required HCF.

**Note:**

(i) Euclid's division lemma and algorithm are so closely interlinked that people often call former as the division algorithm also.

(ii) Euclid's division algorithm is stated for only +ve integers but it can be extended for all integers except zero.

## Euclid's Division Lemma

For given any two positive integers $a$ and $b$, there exist unique integers $q$ and $r$ satisfying
$$a = bq + r,\ 0 \le r < b$$
**Lemma :** A lemma is a proven statement used for proving another statement.

## REAL NUMBERS

## Fundamental Theorem of Arithmetic

Every composite number can be expressed (factorised) as a product of primes, and this factorisation is unique, apart from the order in which the prime factors occur.

The prime factorisation of a natural number is unique, except for the order of its factors. In general, given a composite number $x$, we factorise it as

$x = p_1 p_2 p_3 \ldots\ldots p_n$, where $p_1, p_2, p_3 \ldots\ldots\ldots, p_n$ are primes and written in ascending order, i.e., $p_1 \le p_2 \le p_3 \le \ldots\ldots\le p_n$. If we combine the same primes, we will get powers of primes.

**For Example:**

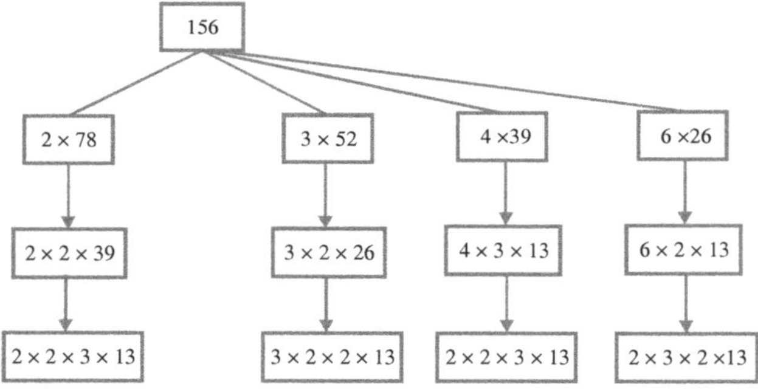

So, in each of the cases prime factors of 156 is $2 \times 2 \times 3 \times 13$

Hence, we can conclude that the prime factorisation of a number is unique.

**Note:**

(i) For two positive integers $a$, $b$
$$\text{HCF}(a, b) \times \text{LCM}(a, b) = a \times b$$

(ii) If $p$ is a prime number and it divides $a^2$, then $p$ also, divides $a$ where '$a$' is the positive integer.

# Map-1

## HCF & LCM of Three Numbers

(i) $\quad \text{LCM}\,(p, q, r) = \dfrac{p \cdot q \cdot r \cdot \text{HCF}(p, q, r)}{\text{HCF}\,(p, q) \cdot \text{HCF}(q, r) \cdot \text{HCF}(p, r)}$

(ii) $\quad \text{HCF}\,(p, q, r) = \dfrac{p \cdot q \cdot r \cdot \text{LCM}(p, q, r)}{\text{LCM}\,(p, q) \cdot \text{LCM}(q, r) \cdot \text{LCM}(p, r)}$

**Note:**
For three positive integers $a$, $b$ and $c$
$\text{HCF}\,(a, b, c) \times \text{LCM}\,(a, b, c) \neq a \times b \times c$

## Irrational Numbers

Number which is not a rational number or whose decimal expansion is non-terminating and non-repeating.

**Note:**

(i) The sum or difference of a rational and an irrational number is irrational, e.g.,

$2 + \sqrt{2}$ is irrational,

$2 - \sqrt{3}$ is irrational.

(ii) The product and quotient of a non-zero rational and irrational number is irrational, e.g.,

$5 \times \sqrt{2}$ is irrational,

$\dfrac{\sqrt{2}}{3}$ is irrational.

## Rational Numbers and Their Decimal Expansion

(i) If denominator of a rational number is of the form $2^n\,5^m$, where $n$, $m$ are non-negative integers then $x$ has decimal expansion which terminates.

(ii) If decimal expansion of rational number terminates then its denominator has prime factorisation of the form $2^n\,5^m$, where $n$, $m$ are non-negative integers.

(iii) If denominator of a rational number is not of the form $2^n\,5^m$, where $n$ and $m$ are non-negative integers then the rational number has decimal expansion which is non-terminating repeating.

Thus we conclude that the decimal expansion of every rational number is either terminating or non-terminating repeating.

# Mind

## Types of Polynomial

| On the basis of number of terms in the polynomial | On the basis of degree of the polynomial |
|---|---|
| **(i) Monomial:** If polynomial has one term | **(i) Linear:** If polynomial has degree one. |
| **(ii) Binomial:** If polynomial has two terms. | **(ii) Quadratic:** If polynomial has degree two. |
| **(iii) Trinomial:** If polynomial has three terms. | **(iii) Cubic:** If polynomial has degree three. |
| | **(iv) Biquadratic:** If polynomial has degree four. |

**Note** that $5, 6, -9$ etc are called constant polynomial as there value is fixed and constant polynomial 0 is called zero polynomial whose degree is not defined.

## Standard Forms of Linear, Quadratic and Cubic Polynomials

**(i) Linear Polynomial:**

$ax + b$, where $a, b$ are real numbers and $a \neq 0$.

**(ii) Quadratic Polynomial:**

$ax^2 + bx + c$, where $a, b, c$ are real numbers & $a \neq 0$.

**(iii) Cubic Polynomials:**

$ax^3 + bx^2 + cx + d$, where $a, b, c, d$ are real numbers and $a \neq 0$.

## Value of a Polynomial

The value of a polynomial $f(x)$ at $x = \alpha$ is obtained by substituting $x = \alpha$ in the given polynomial and is denoted by $f(\alpha)$.

## Zero(es)/Root(s) of Polynomial

$x = r$ is a zero of a polynomial $p(x)$ if $p(r) = 0$.

## Polynomial

An algebraic expression $f(x)$ of the form

$$f(x) = a_0 + a_1 x + a_2 x^2 + .... + a_n x^n,$$

where $a_0, a_1, ....., a_n$ are real numbers and all indices of variable $x$ are non-negative integers is called polynomial in variable $x$.

(i) The highest power of $x$ is called degree of the polynomial.

(ii) $a_0, a_1 x, ...., a_n x^n$ are terms of the polynomial.

(iii) $a_0, a_1, .... a_n$ are co-efficients of the polynomial.

**2**    **1**    **8**

## POLYNOMIALS

**3**    **4**   **5**    **6**    **9**

## Geometrical Meaning of Zeroes of a Polynomial

Zero(es) of a polynomial is/are the $x$-coordinate of the point(s) where graph $y = f(x)$ intersects the $x$-axis.

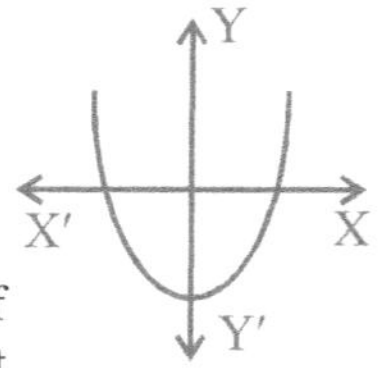

(i) **Linear polynomial:** Graph of linear polynomial is a straight line and has exactly one zero.

(ii) **Quadratic polynomial:** Graph of quadratic polynomial is always a parabola and this polynomial can have atmost two zeroes.

(iii) **Cubic polynomial:** Cubic polynomial can have atmost three zeroes.

# Map-2

**7**

## Relationship between Zeroes and Coefficients of a Polynomial

(i)   Zero of a linear polynomial $ax + b$ is $x = -\dfrac{b}{a}$

(ii)  If $\alpha$ and $\beta$ are the zeroes of the quadratic polynomial $ax^2 + bx + c$, then

$$\alpha + \beta = -\dfrac{b}{a}$$

i.e. sum of zeroes $= -\dfrac{\text{Coefficient of } x}{\text{Coefficient of } x^2}$ and $\alpha\beta = \dfrac{c}{a}$

i.e. product of zeroes $= \dfrac{\text{Constant term}}{\text{Coefficient of } x^2}$

(iii) If $\alpha$, $\beta$ and $\gamma$ are zeroes of the cubic polynomial $ax^3 + bx^2 + cx + d$ then

$$\alpha + \beta + \gamma = -\dfrac{b}{a}$$

i.e. sum of zeroes $= -\dfrac{\text{Coefficient of } x^2}{\text{Coefficient of } x^3}$

$$\alpha\beta + \beta\gamma + \gamma\alpha = \dfrac{c}{a}$$

i.e. sum of product of every two root

$$= \dfrac{\text{Coefficient of } x}{\text{Coefficient of } x^3} \ \& \ \alpha\beta\gamma = -\dfrac{d}{a}$$

i.e. product of roots $= -\dfrac{\text{Constant term}}{\text{Coefficient of } x^3}$

## Division Algorithm

If $p(x)$ and $g(x)$ are any two polynomials with $g(x) \neq 0$, then we can find polynomials $q(x)$ and $r(x)$ such that
$p(x) = g(x) \times q(x) + r(x)$
where either $r(x) = 0$ or degree of $r(x) <$ degree of $g(x)$

## Cases of Quadratic Polynomial

**Case-I :** If a quadratic polynomial $P(x) = ax^2 + bx + c$ has two zeroes, then its graph will intersect the $x$-axis at two distinct points A & B as shown in the figure.

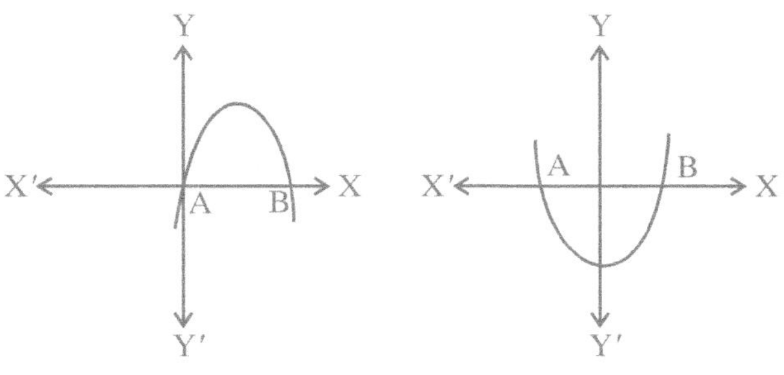

**Case-II :** If a quadratic polynomial $P(x) = ax^2 + bx + c$ has only one zero, then its graph will touch the $x$-axis at only one point A as shown in the figure.

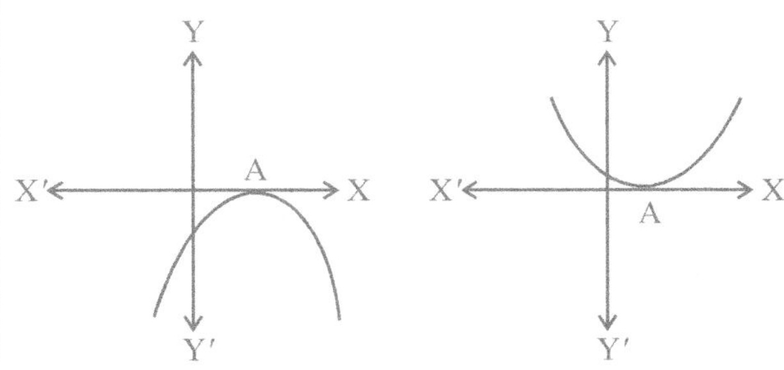

**Case-III:** If a quadratic polynomial $P(x) = ax^2 + bx + c$ has no zero, then its graph will not intersect /touch the $x$-axis at any point as shown in the figure.

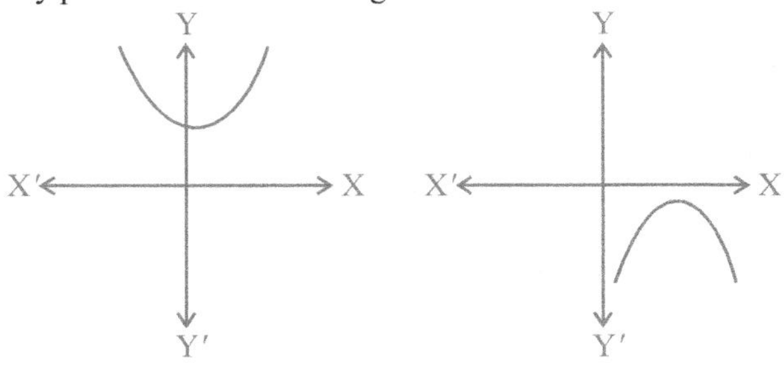

## Representation of Linear Equation In Two Variables

Every linear equation in two variables graphically represents a line and each solution (x, y) of a linear equation in two variables, ax + by + c = 0, corresponds to a point on the line representing the equation, and vice versa.

**2**

## Ploting Linear Equation in Two Variables on the Graph

There are infinitely many solutions of each linear equation. So, we choose at least any two values of one variable & get the value of other variable by substitution. i.e; Consider; $Ax + By + C = 0$
We can write the above linear equation as:
$$y = \frac{-C - Ax}{B}.$$
Here, we can choose any values of $x$ & can find corresponding values of $y$.
After getting the values of $(x, y)$ we plot them on the graph thereby getting the line representing $Ax + By + C = 0$.

## System of a Pair of Linear Equations in Two Variables

An equations of the form Ax + By + C = 0 is called a linear equation in two variables x and y where A, B, C are real numbers.
Two linear equations in the same two variables are called a pair of linear equations in two variables. Standard form of linear equations in two variables.
$$a_1 x + b_1 y + c_1 = 0, \; a_2 x + b_2 y + c_2 = 0$$
where $a_1, a_2, b_1, b_2, c_1, c_2$ are real numbers such that
$$a_1^2 + b_1^2 \neq 0, \; a_2^2 + b_2^2 \neq 0$$

**1**

**3**

# PAIR OF LINEAR EQUATIONS IN TWO VARIABLES

**4**    **5**

**8**

## Method of Solution of a Pair of Linear Equations in Two Variables

Coordinate of the point (x, y) which satisfy the system of pair of linear equations in two variables is the required solution. This is the point where the two lines representing the two equations intersect each other.
There are two methods of finding solution of a pair of Linear equations in two variables.
**(1) Graphical Method :** This method is less convenient when point representing the solution has non-integral co-ordinates.
**(2) Algebraic Method :** This method is more convenient when point representing the solution has non-integral co-ordinates.
This method is further divided into three methods:
(i) Substitution Method,
(ii) Elimination Method and
(iii) Cross Multiplication Method.

## Consistency and Nature of the Graphs

Consider the standard form of linear equations in two variables.
$$a_1 x + b_1 y + c_1 = 0; \; a_2 x + b_2 y + c_2 = 0$$
While solving the above system of equation following three cases arise.

(i) If $\dfrac{a_1}{a_2} \neq \dfrac{b_1}{b_2}$; system is called consistent, having one or unique solution and pair of straight lines representing the above equations intersect at one point only.

(ii) If $\dfrac{a_1}{a_2} = \dfrac{b_1}{b_2} = \dfrac{c_1}{c_2}$; system is called dependent and have infinitely many solution. Pair of lines representing the equations coincide.

(iii) If $\dfrac{a_1}{a_2} = \dfrac{b_1}{b_2} \neq \dfrac{c_1}{c_2}$; system is called inconsistent and has no solution. Pair of lines representing the equations are parallel or do not intersect at any point.

# Map-3

## Graphical Method of Solution

In this method, two equations are plotted separately in a single graph (as discussed in box-3).

**Case-I:**

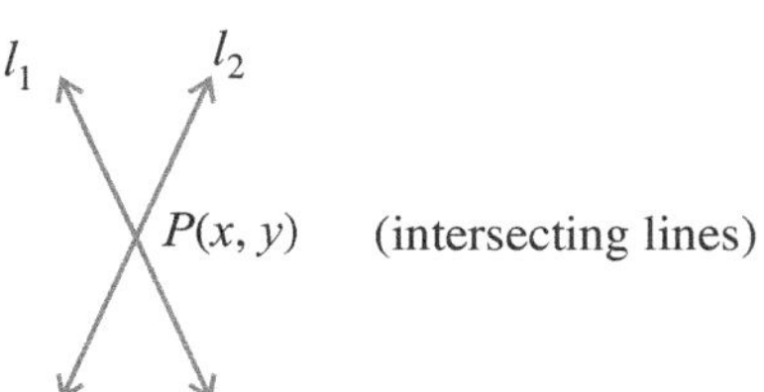


Solution = $P(x, y)$.

**Case-II:**

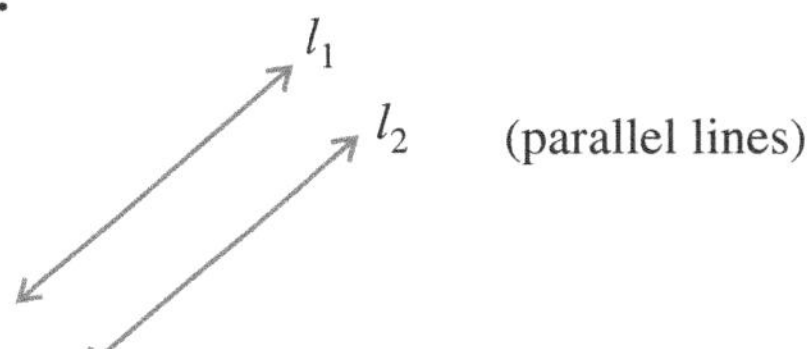


no solution

**Case-III:**

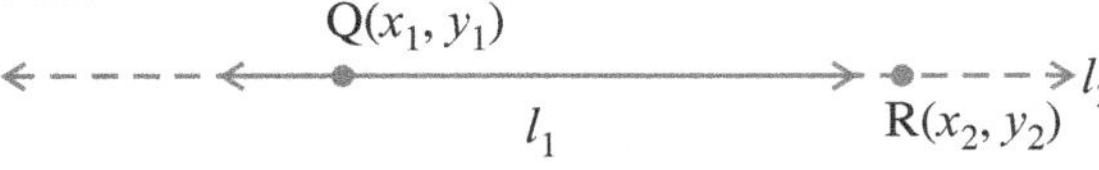


(coincident lines)

Infinite set of solution, some of which are : $Q(x_1, y_1)$ & $R(x_2, y_2)$

## Algebraic Method of Solution

Consider the follwing system of equation
$$a_1 x + b_1 y + c_1 = 0; \quad a_2 x + b_2 y + c_2 = 0$$

There are following three methods under Algebraic method to solve the above system.

**(i) Substitution method**
  (a) Find the value of one variable, say y in terms of x or x in terms of y from one equation.
  (b) Substitute this value in second equation to get equation in one variable and find solution.
  (c) Now substitute the value/solution so obtained in step (b) in the equation got in step (a).

**(ii) Elimination Method**
  (a) If coefficient of any one variable are not same in both the equation multiply both the equation with suitable non-zero constants to make coefficient of any one variable numerically equal.
  (b) Add or subtract the equations so obtained to get equation in one variable and solve it.
  (c) Now substitute the value of the variable got in the above step in either of the original equation to get value of the other variable.

**(iii) Cross multiplication method**
  For the pair of Linear equations intwo variables:
  $$a_1 x + b_1 y + c_1 = 0$$
  $$a_2 x + b_2 y + c_2 = 0$$
  Consider the following diagram.

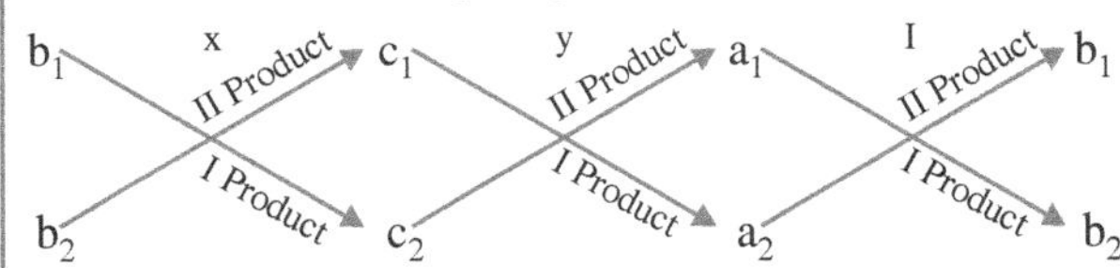


Write equations as $\dfrac{x}{b_1 c_2 - b_2 c_1} = \dfrac{y}{c_1 a_2 - c_2 a_1} = \dfrac{1}{a_1 b_2 - a_2 b_1}$

Solve it to get the solution, provided $a_1 b_2 - a_2 b_1 \neq 0$

## Equations Reducible to a Pair of Linear Equations in Two Variables

Sometimes pair of equations are not linear (or not in standard form), then they are altered so that they reduce to a pair of linear equations in standard form.

For example;
$$\frac{a_1}{x} + \frac{b_1}{y} = c_1 \; ; \; \frac{a_2}{x} - \frac{b_2}{y} = c_2$$

Here we substitute $\dfrac{1}{x} = p$ & $\dfrac{1}{y} = q$, the above equations reduces to:

$$a_1 p + b_1 q = c_1 \; ; \; a_2 p - b_2 q = c_2$$

Now we can use any method to solve them.

# Mind

## Quadratic Equation

Standard from of the quadratic equation in the variable x is an equation of the form $ax^2 + bx + c = 0$, where a, b, c are real numbers and $a \neq 0$.

Any equation of the form $P(x) = 0$, where $P(x)$ is a polynomial of degree 2, is a quadratic equation.

**1**

## Zero(es)/Root(s) of Quadratic Equation

A real number $\alpha$ is said to be a root of the quadratic equation $ax^2 + bx + c = 0$, $a \neq 0$ if $a\alpha^2 + b\alpha + c = 0$.

We can say that $x = \alpha$, is a solution of the quadratic equation or that $\alpha$ satisfies the quadratic equation.

The zeroes of the quadratic polynomial $ax^2 + bx + c$ and the roots of the equation $ax^2 + bx + c = 0$ are same.

A quadratic equation has atmost two roots/zeroes.

**2**

# QUADRATIC EQUATIONS

## Relation Between Zeroes and Co-efficient of a Quadratic Equation

If $\alpha$ and $\beta$ are zeroes of the quadratic equation $ax^2 + bx + c = 0$, where $a, b, c$ are real numebrs and $a \neq 0$, then

$$\alpha + \beta = -\frac{b}{a}$$

$$\Rightarrow \quad \text{sum of zeroes} = -\frac{\text{coefficient of } x}{\text{coefficient of } x^2}$$

$$\text{and } \alpha\beta = \frac{c}{a}$$

$$\Rightarrow \quad \text{product of zeroes} = \frac{\text{constant term}}{\text{coefficient of } x^2}$$

**3**

**4**

## Methods of Solving Quadratic Equation

Following are the methods which are used to solve quadratic equations:
(i)   Factorisation.
(ii)  Completing the square.
(iii) Quadratic Formula.

# Map-4

## Methods of Factorisation

In this method we find the roots of a quadratic equation $(ax^2 + bx + c = 0)$ by factorising LHS it into two linear factors and equating each factor to zero, e.g.,

$$6x^2 - x - 2 = 0$$
$$\Rightarrow \quad 6x^2 + 3x - 4x - 2 = 0 \qquad \qquad ...(i)$$
$$\Rightarrow \quad 3x\,(2x + 1) - 2(2x + 1) = 0$$
$$\Rightarrow \quad (3x - 2)\,(2x + 1) = 0$$
$$\Rightarrow \quad 3x - 2 = 0 \quad \text{or} \quad 2x + 1 = 0$$
$$\Rightarrow \quad x = \frac{2}{3} \quad \text{or} \quad x = \frac{-1}{2}$$

**Necessary Condition** : Product of 1st and last terms of eq. (i) should be equal to product of 2nd and 3rd terms of the same equation.

## Method of Completing the Square

This is the method of converting L.H.S. of a quadratic equation which is not a perfect square into the sum or difference of a perfect square and a constant by adding and subtracting the suitable constant terms. E.g,

(1)
$$x^2 + 4x - 5 = 0$$
$$\Rightarrow \quad x^2 + 2(2)(x) - 5 = 0$$
$$\Rightarrow \quad x^2 + 2(2)(x) + (2)^2 - (2)^2 - 5 = 0$$
$$\Rightarrow \quad (x + 2)^2 - 4 - 5 = 0$$
$$\Rightarrow \quad (x + 2)^2 - 9 = 0$$
$$\Rightarrow \quad x + 2 = \pm 3$$
$$\Rightarrow \quad x = -5, 1$$

(2)
$$3x^2 - 5x + 2 = 0$$
$$\Rightarrow \quad x^2 - \frac{5}{3}x + \frac{2}{3} = 0$$
$$\Rightarrow \quad x^2 - 2\frac{1}{2}\left(\frac{5}{3}\right)x + \frac{2}{3} = 0$$
$$\Rightarrow \quad x^2 - 2\left(\frac{5}{6}\right)x + \frac{2}{3} + \left(\frac{5}{6}\right)^2 - \left(\frac{5}{6}\right)^2 = 0$$
$$\Rightarrow \quad \left(x - \frac{5}{6}\right)^2 + \frac{2}{3} - \frac{25}{36} = 0$$
$$\Rightarrow \quad \left(x - \frac{5}{6}\right)^2 = \frac{1}{36}$$
$$\Rightarrow \quad x - \frac{5}{6} = \pm \frac{1}{6}$$
$$\Rightarrow \quad x = 1, \frac{2}{3}.$$

## Quadratic Formula

Consider a quadratic equation:
$ax^2 + bx + c = 0.$
If $b^2 - 4ac \geq 0$, then the roots of the above equation are given by:

$$x = \frac{-b \pm \sqrt{b^2 - 4ac}}{2a}$$

## Nature of Roots

For quadratic equation $ax^2 + bx + c = 0$ $(a \neq 0)$, value of $(b^2 - 4ac)$ is called discriminant of the equation and denoted as D.

$$\therefore D = b^2 - 4ac$$

Discriminant is very important in finding nature of the roots.

(i)   If $D = 0$, then roots are real and equal.
(ii)  If $D > 0$, then roots are real and unequal
(iii) If $D < 0$, then roots are not real.

# Mind

## Arithmetic Progression (AP)

Consider
(i)　　1, 2, 3, 4, ..........
(ii)　　3, 3, 3, 3, ..........
(i) and (ii) are the sequence of numbers, each number in these sequences is called a term.
An arithmetic progression (AP) is a sequence of numbers in which each term is obtained by adding a fixed number '$d$' to the preceeding term, except the first term.
The fixed number is caled the common difference. It can be positive, negative or zero.
Any Arithmetic progression can be represented as :
$a, a + d, a + 2d, a + 3d,$ ......
where '$a$' is the first term & '$d$' is the common difference.
Arithmetic progressions which does not have a last term are called Infinite Arithmetic Progression. e.g.;
6, 9, 12, 15, ..................

# ARITHMETIC PROGRESSIONS

## Formula for Common Difference (d)

A sequence of numbers $a_1, a_2, a_3$...... is an AP if the difference $a_2 - a_1, a_3 - a_2, a_4 - a_3$.... gives the same value, i.e. if $a_{k+1} - a_k$ is the same for different values of $k$. The difference $(a_{k+1} - a_k)$ is called common difference (d). Here $a_{k+1}$ & $a_k$ are the $(k + 1)$th & kth terms respectively.

$\therefore d = a_2 - a_1 = a_3 - a_2 = a_4 - a_3$........

# Map-5

## $n^{th}$ Term (or General Term) of an Arithmetic Progressions

In an AP, with first term 'a' and common difference $d$, the $n^{th}$ term (or the general term) is given by,
$$a_n = a + (n-1)d$$
**Note** that an AP can be finite or infinite according to as the number of terms are finite or infinite.
If there are m terms in an AP, then $a_m$ is the last term & is sometimes denoted by '$l$'.

**3**

## Sum of the FIRST 'n' Terms of an A.P.

(i) The sum of the first n terms of an A.P. is given by
$$S_n = \frac{n}{2}[2a + (n-1)d],$$
where a is the first term and d is the common difference.

(ii) If $l$ is the last term of the finite A.P. say the $n^{th}$ term, then the sum of all terms of the A.P. is given by,
$$S_n = \frac{n}{2}[a + l]$$

**Note** that sum of first $n$ positive integers is given by
$$S_n = \frac{n(n+1)}{2}$$

**4**

## Arithmetic Mean Between Two Numbers

If $a, b, c$ are in $AP$. Then $b$ is called the arithmetic mean of $a$ & $c$ and is given by
$$b = \frac{a+c}{2}$$

**5**

# Mind

## Similar Figures

Two figures having the same shape but not necessarily the same size are called similar figures

Two figures having the same shape as well as same size are called congruent figures.

**Note** that all congruent figures are similar but the similar figures need not be congruent.

**1**

## Similarity of Polygons

Two polygons of the same number of sides are similar if
(i)   their corresponding angles are equal and
(ii)  their corresponding sides are in the same ratio (or proportion).

**2**

## Similarity of Triangles

Two trianlges are similar if
(i)   their corresponding angles are equal and
(ii)  their corresponding sides are in the same ratio (or proportion).

**Note :** If the corresponding angles of two triangles are equal, then they are known as equiangular triangles.

The ratio of any two corresponding sides in two equiangular triangles is always the same.

**3**

## Basic Proportionality Theorem (BPT) and its Converse

**Basic Proportionality Theorem**

If a line is drawn parallel to one side of a triangle to intersect the other two sides in distinct points, then other two sides are divided in the same ratio. Thus in $\triangle ABC$, if $DE \parallel BC$, then

$$\frac{AD}{DB} = \frac{AE}{EX}$$

**Converse of BPT**

If a line divides any two sides of a triangle in the same ratio, then the line is parallel to the third side,

**4**

# Map-6

**5**

## Criteria For Similarity of Triangles

**(i)** **AAA Similarity Criterion :** If in two triangles, corresponding angles are equal, then their corresponding sides are in the same ratio and hence the two triangles are similar.

**(ii)** **AA Similarity Criterion :** If in two triangles, two angles of one triangle are respectively equal to the two angles of the other triangle, then the two triangles are similar.

**(iii)** **SSS Similarity Criterion :** If in two triangles, corresponding sides are in the same ratio then their correspoding angles are equal and hence the triangles are similar.

**(iv)** **SAS Similarity Criterion :** If one angle of a triangle is equal to one angle of another triangle and the sides including these angles are in the same ratio (proportion), then the two triangles are similar.

**6**

## Areas of Similar Triangles

The ratio of the areas of two similar triangles is equal to the ratio of the squares fo their corresponding sides thus if $\triangle ABC - \triangle PQR$, then

$$\frac{\text{Area } (\triangle ABC)}{\text{Area } (\triangle PQR)} = \frac{AB^2}{PQ^2} = \frac{BC^2}{QR^2} = \frac{AC^2}{PR^2}$$

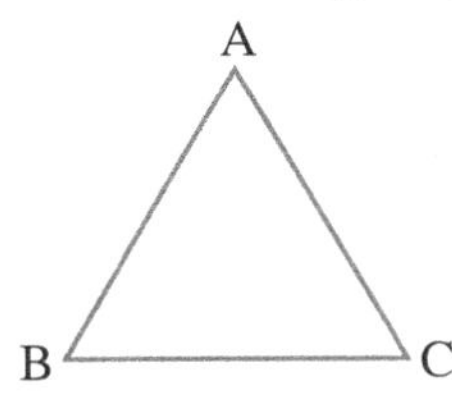


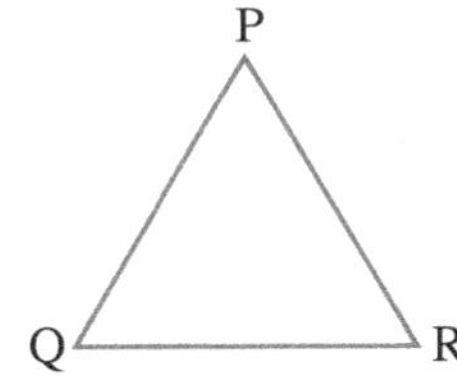


**7**

## Pythagoras Theorem and its Converse

**(i)** If perpendicular is drawn from the vertex of the right angle of a right triangle to the hypotenuse then the triangles on both sides of the perpendicular are similar to the whole triangle and also to each other.

**(ii)** **Pythagoras Theorem :** In a right triangle, the square of the hypotenuse is equal to the sum of the squares of the other two sides. Thus in right $\triangle ABC$ right angled at B
$$AC^2 = AB^2 + BC^2$$

**(iii)** **Converse of Pythagoras Theorem :** If in a trinagle, square of one side is equal to the sum of the squares of the other two sides, then the angle opposite the first side is a right angle.

**Mind**

## Coordinate of a Point in XY- Plane

**1**

The perpendicular distance of $x$ a point from the $y$-axis is called its $x$-coordinate or abscissa. The perpendicular distance $y$ of a point from the $x$-axis is called its $y$-coordinate or ordinate. The $x$ and $y$ taken together in order is called coordinate of a point denoted by $(x, y)$. The coordinate of the points on $x$-axis are of the form $(x, 0)$ and the points on the $y$-axis are of the form $(0, y)$. Coordinate of origin is $(0, 0)$.

## Sign-conventions in the XY-Plane

**2**

The $x$ and $y$-axis divide the plane into four parts known as quadrants denoted by I, II, III and IV. The sign of $x$-and $y$-coordinates in each of the quadrant is shown below:

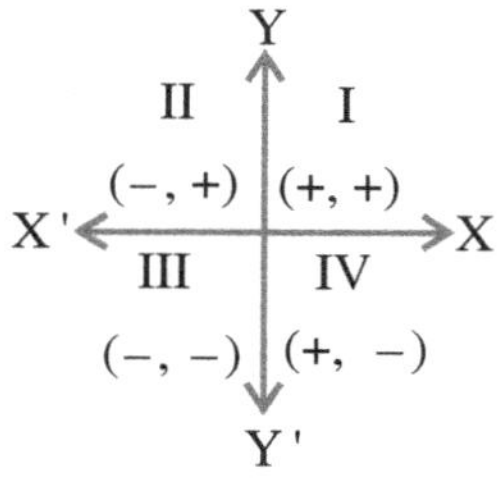

$$
\begin{array}{c|c}
\text{II} & \text{I} \\
(-, +) & (+, +) \\
\hline
\text{III} & \text{IV} \\
(-, -) & (+, -)
\end{array}
$$

# COORDINATE GEOMETRY

## Distance Formula

**3**

The distance between any two points $P(x_1, y_1)$ and $Q(x_2, y_2)$ in the plane is given by,

$$PQ = \sqrt{(x_1 - x_2)^2 + (y_1 - y_2)^2}$$

Also the distance of the point $P(x_1, y_1)$ from the origin is

$$\sqrt{x_1^2 + y_1^2}$$

# Map-7

## Section Formula

**(i)**

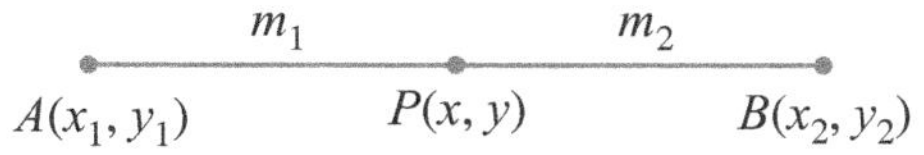

$$\underset{A(x_1, y_1)}{\bullet}\overset{m_1}{\rule{3cm}{0.4pt}}\underset{P(x, y)}{\bullet}\overset{m_2}{\rule{3cm}{0.4pt}}\underset{B(x_2, y_2)}{\bullet}$$

The coordinates of the point $P(x, y)$ which divides the line segment joining the points $A(x_1, y_1)$ and $B(x_2, y_2)$ internally in the ratio $m_1 : m_2$ i.e., $\dfrac{PA}{PB} = \dfrac{m_1}{m_2}$ are

$$\left( \frac{m_1 x_2 + m_2 x_1}{m_1 + m_2}, \frac{m_1 y_2 + m_2 y_1}{m_1 + m_2} \right)$$

**(ii)**

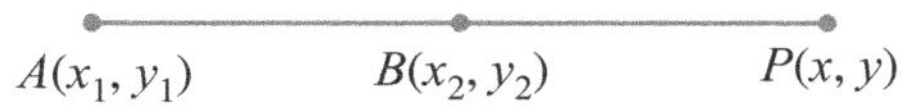

$$\underset{A(x_1, y_1)}{\bullet}\rule{3cm}{0.4pt}\underset{B(x_2, y_2)}{\bullet}\rule{3cm}{0.4pt}\underset{P(x, y)}{\bullet}$$

The coordinates of the point $P(x, y)$ which divides the line segment joining the points $A(x_1, y_1)$ and $B(x_2, y_2)$ externally in the ratio, $m_1 : m_2$ i.e., $\dfrac{PA}{PB} = \dfrac{m_1}{m_2}$ are

$$\left( \frac{m_1 x_2 - m_2 x_1}{m_1 - m_2}, \frac{m_1 y_2 - m_2 y_1}{m_1 - m_2} \right)$$

**(iii)** If the ratio in which $P$ divides $AB$ is $K : 1$, then the coordinates of the point $P$ will be

$$\left( \frac{Kx_2 + x_1}{K + 1}, \frac{Ky_2 + y_1}{K + 1} \right)$$

## Mid-point Formula

The coordinates of the mid point $P$ of the line segment joining the points $A(x_1, y_1)$ and $B(x_2, y_2)$ is

$$\left( \frac{x_1 + x_2}{2}, \frac{y_1 + y_2}{2} \right)$$

## Area of a Triangle

The area of $\Delta ABC$ formed by the vertices $A(x_1, y_1)$, $B(x_2, y_2)$ and $C(x_3, y_3)$ is given by

$$\frac{1}{2} \left| x_1(y_2 - y_3) + x_2(y_3 - y_1) + x_3(y_1 - y_2) \right|$$

**Note:**

(i) Area of triangle = $\dfrac{1}{2} \times$ base $\times$ Altitude
(ii) Area of polygon can be calculated by dividing it into the triangular region.
(iii) If three points are collinear then area of the triangle formed by them is zero.

# Mind

## Trigonometry

Trigonometry is the study of relationships between the sides and angles of a right angled triangle.

**1**

## Trigonometric Ratios

Trigonometric ratios of an acute angle in a right triangle express the relationship between the angle and the length of its sides.

Let $\triangle ABC$ be a triangle right angled at $B$. Then the trigonometric ratios of the angle $A$ in right $\triangle ABC$ are defined as follows:

**2**

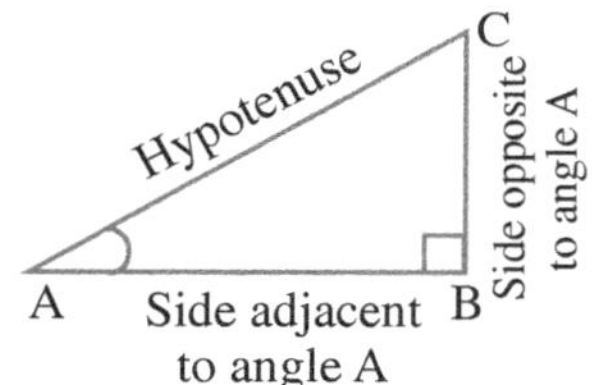


sine of $\angle A$ i.e. $\sin A = \dfrac{\text{Side opposite to } \angle A}{\text{hypotenuse}} = \dfrac{BC}{AC}$

cosine of $\angle A$ i.e. $\cos A = \dfrac{\text{Side adjacent to } \angle A}{\text{hypotenuse}} = \dfrac{AB}{AC}$

tangent of $\angle A$ i.e. $\tan A = \dfrac{\text{Side opposite to } \angle A}{\text{Side adjacent to } \angle A} = \dfrac{BC}{AB}$

cosecant of $\angle A$ i.e. $\operatorname{cosec} A = \dfrac{1}{\text{sine of } \angle A} = \dfrac{\text{hypotenuse}}{\text{Side opposite to } \angle A} = \dfrac{AC}{BC}$

secant of $\angle A$ i.e. $\sec A = \dfrac{1}{\text{cosine of } \angle A} = \dfrac{\text{hypotenuse}}{\text{Side adjacent } \angle A} = \dfrac{AC}{AB}$

cotangent of $\angle A$ i.e. $\cot A = \dfrac{1}{\text{tangent of } \angle A} = \dfrac{\text{side adjacent to } \angle A}{\text{Side opposite to } \angle A}$

$$= \dfrac{AB}{BC}$$

(i) $\sin A . \operatorname{cosec} A = 1$　(ii) $\cos A . \sec A = 1$

(iii) $\tan A . \cot A = 1$　(iv) $\tan A = \dfrac{\sin A}{\cos A}$　(v) $\cot A = \dfrac{\cos A}{\sin A}$

**Note:**

The values of the trigonometric ratios of an angle do not vary with the lengths of the sides of the triangle, if the angle remains same.

## INTRODUCTION TO TRIGONOMETRY

# Map-8

## Trigonometric Ratios of Some Specific Angles

| $\angle A$ | $0°$ | $30°$ | $45°$ | $60°$ | $90°$ |
|---|---|---|---|---|---|
| $\sin A$ | $0$ | $\dfrac{1}{2}$ | $\dfrac{1}{\sqrt{2}}$ | $\dfrac{\sqrt{3}}{2}$ | $1$ |
| $\cos A$ | $1$ | $\dfrac{\sqrt{3}}{2}$ | $\dfrac{1}{\sqrt{2}}$ | $\dfrac{1}{2}$ | $0$ |
| $\tan A$ | $0$ | $\dfrac{1}{\sqrt{3}}$ | $1$ | $\sqrt{3}$ | Not defined |
| $\operatorname{cosec} A$ | Not defined | $2$ | $\sqrt{2}$ | $\dfrac{2}{\sqrt{3}}$ | $1$ |
| $\sec A$ | $1$ | $\dfrac{2}{\sqrt{3}}$ | $\sqrt{2}$ | $2$ | Not defined |
| $\cot A$ | Not defined | $\sqrt{3}$ | $1$ | $\dfrac{1}{\sqrt{3}}$ | $0$ |

## Trigonometric Ratios for Complementary Angles

$\sin (90° - A) = \cos A$
$\cos (90° - A) = \sin A$
$\tan (90° - A) = \cot A$
$\cot (90° - A) = \tan A$
$\sec (90° - A) = \operatorname{cosec} A$
$\operatorname{cosec} (90° - A) = \sec A$
**Note:**
Here $(90° - A)$ is the complementary angle of A.

## Trigonometric Identities

An equation involving trigonometric ratios of an angle is called a trigonometric identity, if it is true for all values of the angle(s) involved.
(i)   $\sin^2\theta + \cos^2\theta = 1$   [for $0° \leq \theta \leq 90°$]
(ii)   $\sec^2\theta - \tan^2\theta = 1$   [for $0° \leq \theta \leq 90°$]
(iii)   $\operatorname{cosec}^2\theta - \cot^2\theta = 1$   [for $0° < \theta \leq 90°$]

## Mind

### Introduction

The height or length of an object or the distance between two distant objects can be determined with the help of trigonometric ratios.

**1**

## SOME APPLICATION OF TRIGONOMETRY

### Line of Sight and Angle of Elevation

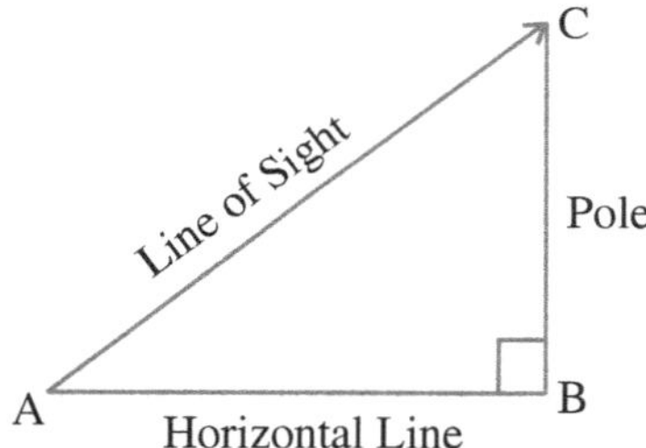


**2**

In the above figure, the line AC drawn from the eye of an observer at A to the top of the pole 'C' is called the **line of sight**. The observer is looking at the top of the pole. The angle BAC, so formed by the line of sight with the horizontal, is called the **angle of elevation** of the top of the pole from the eye of an observer.

# Map-9

## Angle of Depression

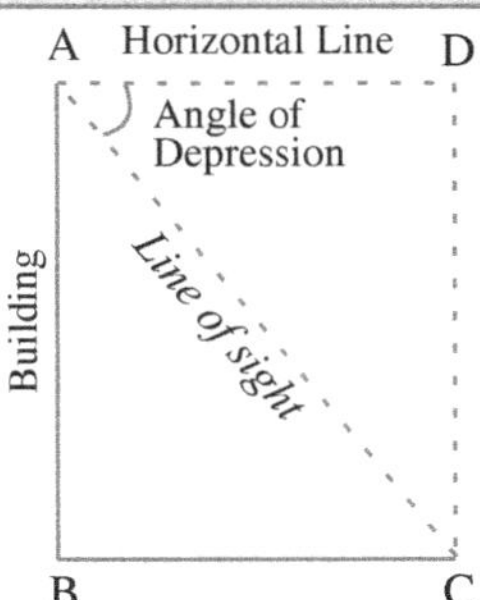


In the above figure, the line AC, is the **line of sight** as the observer is looking downwards from the top of the building at A towards the object at C. Here angle DAC, so formed by the line of sight with the horizontal, when the observer is lowering his/her head is called **Angle of depression.**

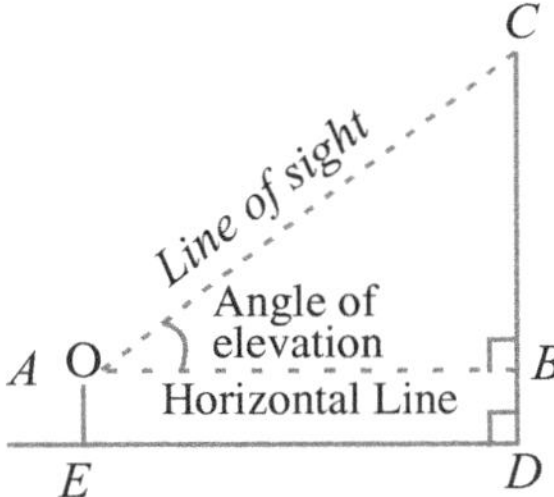


From the above figure, if we want to find the height CD of the pole without actually measuring it, we need the following information:

(i)     Distance ED of the observer from the pole.

(ii)    the angle of elevation $\angle$ BAC, of the top of the pole.

(iii)   the height AE of the observer if it is considerable.

Assuming that the above three conditions are known we can determine the height of the pole in the following way.

In the figure, CD = CB + BD. Here, BD = AE, which is the height of the observer.

To find BC, we will use trigonometric ratios of $\angle$ BAC or $\angle$A.

In $\triangle$ABC, the side BC is the opposite side to the known $\angle$ A. Now we use either tan A or cot A, as these trigonometric ratios involve AB and BC to find BC.

Therefore,  $\tan A = \dfrac{BC}{AB}$ *or* $\cot A = \dfrac{AB}{BC}$, which on solving would give us

BC. By adding AE to BC, you will get the height of the pole.

# Mind

## Line and a Circle

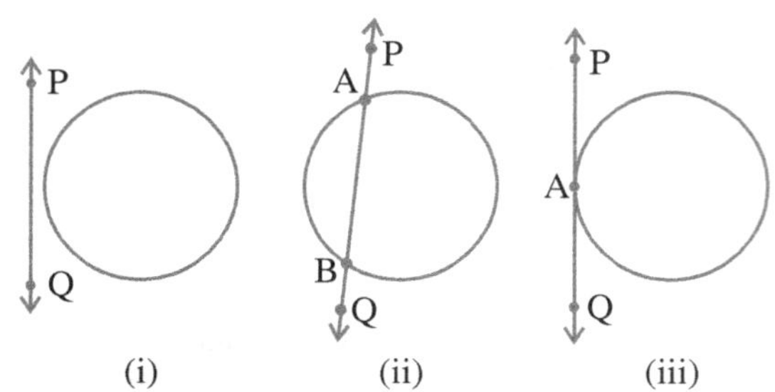



In Fig. (i), the line PQ and the circle have no common point. In this case, PQ is called a non-intersecting line with respect to the circle. In Fig. (ii), there are two common points A and B that the line PQ and the circle have. In this case, we call the line PQ a secant of the circle. In Fig. (iii), there is only one point A which is common to the line PQ and the circle. In this case, the line is called a tangent to the circle.

## Introduction

A circle is a set of all points in a plane at a fixed distance from a fixed point in a plane. The fixed point is called the centre of the circle. The fixed distance is called the radius of the circle.

**1**

**2**

## CIRCLES

## Tangent

A tangent to a circle is a straight line which touches the circle at only one point. The point where the tangent touches the circle is called point of contact of the tangent to the circle.

A tangent to a circle is a special case of a secant, when the two ends points of its corresponding chord coincides.

**Theorem:** Tangent at any point on a circle is perpendicular to the radius through the point of contact.

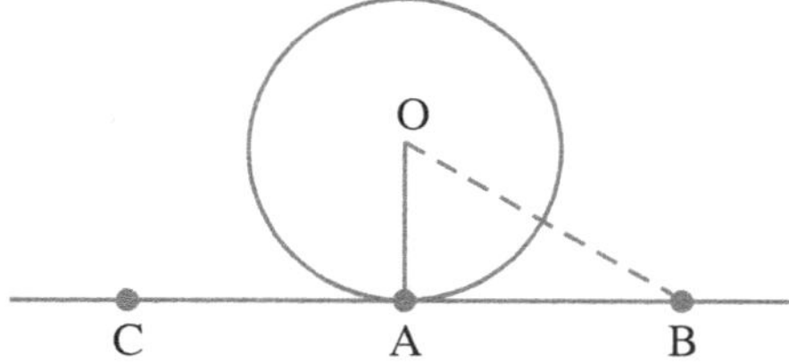



CB is the tangent to the given circle touching at A and OA is the radius.

∴    $\angle OAB = 90°$

(i)    At any point on the circle there can be one and only one tangent.

(ii)    The line containing the radius through the point of contact is called the normal to the circle at the point.

**3**

# Map-10

## 4   Number of Tangents from a Point to Circle

(i) No tangent can be drawn from the point lying inside the circle, as shown in fig. (i).

(ii) One and only one tangent can be drawn from a point lying on the circle, as shown in fig. (ii).

(iii) Only two tangents can be drawn from an exterior point to a circle, as shown in fig. (iii).

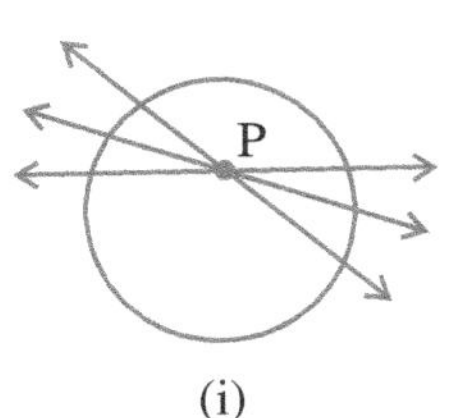
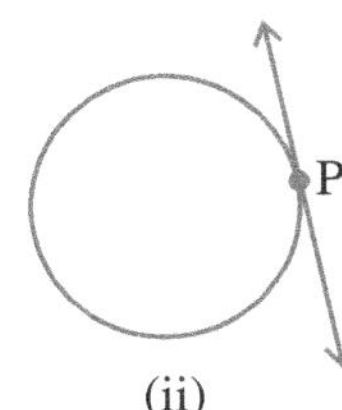
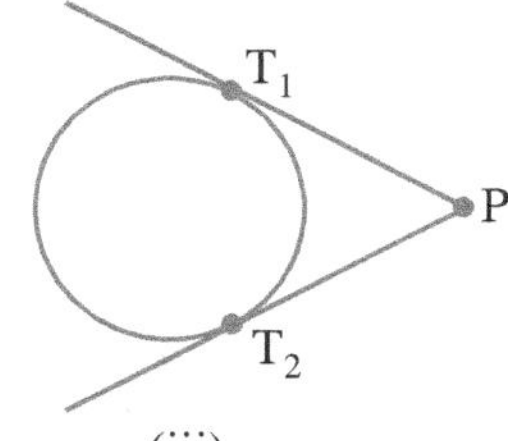


## 5   Length of a Tangent

The length of the segment of a tangent from an external point to the point of contact with the circle is called the **length of the tangent.**

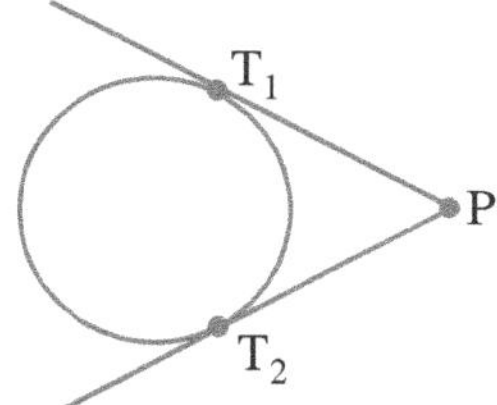


In the given figure, $T_1$ & $T_2$ are the points of contact of the tangents $PT_1$ & $PT_2$ respectively from the external point P.

## 6   Theorem Related to Length of Tangents From the External Points

The lengths of tangents drawn from an external point to a circle are equal.

i.e.,

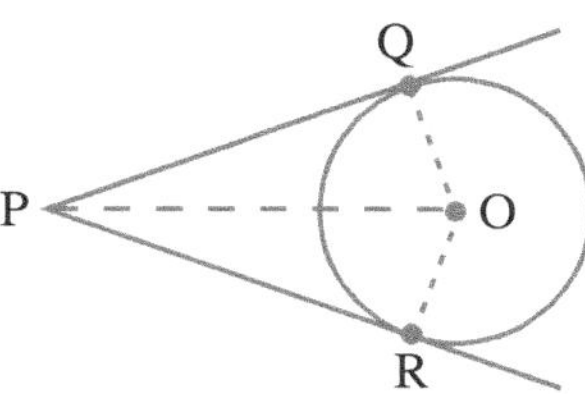


Here, PQ & PR are the two tangents drawn from P to the circle.

Here OP is the angle bisector of $\angle QPR$, i.e., the centre lies on the bisector of the angle between the two tangents.

# Mind

**CONSTRUCTIONS**

## 1 Construction

Construction implies drawing geometrical figures accurately such that triangles, quadrilateral and circles with the help of ruler and compass.

## 2 Division of a Line Segment

A line segment can be divided in a given ratio (both internally and externally)

**Example:**

Divide a line segment of length 12 cm internally in the ratio 3 : 2.

**Solution :**

**Steps of construction :**

(i)    Draw a line segment AB = 12 cm. by using a ruler.

(ii)   Draw a ray making a suitable acute angle $\angle$BAX with AB.

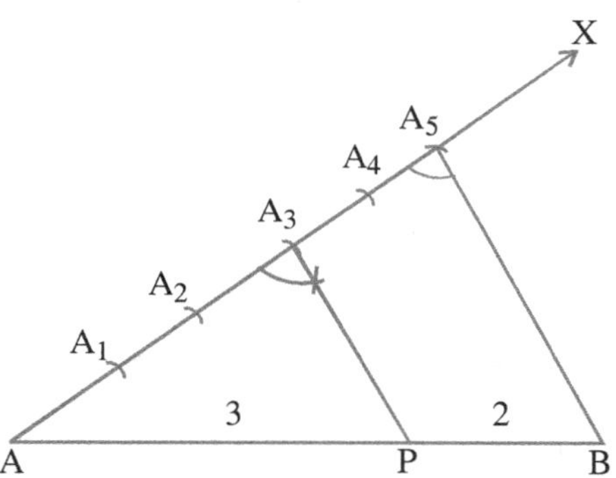


(iii)  Along AX, draw 5 ( = 3 + 2) arcs intersecting the ray AX at $A_1$, $A_2$, $A_3$, $A_4$ and $A_5$ such that

$$AA_1 = A_1A_2 = A_2A_3 = A_3A_4 = A_4A_5$$

(iv)  Join $BA_5$.

(v)   Through $A_3$ draw a line $A_3P$ parallel to $A_5B$ making $\angle AA_3P = \angle AA_5B$, intersecting AB at point P.

The point P so obtained is the required point, which divides AB internally in the ratio 3 : 2.

**4**

# Map-11

## Similar Triangles

**3**

(i)   This Construction involves two different situation.
    (a)  Construction of a similar triangle smaller than the given triangle.
    (b)  Construction of a similar triangle greater than the given triangle.

(ii)  The ratio of sides of the triangle to be constructed with the corresponding sides of the given triangle is called scale factor.

**Example:**
Draw a triangle ABC with side BC = 7 cm. $\angle B = 45°$, $\angle A = 105°$. Construct a triangle whose sides are (4/3) times the corresponding side of $\triangle ABC$.

**Solution :**

**Steps of construction :**

(i)   Draw BC = 7 cm.

(ii)  Draw a ray BX and CY such that $\angle CBX = 45°$ and
      $\angle BCY = 180° - (45° + 105°) = 30°$
      Suppose BX and CY intersect each other at A.
      $\triangle ABC$ so obtained is the given triangle.

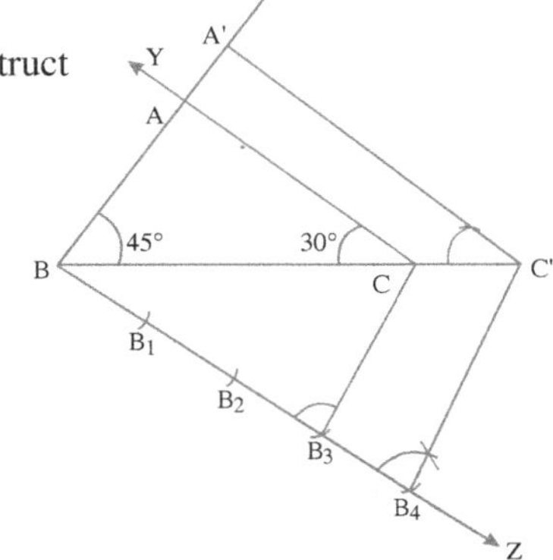


(iii) Draw a ray BZ making a suitable acute angle with  BC on opposite side of vertex A with respect to BC.

(iv) Draw four (greater of 4 and 3 in 4/3) arcs intersecting the ray BZ at $B_1, B_2, B_3, B_4$ such that $BB_1 = B_1B_2 = B_2B_3 = B_3B_4$.

(v)  Join $B_3$ to C and draw a line through $B_4$ parallel to $B_3C$, intersecting the extended line segment BC at C′.

(vi) Draw a line through C′ parallel to CA intersecting the extended line segment BA at A′.
     Triangle A′BC′ so obtained is the required triangle.

## Tangents to a Circle

Two tangents can be drawn to a given circle from a point outside it.

**Example:**
Draw a circle of radius 4 cm. Take a point P outside the circle. Without using the centre of the circle, draw two tangents to the circle from point P.

**Solution :**

**Steps of construction :**

(i)   Draw a circle of radius 4 cm.

(ii)  Take a point P outside the circle and draw a secant PAB, intersecting the circle at A and B.

(iii) Produce AP to C such that AP = CP.

(iv) Draw a semi-circle with CB as diameter.

(v)  Draw PD $\perp$ CB, intersecting the semi-circle at D.

(vi) With P as centre and PD as radius draw arcs to intersect the given circle at T and T′.

(vii) Join PT and PT′. Then, PT and PT′ are the required tangents.

**Note:**
If centre of a circle is not given, then it can be located by finding point of intersection of perpendicular bisector, of any two nonparallel chords of a circle.

# Mind

## Terms Related To Circle

(i) **Chord:** A line segment joining any two points on a circle.

(ii) **Arc:** A piece of a circle between two points on the circle is called an **arc.**

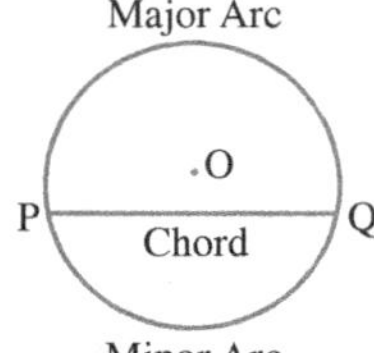


The arc less than the semicircular arc is called **minor arc** and the one greater than the semi-circular arc is called **major arc.**

(iii) **Sector:** The portion of a circular region enclosed by two radii and the corresponding arc is called a sector of the circle.

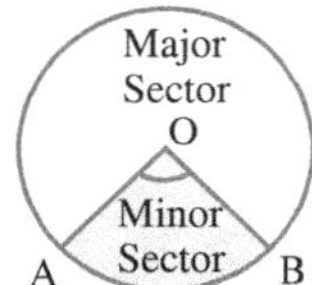


Sector smaller than the semi-circle is called **minor sector** and the sector larger than the semi-circle is called **major sector.**

(iv) **Segment:** The portion of a circular region enclosed between a chord and the corresponding arc is called a segment of the circle.

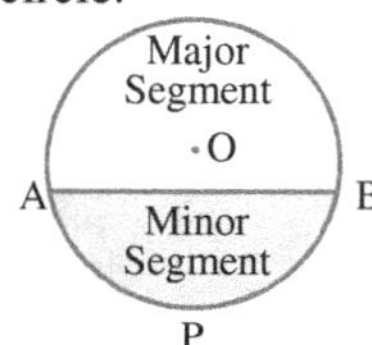


The segment bounded by the chord and the minor arc intercepted by the chord is called **minor segment** and the segment bounded by the chord and the major arc intercepted by the chord is called **major segment.**

## Circle

The set of all points in a plane which are at a fixed distance from a fixed point in the plane is called circle. The fixed point is called centre and the fixed distance is called radius of the circle.

**2**

**1**

**3**

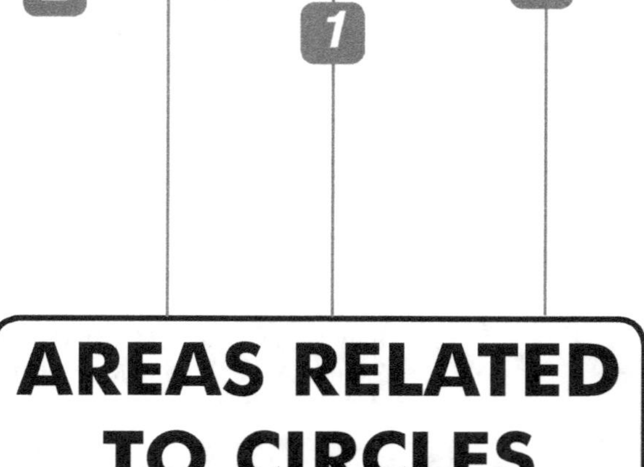

# Map-12

## Circumference and Area of a Circle

(i) The circumference of a circle is defined as distance covered by travelling once around a circle and is given by $C = 2\pi r = \pi d$
where r = radius of the circle and
d = diameter of the circle.

(ii) The Area of a circle of radius r is given by,
$A = \pi r^2 = \dfrac{\pi}{4}d^2$ where, d = diameter of the circle.

(iii) **Area of a circular ring:**
The area of the circular path or ring is given by the difference of the area of outer circle and the area of inner circle.
Area of circular ring $= \pi(R^2 - r^2)$

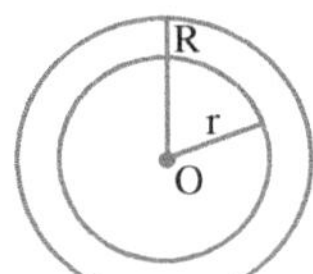

## Length of an Arc and Area of Sector

(i) The length of an arc of a sector of an angle θ is given by,
$$l = \dfrac{\theta}{360} \times 2\pi r$$

Perimeter of sector $AOB$
$$= OA + OB + \widehat{AB} \;=\; 2r + \dfrac{\theta}{360} \times 2\pi r$$

(ii) The area of the sector AOB of angle θ is given by,
$$= \dfrac{\theta}{360^\circ} \times \pi r^2$$

This is the area of minor sector.
∴ area of major sector AOB
$= \pi r^2 -$ Area of minor sector AOB

## Area of a Segment

(i) Area of segment APB
= Area (sector OAPB)
− Area (ΔOAB)
$$= \dfrac{\theta}{360} \times \pi r^2 - \text{area of } \Delta OAB$$

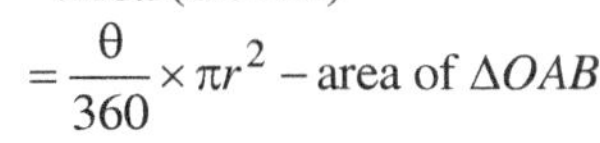

This is the area of minor segment.
∴ area of major segment AQB
$= \pi r^2 -$ Area of minor segment APB

(ii) If θ is the central angle, then the area of segment APB
$$= \dfrac{\theta}{360} \times \pi r^2 - r^2 \sin\dfrac{\theta}{2}\cos\dfrac{\theta}{2}$$

**Mind**

## Surface Areas and Volumes of Solids

(i) **Cuboid:**
Volume $= l \times b \times h$
Total surface area
$= 2[lb + bh + hl]$
Lateral surface area
$= 2[bh + hl]$
Diagonal of the coboid $= \sqrt{\ell^2 + b^2 + h^2}$
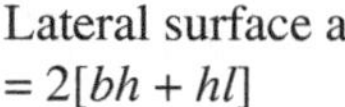

(ii) **Cube:**
Volume $= a^3$
Total surface area $= 6a^2$
Lateral surface area $= 4a^2$
Diagonal of a cube $= \sqrt{3}a$

(iii) **Cylinder:**
(a) Right circular cylinder:
Volume $= \pi r^2 h$
Curved Surface Area $= 2\pi rh$
Total Surface Area $= 2\pi rh + 2\pi r^2 = 2\pi r(r + h)$
(b) Right circular hollow cylinder:
Let $r$ and $R$
be internal & external radii.
Volume $= \pi(R^2 - r^2)h$
Curved Surface Area $= 2\pi(R + r)h$
Total Surface Area $= 2\pi(R + r)h + 2\pi(R^2 - r^2)$
$= 2\pi(R + r)(h + R - r)$

(iv) **Right circular cone:**
Slant height, $l = \sqrt{r^2 + h^2}$
Volume $= \dfrac{1}{3}\pi r^2 h$
Curved Surface Area $= \pi rl$
Total Surface Area $= \pi rl + \pi r^2$

**1**   **3**

# Surface Areas and Volumes

**2**   **6**

## Surface Areas and Volumes of Sphere and Hemisphere

(i) **Sphere:**
Volume $= \dfrac{4}{3}\pi r^3$
Surface area $= 4\pi r^2$

(ii) **Hemisphere:**
Volume $= \dfrac{2}{3}\pi r^3$
C.S.A $= 2\pi r^2$
T.S.A $= 3\pi r^2$

(iii) **Hemispherical shell:**
Volume $= \dfrac{2}{3}\pi(R^3 - r^3)$
Curved Surface Area $= 2\pi(R^2 + r^2)$
Total Surface Area $= 2\pi(r^2 + R^2) + \pi(R^2 - r^2)$
$= \pi(r^2 + 3R^2)$

# Map-13

## Surface Areas of a Combination of Solids

The surface area of a solid which is a combination of two or more solids is calculated by adding the surface areas of the individual solids which are visible in the new solid formed.

For Example:

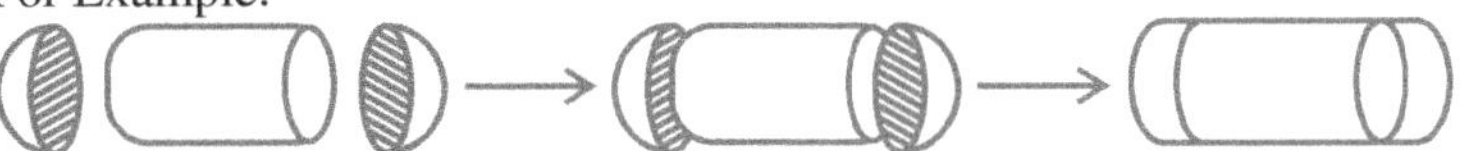

If we consider the surface of the newly formed object as given in the figure above, we would be able to see only the curved surfaces of the two hemispheres and the curved surface of the cylinder.

So, the total surface area of the new solid is the sum of the curved surface areas of each of the individual parts. This gives, TSA of new solid = CSA of one hemisphere + CSA of cylinder + CSA of other hemisphere

## Volume of a Combination of Solids

Whenever solid is formed by combining two or more solids, then the amount of matter present in the new solid is equal to the sum of amounts of matter in the constituting solids. Volume of new solid = sum of the volumes of the individual solids

## Frustum of a Cone

When we slice (or cut) through a cone with a plane parallel to its base (see below figure ) and remove the cone that is formed on one side of that plane, the part that is now left over on the other side of the plane is called a **frustum of the cone**.

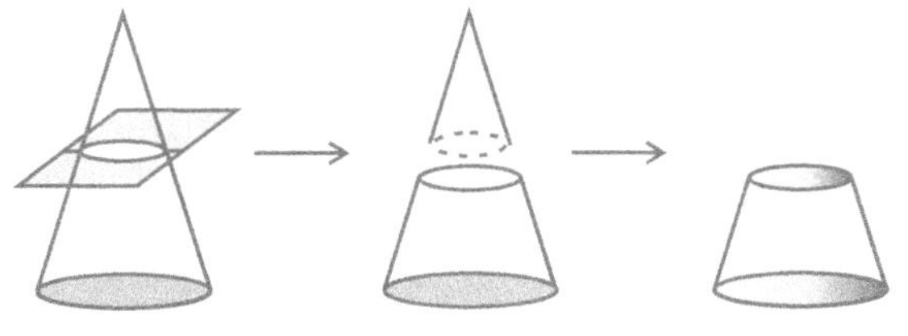

A cone sliced by a plane parallel to base — The two parts separated — Frustum of a cone

(i) Volume of the frustum of cone
$$= \frac{1}{3}\pi h(r_1^2 + r_2^2 + r_1 r_2)$$

(ii) C.S.A. of the frustum of cone
$$= \pi(r_1 + r_2)l,$$
where $l = \sqrt{h^2 + (r_1 - r_2)^2}$

(iii) T.S.A. of the frustum of cone
$$l = \sqrt{h^2 + (r_1 - r_2)^2}$$

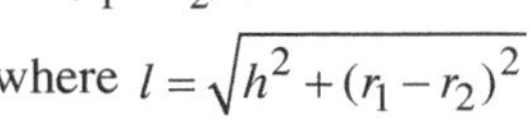

## Conversion of Solid form One Shape to Another

(i) When a solid is converted from one shape to other, then its volume remains same only its shape and size changes.

(ii) If a solid is converted into a number of small identical solids, then Number of small items
$$= \frac{\text{Volume of larger object}}{\text{Volume of smaller object}}$$

# Mind

## Basic Terms

**Class limits :** Suppose marks obtained by all of the students are divided into class intervals $25 - 35$, $35 - 45$ and so interval on.

In class interval $25 - 35$, 25 is called lower class limit and 35 is called upper class limit.

**Class size :** The difference between upper and lower class limit.

**Class mark:** It is given by

$\dfrac{1}{2} \times$ (Upper class limit +Lower class limit)

## Ungrouped and Grouped Data

The data obtained in original form are called **raw data** or **ungrouped data**.

To put the data in a more condensed form, we make groups of suitable size, and mention the frequency of each group. Such a table is called **grouped frequency distribution table**, and the data so obtained is called **grouped data**.

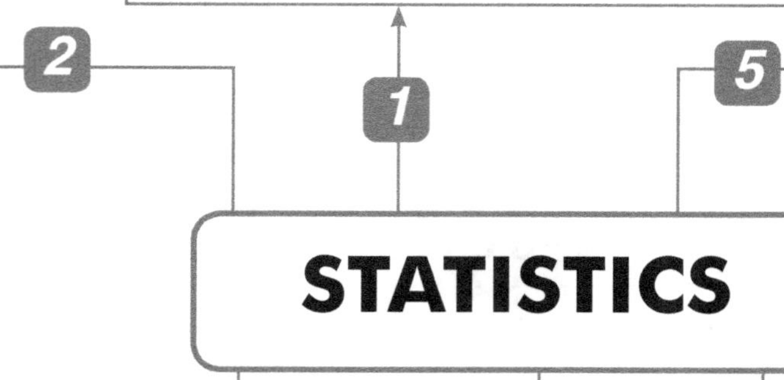

## STATISTICS

## Mean

**For Ungrouped Data:**
Consider 'n' observations in ungrouped data as: $x_1$, $x_2$, $x_3$,............, $x_n$. The mean of these observations is:

$$\text{Mean} = \frac{\text{Sum of the value of all observations}}{\text{Total number of observations}}.$$

Or $\quad \overline{x} = \dfrac{\sum x_i}{x}$

**(i) Direct method:**

$$\text{Mean } (\overline{x}) = \frac{\sum x_i f_i}{\sum f_i}$$

Where '$f_i$' is the frequency corresponding to the class mark '$x_i$'

**(ii) Assumed mean method:**

$$\text{Mean } (\overline{x}) = A + \frac{\sum f_i d_i}{\sum f_i},$$

where $A$ is assumed mean & $d_i = x_i - A$

**(iii) Step deviation method:**

$$\text{Mean } (\overline{x}) = A + \left( \frac{\sum f_i u_i}{\sum f_i} \right) h,$$

where $u_i = \dfrac{x_i - A}{h}$ and '$f_i$' is the frequency corresponding to the class mark '$x_i$'.

## Mode

**(i) For Ungrouped Data:**
The mode is that observation which occurs most frequently, i.e, an observation with maximum frequency.

**(ii) For Grouped Data:**

$$\text{Mode} = l + \frac{f_1 - f_0}{2 f_1 - f_0 - f_2} \times h, \text{ where}$$

$l$ = lower limit of the modal class,
$f_1$ = frequency of the modal class,
$f_2$ = frequency of the class suceeding the modal class,
$h$ = size ofthe class interval,
$f_0$ = frequency of the class preceeding the modal class.
The class with the maximum frequency is called modal class.

# Map-14

## Median

Median is a measure of central tendency which gives the value of the middle-most observation in the data.

**(i) For Ungrouped Data:**

Arrange the data in ascending order.

If number of data $n$ is odd, then the median is $\left(\dfrac{n+1}{2}\right)^{th}$ observation.

If number of data $n$ is even, then the median is the average of $\left(\dfrac{n}{2}\right)^{th}$ and $\left(\dfrac{n}{2}+1\right)^{th}$ observations.

**(ii) For Grouped Data:**

$$\text{Median} = l + \left[\dfrac{\dfrac{n}{2} - cf}{f}\right] \times h, \text{ where}$$

$l$ = lower limit of the median class,
c.f = cumulative frequency of the class proceeding the median class,
$f$ = frequency of the median class,
$h$ = class size,
n = number of observations.
The class whose cumulative frequency is greater than (and nearest to) $\dfrac{n}{2}$ is called median class.

## Relationship Between Mean, Mode and Median

3 Median = Mode + 2 Mean

## Cumulative Frequency Curve (Ogive)

(i) The smooth free hand curve is formed by joining the points $(x_i, f_i)$ where $x_i$ is the upper limit of a class and $f_i$ is the corresponding c.f. The curve so obtained is called a cumulative frequency curve, or an ogive of the less than type.

(ii) The smooth free hand curve is formed by joining the points $(x_i, f_i)$ where $x_i$ is the lower limit of a class and $f_i$ is the corresponding c.f. The curve so obtained is called a cumulative frequency curve, or an ogive of the more than type.

## Median by Graph

(i) Draw the ogive of the less than type and ogive of the more than type on the same axis. The two ogives will intersect each other at a point. From this point, if we draw a perpendicular on the x-axis, the point at which it cuts the x-axis gives us the median.

(ii) Draw the ogive of the less than type, then locate $\dfrac{n}{2}$ on the y-axis (n = number of observations).

From this point on y-axis, draw a line parallel to x-axis cutting the less than ogive at a point. From this point draw a perpendicular on the x-axis, the point at which the perpendicular cuts the x-axis gives us the median.

 

**Mind**

## Probability - An Experimental (Empirical) Approach

Let n be the total number of trials. The empirical probability of an event E happening, is given by

$$P(E) = \frac{\text{Number of trials in which the event happened}}{\text{The total number of trials.}}$$

**1**

## Rational Numbers and Their

(i) **Experiment :** An operation which can produce some well defined outcomes is known as experiment

(ii) **Trial :** Performing of an experiment is called trial.

(iii) **Equally likely outcomes :** Outcomes of trial are equally likely if there is no reason to accecept one in preference to the others.

(iv) **Sample space :** The set of all possible outcomes of an experiment is called sample space.

(v) **Elementary event :** An event having only one outcome

**Note** that the sum of probabilities of all the elementary events of an experiment is 1.

**2**

# PROBABILITY

**3**

## Probability - A Theoretical Approach (Classical Probability)

If an event 'A' can happen in 'm' ways and does not happen in 'n' ways, then the probability of occurence of event 'A' denoted by P (A) is given by

Number of favourable outcomes m

$$P(A) = \frac{\text{Number of favorable outcomes}}{\text{Number of all possible outcomes}} = \frac{m}{m+n}$$

and the probability of not happening of A, denoted by $P(\overline{A})$ is given by

$$P(\overline{A}) = \frac{\text{Number of unfavourable outcomes}}{\text{Number of all possible outcomes}} = \frac{n}{m+n}$$

# Map-15

## Probability of Impossible and Sure Events

The probability of an event which is impossible to occur is 0 and such an event is called **impossible event.**
i.e; for impossible event 'I', $P(I) = 0$
The probability of an event which is sure or certain to occur is 1 and such an event is called **sure event** or **certain event.**
i.e; for sure event or certain event 's', $P(s) = 1$

## Range of the Probability of an Event

From the definition of the probability P(E), we see that the numerator (number of outcomes favourable to the event E) is always equal or greater than 0 but less than or equal to the denominator (the number of all possible outcomes). Therefore,
$$0 \leq P(E) \leq 1$$

## Complementary Events

The event representing ('not E) is called the complement of event 'E' and we say that the events E and $\bar{E}$ are complementary events,
$$P(E) + P(\bar{E}) = 1$$
$$\text{OR}$$
$$P(E) = 1 - P(\bar{E})$$

# CHAPTERWISE
# MIND MAPS
# SCIENCE

# MIND

## CHEMICAL REACTIONS AND EQUATIONS

### Chemical Equation

The representation of chemical reaction by means of symbols of substances in the form of formulae is called chemical equation.

For example

$$N_2 + 3H_2 \rightleftharpoons 2NH_3$$

### Balanced Chemical Equation

A balanced chemical equation has equal number of atom of each element participating in the reaction on both left and right hand sides of the reaction.

According to **Law of Conservation of Mass**, total mass of the elements present in the products of a chemical reaction has to be equal to the total mass of the element present in the reactants.

### Balancing Of A Chemical Equation

| Total No of Atoms = on R.H.S | | Total no of Atoms on L.H.S. |
|---|---|---|
| | $Fe_3O_4 + H_2 \longrightarrow$ | $Fe + H_2O$ |
| [Fe] | $Fe_3O_4 + H_2 \longrightarrow$ | $3Fe + H_2O$ |
| [O] | $Fe_3O_4 + H_2 \longrightarrow$ | $3Fe + 4H_2O$ |
| [H] | $Fe_3O_4 + 4H_2 \longrightarrow$ | $3Fe + 4H_2O$ |

### Oxidation In Everyday Life

### Rusting

When iron reacts with oxygen moisture it forms a red subst called rust.

### Corrosion

Metals on coming in contact oxygen, water, acids or g presents in air changes its sur This is called corrosion for e.g. b coating on silver and green coa on copper.

**Prevention** - painting, galvanization, oiling, greasing

### Rancidity

Oil and fats on exposure to air s a change in taste and smell. property is known as rancidity.

**Prevention** – adding antioxida Vacuum packing, refrigerat flushing food with nitrogen

# MAP-1

## Types Of Chemical Reactions

The transformation of chemical substance into a new chemical substance by making and breaking of bonds between different atom is known a chemical reaction.

## Combination Reaction

When two elements or one compound and one element or two compounds combines to form a new product.
For example
- $H_2 + Cl_2 \longrightarrow 2HCl$
- $Zn + CuSO_4 \rightarrow ZnSO_4 + Cu$
- $NaOH + H_2SO_4 \rightarrow Na_2SO_4 + H_2O$

## Exothermic Reactions

Reactions producing energy are called exothermic reactions.
Most of the combination reactions are exothermic in nature.
For example : $CaO + H_2O \rightarrow Ca(OH)_2 + Heat$

## Oxidation

Gain of oxygen or removal of hydrogen is called oxidation eg.
- $Zn + O_2 \rightarrow ZnO$
- $Mn + HCl \rightarrow MnCl_2 + H_2$

## Reduction

Gain of hydrogen or removal of oxygen is called reduction.
e.g. $CuO + H_2 \rightarrow Cu + H_2O$

## Redox Reactions

A chemical reaction in which both oxidation and reduction takes place simultaneously are called redox reactions.
For example
$CuO + H_2 \longrightarrow Cu + H_2O$

## Decomposition Reaction

When a compound split into two or more simple products for example
$$Ca(OH)_2 \xrightarrow{\Delta} CaO + H_2O$$
Decomposition reaction require energy either in the form of heat, light or electricity for decomposing the reactions

## Endothermic Reactions

Reactions which require energy to occur are known as endo thermic reactions.
For example :
$$2AgBr \xrightarrow{heat} 2Ag + Br_2$$

## Displacement Reactions

It takes place when a more reactive metal displaces a less reactive metal. For Example :
$Fe + CuSO_4 \longrightarrow FeSO_4 + Cu$

## Double Displacement Reactions

In this reactions ions are exchanged between two reactants and forming new compounds.

## Precipitation Reaction :

In some reactions, an insoluble mass is formed which is known as precipitate and such reactions are called precipitation reaction.

**For Example**
$Na_2SO_4 + BaCl_2 \rightarrow 2NaCl + BaSO_4$
                                                    Precipitate

# MIND

## Chemical Properties Of Bases

- Bases + Metals → Salt + $H_2$

  $2NaOH + Zn \rightarrow Na_2ZnO_2 + H_2$
- Bases + Acids → Salt + Water

  $KOH + HCl \rightarrow KCl + H_2O$
- Base + Non–metallic oxide →

                       Salt + water

  $2NaOH + CO_2 \rightarrow Na_2CO3 + H_2O$

## Chemical Properties Of Acids

- Acids + Metal → Salt + $H_2$

  e.g. $H_2SO_4 + Zn \rightarrow ZnSO_4 + H_2$
- Acids + Metal Carbonate/Metal hydrogen

  Carbonate = Salt + $CO_2$

  e.g $NaHCO_3 + HCl \rightarrow NaCl + H_2O + CO_2$
- Acids + Bases → Salt + water

  $NaOH + HCl \rightarrow NaCl + H_2O$
- Acids + Metal oxide → Salt + Water

  $H_2SO_4 + CuO \rightarrow CuSO_4 + H_2O$

## Acids

- Produce $[H^+]$ in $H_2O$
- Sour taste
- Turns blue litmus red
- Acts as electrolyte in solution

## Salt

Salt is formed by combinatio
a c i d  a n d  b a s e  t h r o u
neutralization reaction.

**Water of Crystallization :**
It is the fixed number of w
molecules present in
formula unit of a salt e.g.

$CuSO_4 . 5H_2O$, $Na_2CO_3 . 10H$

## Bases

- Produce $[OH^-]$ in $H_2O$
- Bitter taste
- Turns red litmus blue
- Acts as electrolyte in solution
- Water soluble bases are known as alkali

## ACIDS BASES AND SALTS

| Indicators | Color in Acidic medium | Color in Basic Medium |
|---|---|---|
| Litmus solution | Red | Blue |
| Methyl orange | Pink | Orange |
| Phenolphthalein | Colourless | Pink |
| Methyl red | Yellow | Red |

## Indicators

These are the substances which indicate the acidi
basic nature of the solution by their colour change

## Strength of Acids & Bases in Solutio

pH scale is used for measuring hydrogen
concentration in solution.

**Importance of pH**

- Some animals like bee and plants like ne
  secretes highly acidic substance for self defense
- Lower pH of sour & sweet food can cause too
  decay. The pH of mouth should be more than 5.5
- The inner lining of stomach protects   vital ce
  from the acidic pH which is   developed by H
  secreted by stomach.
  The optimum pH range for human body is 7 to 7

| | | |
|---|---|---|
| $\pi H = 7$ | Neutral Solution | $H_3O^+ = OH^-$ |
| $\pi H > 7$ | Basic Solution | $OH^- > H_3O^+$ |
| $\pi H < 7$ | Acidic Solution | $OH^- < H_3O+$ |

# MAP-2

| pH | Acid | Base | Salt | Example |
|----|------|------|------|---------|
| 7 | Strong | Strong | Neutral | $NaOH + H_2SO_4 \rightarrow Na_2SO_4 + H_2O$ |
| < 7 | Strong | Weak | Acidic | $HCl + NH_4OH \rightarrow NH_4Cl + H_2O$ |
| > 7 | Weak | Strong | Basic | $CH_3COOH + KOH \rightarrow CH_3COOK + H_2O$ |
| < 7 | Weak | Weak | Weak | $CH_3COOH + NH_4OH \rightarrow CH_3COONH_4 + H_2O$ |

## Types of Salts

The acidic & basic nature of salts depends on the acid and base combined in neutralization reaction.

## Some Important Salts

### Plaster of Paris ($CaSO_4 \cdot \frac{1}{2} H_2O$)

- $CaSO_4 \cdot 2H_2O \xrightarrow{373K} CaSO_4 \frac{1}{2} H_2O + \frac{3}{2} H_2O$
  Gypsum                      Plaster of Paris
- Used for making toys, material for decor action, smooth surfaces.

### Bleaching Powder ($CaOCl_2$) :

- $Ca(OH)_2 + Cl_2 \longrightarrow CaOCl_2 + H_2O$
  dry slaked lime

Used
- as an oxidising agent in chemical industry.
- In disinfecting water.

## Sodium Hydroxide (NaOH)

- Prepared by chlor alkali process
- $NaCl + H_2O \xrightarrow{\text{Electricity}} NaOH + Cl_2 + H_2$
  (brine)                              near the        at anode
                                       cathode         at cathode

### Common Salt NaCl :

- Main source is sea water.
- Also exists in the form of rock hence also known as rock salt.
- Important component of food.
- Used in preparation of sodium hydroxide, baking soda & washing soda.

## Washing Soda ($Na_2CO_3 \cdot 10H_2O$) :

- $Na_2CO_3 + 10H_2O \rightarrow Na_2CO_3 \cdot 10H_2O$
- Used in glass, soap & paper indusby, removing Permanent hardness of water and cleaning agent

### Baking Soda ($NaHCO_3$)

- $NaCl + H_2O + CO_2 + NH_3 \longrightarrow NH_4Cl + NaHCO_3$
- Mild non – corrosive
- $2NaHCO_3 \xrightarrow{\Delta} Na_2CO_3 + H_2O + CO_2$
- Used as in baking cakes as antacid
- Fire extinguisher

## Addition of Acids or Bases to Water

Always add acid to water and not water to acid because this process is highly exothermic. The acid must be added slowly to water by constant shirring on. Adding water to a concentrated acid, the heat generated may cause the mixture to splash out and cause burns.

# MIND

## METAL AND NON-METALS

There 92 well known naturally occurring minerals of which 70 are metals and rest 20 are the non-metals.

### Physical Properties of Metals & Non-Metals

| Property | Metals | Non-Metals |
|---|---|---|
| Luster | They have shining surface. | They do not have shining surface except iodine. |
| Hardness | Generally hard except sodium, lithium & potassium .These are soft and can be cut with knife. | Generally soft except diamond (hardest natural substance) |
| State | Exist as solids except mercury. | Exist as solids or gases except bromine. |
| Malleability | Can be beaten into thin sheets. Gold & silver are the most malleable metals. | Non-malleable |
| Ductility | Can be drawn into thin wires. | Non-ductile |
| Conductor of heat & electricity | Good conductors of heat and electricity. Ag & Cu are best conductors of heat and Pb & Hg are poor conductor of heat. | Poor conductor of heat and electricity except graphite. |
| Density | High density & high melting point except Na & K. | Low density & melting point. |
| Sonorous | Produce sound on striking a hard surface. | Not sonorous |
| Oxides | Metallic oxides are basic in nature. | Non-metallic oxides are acidic in nature. |

### Reaction between Metals and Non Metals

- Reactivity of an element can be explained as tendency to attain a completely filled outermost shell.
- Metals have 1, 2 or 3 e- in outermost shell and thus it is easier for them to loss e- rather than to gain. They loss e- & gains positive charge & are termed as cation.
- In contrast, non-metals have 4-8 e- in outermost shell & thus they gain e- to achieve their octet. They gain e- as well as negative charge & termed as anion.
- Cations & anions attract each other & are held by strong electrostatic force of attraction.
- The compounds formed by the transfer of electrons from metal to non-non-metal are known as ionic compounds or electrovalent compound.

$$Na \cdot \ddot{\underset{..}{Cl}} : \longrightarrow [Na]^+ [\ddot{\underset{..}{Cl}} :]^-$$

### Chemical Properties of Metals

| | | |
|---|---|---|
| Reaction with Oxygen | Metal + Oxygen → Metal oxide (basic)<br>$2Cu + O_2 \rightarrow 2CuO$<br>$4Al + 3O_2 \rightarrow 2Al_2O_3$<br>Zn & Al form amphoteric oxides i.e. they react with both acids & bases to produce salt & water.<br>$Al_2O_3 + 6HCl \rightarrow 2AlCl_3 + 3H_2O$<br>$Al_2O_3 + 2NaOH \rightarrow 2NaAlO_2 + H_2O$<br>Metal oxides are insoluble in water but some of them dissolve in water to form alkalis.<br>$Na_2O(s) + H_2O(l) \rightarrow 2NaOH(aq)$ | Na & K are vigorou[s] elements & are kep[t] immersed in kerose[ne] oil.<br><br>Protective metal ox[ide] layer prevents the m[etal] from further oxidat[ion] such as found in Al [&] Pb etc.<br><br>Cu doesn't burn but [the] metal coated with C[uO] black colored layer. Ag & Au do not rea[ct] with $O_2$. |
| Reaction with Water | Metals + Water → Metal Oxides + $H_2$<br>Metal Oxides + $H_2O \rightarrow$ Metal Hydroxide<br>$2Na(s) + 2H_2O(l) \rightarrow 2NaOH(aq) + H_2(g) + E$<br>$2K(s) + 2H_2O(l) \rightarrow 2KOH(aq) + H_2(g) + E$ | Na & K: react viole[ntly] with cold water.<br>Ca: reacts less violently.<br>Mg: reacts with hot water.<br>Al, Fe, Zn react wit[h] steam to from meta[l] hydroxide & $H_2$. |
| Reaction with dilute Acids | Metal + Dilute Acid → Salt + $H_2$<br>$Mg(s) + 2HCl(aq) \rightarrow MgCl_2(aq) + H_2(g)$<br>Metal + $HNO_3 \rightarrow H_2$ not evolved<br>**Reason-** $HNO_3$ is strong oxidizing agent & oxidized $H_2$ to water. | Mg & Mn react wit[h] very dil. HCl to evo[lve] $H_2$ gas.<br>The reactivity decreases in the ord[er] Mg> Al> Zn> Fe.<br>Cu doesn't react wit[h] dil. HCl. |
| Reaction with Solutions of other Metal Salts | Reactive metals can displace less reactive metals from their compounds in solution or molten state.<br>Metals A+ Salt solution of B→ salt of A+ Metal B<br>$CuSO_4(aq) + Zn(s) \rightarrow ZnSO_4(aq) + Cu(s)$ | Reactivity Series: L[ist] of metals in order o[f] their decreasing activities.<br>K > Na> Ca > Mg > [Al] > Zn > Fe > Pb > H [>] Cu > Hg > Ag> Au. |

# MAP-3

## Occurrence of Metals

The elements or compounds, which occur naturally in the earth's crust, are known as **minerals.**

At some places, minerals contain a very high percentage of a particular metal and the metal can be profitably extracted from it. These minerals are called **ores.**

## Corrosion

Corrosion is the deterioration of materials by chemical interaction with their environment for e.g. darkening of silver articles when exposed to air, gaining of green coat on copper, rusting of iron.

**Prevention:** The rusting of iron can be prevented by painting, oiling, greasing, galvanising, chrome plating, anodising or making alloys.

- Galvanisation is a method of protecting steel and iron from rusting by coating them with a thin layer of zinc.
- Alloy is a homogeneous mixture of two or more metals, or a metal & nonmetal. For e.g. stainless steel (alloy of Fe, Ni, & Cr), amalgam (alloy of Hg), brass (alloy of Cu & Zn) etc. The electrical conductivity & melting point of an alloy is less than that of pure metals.

## Extracting Metals Low in the Activity Series

- These metals are the least reactive & are often found in a free state for e.g. Au, Ag, Pt & Cu are found in the free state.
- However, Cu & Ag are also found in the combined state as their sulphide or oxide ores.
- The oxides of these metals can be reduced to metals by heating alone. For e.g. cinnabar (HgS), ore of mercury it is heated in air to converted it in mercuric oxide (HgO) which is then reduced to mercury by further heating.
- $2HgS(s) + 3O_2(g) \xrightarrow{Heat} 2HgO(s) + 2SO_2(g)$
- $2HgO(s) \xrightarrow{Heat} 2Hg(l) + O_2(g)$
- Another instance is reduction of $Cu_2S$ (ore of copper) to copper by heating.
- $2Cu_2S + 3O_2(g) \xrightarrow{Heat} 2Cu_2O(s) + 2SO_2(g)$
- $2Cu_2O + Cu_2S \xrightarrow{Heat} 6Cu(s) + SO_2$

## Extracting Metals Middle in the Activity Series

- These metals such as Fe, Zn, Pb, Cu, etc are moderately reactive & are usually present as sulphides or carbonates in nature.
- The sulphide ores are converted into oxides by heating strongly in the presence of excess air which is known as roasting.
- The carbonate ores are changed into oxides by heating strongly in limited air which is known as calcination.
- The metal oxides are then reduced to the corresponding metals by using suitable reducing agents such as carbon.
- For e.g. extraction of Zn
- **Roasting:** $2ZnS(s) + 3O_2(g) \xrightarrow{Heat} 2ZnO(s) + 2SO_2(g)$
- **Calcination:** $ZnCO_3(s) \xrightarrow{Heat} ZnO(s) + CO_2(g)$
- **Reduction:** $ZnO(s) + C(s) \rightarrow Zn(s) + CO(g)$
- Sometimes displacement reactions can also be used in place of reduction & highly reactive metals such as Na, Ca, Al, etc., are used as reducing agents.
- For e.g. $3MnO_2(s) + 4Al(s) \rightarrow 3Mn(l) + 2Al_2O_3(s) + Heat$
- $Fe_2O_3(s) + 2Al(s) \rightarrow 2Fe(l) + Al_2O_3(s) + Heat$
- This reaction is used to join railway tracks or cracked machine parts and is known as the **thermit reaction.**

## Enrichment of Ores

Ores mined from the earth are usually contaminated with large amounts of impurities such as soil, sand, etc., called **gangue.** The impurities must be removed from the ore prior to the extraction of the metal.

The processes used for removing the gangue from the ore are based on the differences between physical or chemical properties of the gangue and the ore.

## Extraction of Metals

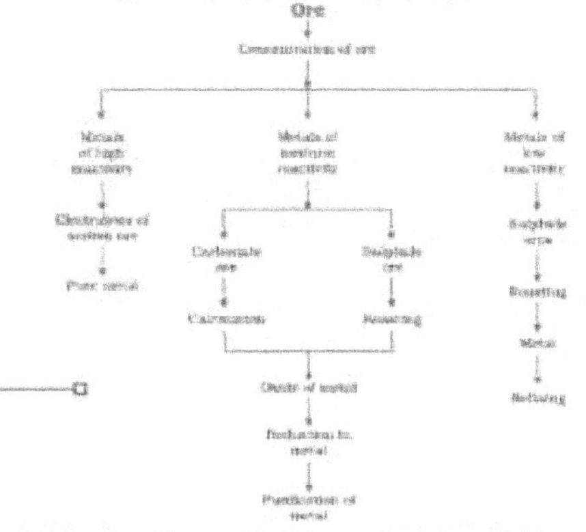


**Figure:** Steps involved in the extraction of metals from ores

## Extracting Metals towards the Top of the Activity Series

These metals are highly reactive & are obtained by electrolytic reduction. For e.g. Na, Mg, & Ca are obtained by the electrolysis of their molten chlorides.

The metals are deposited at the cathode whereas chlorine is liberated at anode.

At cathode $Na^+ + e^- \rightarrow Na$

At anode $2Cl^- \rightarrow Cl_2 + 2e^-$

Similarly, aluminium is obtained by the electrolytic reduction of aluminium oxide.

## Refining of Metals

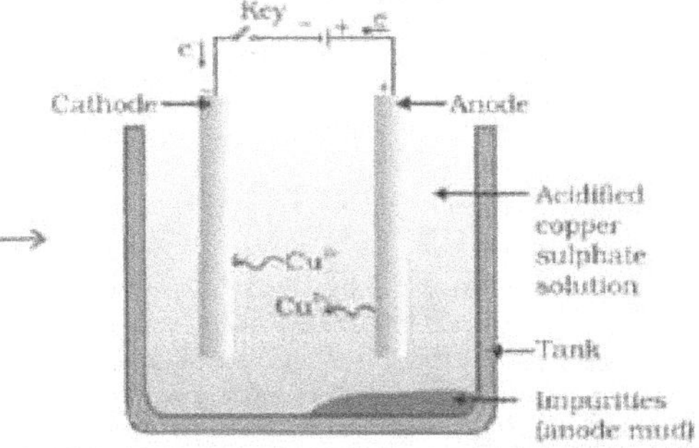

# MIND

## CARBON AND ITS COMPOUNDS

Carbon is an important constituent of the foods, fuels, household and commercial articles, textile fabrics, perfume explosives, dyes, war gases etc. The Earth's crust has only 0.02% carbon in the form of minerals (like petroleum, c carbonates and hydrogen carbonates) and the atmosphere comprises of only 0.03% of carbon dioxide

### Allotropes of Carbon

An element, in different forms, having different physical properties but similar chemical properties is known as allotropes of that element.

Carbon has three well known allotropes which are graphite, diamond and buck minster fullerene.

**Graphite:**
- In graphite, each carbon atom is bonded to three other carbon atoms in the same plane giving a hexagonal array.
- One of these bonds is a double-bond, and thus the valency of carbon is satisfied.
- Graphite structure is formed by the hexagonal arrays being placed in layers one above the other.
- Unlike other non-metals graphite is a very good conductor of electricity.

**Diamond:**
- In diamond, each carbon atom is bonded to four other carbon atoms forming a rigid three-dimensional structure.
- Diamond is the hardest substance known while graphite is smooth and slippery.
- Diamonds can be synthesised by subjecting pure carbon to very high pressure and temperature.
- These synthetic diamonds are small but are otherwise indistinguishable from natural diamonds.

**Fullerene:**
This is another class of carbon allotropes. The first one to be identified was C-60 which has carbon atoms arranged in the shape of a football. Since this looked like the geodesic dome designed by the US architect Buckminster Fuller, the molecule was named fullerene.

### Saturated and Unsaturated Hydrocarbons

**Saturated hydrocarbons:** Compounds in which carbon-carbon atoms & carbon-hydrogen atoms are held together by single bonds. General formula is $C_nH_{2n+2}$.

**Unsaturated hydrocarbons:** Compounds consist of a single, double or triple bond between carbon-carbon atoms.

These double-bonded compounds are called alkenes & the triple-bonded compounds are called alkynes.

The general formula for alkenes is $C_nH_{2n}$ & for alkynes the same is $C_nH_{2n-2}$.

**Cycloalkanes:** These hydrocarbons possess one or multiple carbon rings. The hydrogen atom is attached to the carbon ring.

**Aromatic hydrocarbons:** These are also called as arenes. Arenes are compounds which consist of at least one aromatic ring.

### Bonding in Carbon

- Atomic number of carbon = 6
- Electronic configuration has 2 electrons in K and 4 electrons in L shell.
- Carbon **shares its four** valence electrons other atoms of carbon or with atoms of elements. **These electrons contributed b atoms, for mutual sharing in order to ac the stable noble gas configuration is covalency of that atom.**
- **Hence, carbon shows tetracovalency.**
- The simplest molecule formed by shari electrons (i.e., covalent bonds), ca represented by electron dot structure.

### Versatile Nature of Carbon

- **Catenation:** It is the unique property o linkage of carbon atoms by means of co bonds to form straight chains, or branched c or the rings of different sizes.
- **Tetracovalency:** Due to small size, and pr of four valence electrons, carbon can form bonds with other carbon atoms, hydr oxygen, nitrogen, or sulphur, etc. For exa compounds of carbon with hydrogen are hydrocarbons.
- **Multiple Bond Formation:** Due to small s forms multiple bonds (i.e., double bonds or bonds) with other elements as well as with it atoms.
- **Isomerism:** The phenomenon by means of the carbon compounds with same mole formula show different structures, and prope

**Soaps:** Ester of higher fatty acids is called soap manufactured by the reaction of easter of h fatty acid with sodium hydroxide. The sodium s formed has cleansing property.

**Detergents:** Soap cannot form lather in hard v To overcome this problem, detergents introduced. Detergent is also known as soa soap. Detergent is sodium salt of benzene sulp acid or sodium salt of long chain alkyl hydr sulphate.

# MAP-4

## Nomenclature of Carbon Compounds: IUPAC Name

Rules for Nomenclature of Organic Compounds:

- Identify the number of carbon atoms in the compound & name the compound according to the number of carbon atoms.
- If any functional group is present, add a 'prefix' or 'suffix' specified for the functional group with the name of the parent compound.
- Prefix is added for only Halo group and for rest of the functional groups suffix is added.
- If the name of the functional group is to be given as a suffix, the name of the carbon chain is modified by deleting the final 'e' and adding the appropriate suffix.
- In the case of unsaturated hydrocarbon if double bond is present in the carbon chain, then 'ene' will be added in the parent name of compound after omitting 'ane' and if triple bond is present in the carbon chain, then 'yne' will be added.

## Properties of Ethanol

- Ethanol exists in liquid state at room temperature.
- Mixture of alcohol to ethane results in the formation of ethanol & it is the active ingredient of all alcoholic drinks. Even a small quantity of ethanol if consumed can causes drunkenness.
- Being a good solvent, it is also used in medicines like tincture of iodine, cough syrups, and many other tonics.
- Reaction with sodium –

$$2Na + 2CH_3CH_2OH \longrightarrow 2CH_3CH_2ONa + H_2$$

　Ethanol　　　　　　　　Sodium Ethoxide

- Reaction to give unsaturated hydrocarbon:

$$2CH_3CH_2OH \xrightarrow[\text{H}_2\text{SO}_4]{\text{Hot Conc.}} 2CH_2 = CH_2 + H_2O$$

　Ethanol　　　　　　　　　　Ethene

## Properties of Ethanoic Acid

- Ethanoic acid commonly known as acetic acid belongs to a group of carboxylic acids.
- Vinegar used in our day to day life is a 5-8% solution of acetic acid in water. It is extensively used as a preservative in pickles.
- Pure ethanoic acid has a melting point of 290 K due to which it often freezes in cold climates giving rise to its name as glacial acetic acid.
- Esterification reaction:

$$CH_3COOH + CH_3CH_2OH \xrightarrow{\text{Acid}} CH_3COCH_2CH_3$$

　Ethanoic Acid　　Ethanol　　　　　　　O Ester

- Reaction with a base: $NaOH + CH_3COOH \longrightarrow$
$$CH_3COONa + H_2O$$

- Reaction with carbonates and hydrogen carbonates:

$$2CH_3COOH + NA_2CO_3 \longrightarrow 2CH_3COONa + H_2O + CO_2$$

$$CH_3COOH + NaHCO_3 \longrightarrow CH_3COONa + H_2O + CO_2$$

## Homologous Series

- A series of carbon compounds in which same functional group substitutes the hydrogen atom is called a homologous series.
- These compounds have similar chemical properties due to the presence of same kind of functional group. For e.g. series of alkanes i.e. methane, ethane, propane, butane and so on is a homologous series.
- Similarly the series of alkene & alkynes also forms homologous series.
- The series like methanol, ethanol, propanol, butanol and so on is also a homologous series. The functional group attached to these compounds is alcohol.
- With the increase in molecular mass in a homologous series the physical properties like melting points, boiling points & solubility in a particular solvent increases.
- But the chemical properties of a homologous series determined by the functional group remain same.

## Chemical Properties of Carbon Compounds

**Combustion Reactions:** When Carbon & its compounds burn in the presence of Oxygen (or air), they give $CO_2$, heat & light.
E.g.: $C + O_2 \rightarrow CO_2 + Heat + Light$.

**Oxidation Reactions:** Though combustion is generally an oxidation reaction, **not all oxidation reactions are combustion reactions.** Oxidation is also carried out by using oxidizing agents (Oxidants).

**Addition reactions:** Unsaturated organic compounds, like alkenes and alkynes, undergo addition reactions to become saturated in nature.
E.g. $CH_2=CH_2 + H_2 + $ (Nickel catalyst) $\rightarrow CH_3 - CH_3$

**Substitution Reaction:** A Substitution reaction is one in which an atom or a group of atoms (functional group) in the compound are replaced by another atom (or group of atoms). Substitution reactions are single displacement reactions.
E.g.: $CH_4 + Cl_2 + Sunlight \rightarrow CH_3Cl + HCl$

## Functional Groups In Carbon Compounds

| Heteroatom | Functional group | Formula of functional group | Suffix |
|---|---|---|---|
| Cl/Br | Halo-(chloro/bromo) | $-Cl, -Br$ | (Named as prefix) |
| Oxygen | 1. Alcohols | $-OH$ | –ol |
| | 2. Aldehyde | $-\overset{\text{H}}{\underset{\text{O}}{C}}$ | –al |
| | 3. Ketone | $-\overset{|}{\underset{|}{C}}=O$ | –one |
| | 4. Carboxylic acid | $-\overset{|}{C}-OH$ | –oic acid |
| | 5. Esters | $-\overset{|}{C}-OR$ | –oate |
| Nitrogen | 1. Amino | $-NH_2$ | (Named as prefix) |
| | 2. Nitro | $-NH_2$ | (Named as prefix) |

# MIND

## Periodic Classification Of Elements

### Dobereiners's Triads

- Dobereiner found that when elements are arranged into groups of three in the order of their increasing atomic mass, the atomic mass of the element; which comes in the middle, is the arithmetic mean of rest of the two.
- He arranged three elements in one group which is known as Dobereiner's Triads. For e.g.:
  (Li) 7.0 (Na) 23.0 (K) 39.0
  (Ca) 40.0 (Sr) 87.5 (Ba) 137.0
- Here atomic mass of sodium is equal to arithmetic mean of atomic masses of lihtium and potassium. Similarly, atomic mass of strontium is equal to arithmetic mean of atomic masses of calcium and barium

### Limitations of Doberiner's Triads

- He could identify only a few such triads and so the law could not gain importance.
- In the triad of Fe, Co, Ni, all the three elements have a nearly equal atomic mass and thus it does not follow the above law.

### Mendeleev's Periodic Classification

- Mendeleev periodic law, states that 'the properties of elements are the periodic function of their atomic masses'.
- Mendeleev's periodic table contains vertical columns called 'groups' and horizontal rows called 'periods'.

### Characteristics of the Mendeleev's Periodic Table

- The elements are arranged in vertical rows called groups and horizontal rows called periods.
- There are eight groups indicated by Roman Numerals I, II, III, IV, V, VI, VII, VIII. The elements belonging to first seven groups have been divided into sub-groups designated as A and B on the basis of similarities. Group VIII consists of nine elements arranged in three triads.
- There are six periods (numbered 1, 2, 3, 4, 5 and 6).

### Newlands' Law of Octaves

- According to this law "if elements are arranged in the increasing order of their atomic mass, property of every eighth element repeats."
- The arrangement of elements in Newlands' Octaves resembles the musical notes.

### Limitation of Newlands' Octaves

- Law of Octaves could be valid up to calcium only as after calcium, elements do not obey the rule of Octaves.
- It was assumed by Newlands that only elements existed in nature and no more elements would be discovered in the future
- More than one element had to be placed in some of the groups; in order to place the elements having similar properties in one group. But in order to do so, he also put some dissimilar elements in same group.
- Iron; which has similar property as cobalt and nickel, was placed far from them.
- Cobalt and nickel were placed in the group with chlorine and fluorine in spite of having different properties.

### Limitation of Mendeleev's Periodic Table

- Some elements in Mendeleev's Table have not been arranged in the increasing order of their atomic masses. For example, Co and Ni.
- Hydrogen forms similar compounds as Group 1 elements. However, it also forms similar diatomic molecules as Group 7 elements ($H_2$, $F_2$, $Cl_2$, $I_2$). Hence, it could not be assigned a fixed position in the table.
- Isotopes posed a challenge to Mendeleev's table. For example, Cl has two major isotopes – Cl-35 and Cl-37.

### Merits of Mendeleev's Periodic Table

- Mendeleev left some blank spaces in his periodic table in order to place the elements having similar properties in the same group.
- Mendeleev predicted the discovery of some elements and named them as eka-boron, eka-aluminium and eka-silicon.
- One of the strengths of Mendeleev's periodic table was that, when inert gases were discovered, they could be placed in a new group without disturbing the existing order.

# MAP-5

## Modern Periodic Table

In 1913, Henry Moseley showed that atomic number of an element is a more fundamental property than its atomic mass. According to this law "properties of elements are a periodic function of their atomic number".

## Trends in Modern Periodic Table

| Property | Valency | Atomic Size | Metallic Character | Nonmetallic Character | Electronegativity |
|---|---|---|---|---|---|
| Variation in period | Increases from 1 to 4 then decreases to zero | Decreases | Decreases | Increases | Increases |
| Reason | No. of atomic shells remains the same & atomic number increases by 1 unit. | This is due to an increase in nuclear charge which tends to pull the electrons closer to the nucleus and reduces the size of the atom. | Effective nuclear charge increases. Hence tendency to lose electron decreases. | Effective nuclear charge increases. Hence tendency to gain electron increases | |
| Variation in group | Remains same | Increases | Increases | Decreases | Decreases |
| Reason | | New shells are being added as we go down the group. This increases the distance between the outermost electrons and the nucleus so that the atomic size increases in spite of the increase in nuclear charge. | Effective nuclear charge decreases | Effective nuclear charge decreases. Hence tendency to gain electron decreases | |

## Position of Elements in the Modern Periodic Table

### Position of Elements

| No of Valence Electrons | Group | No. of Shell | Period |
|---|---|---|---|
| 1 | 1 | 1 | 1 |
| 2 | 2 | 2 | 2 |
| 3 | 13 | 3 | 3 |
| 4 | 14 | 4 | 4 |
| 5 | 15 | 5 | 5 |
| 6 | 16 | 6 | 6 |
| 7 | 17 | 7 | 7 |
| 8 | 18 | | |

Elements are placed in groups according to the number of valence electrons and placed in periods according to the number of shells present in them.

Helium has valence electrons equal to 2, but it is placed in group number 18 because it is a noble gas and has completely filled outermost shell.

## MIND

### Nutrition

Nutrition is the process by which source of energy (food) is transferred from outside the body of the organism to the inside. Most of the food sources are also carbon-based on Earth and depending on the complexity of these carbon sources different organisms use different kinds of nutritional processes.

**Autotrophic Nutrition:** Carbon and energy requirements of the autotrophic organism are fulfilled by photosynthesis.
- It is the process by which autotrophs convert carbon dioxide & water into carbohydrate in the presence of sunlight and chlorophyll. Oxygen is the byproduct.
- The following events occur during this process:
  - Absorption of light energy by chlorophyll.
  - Conversion of light energy to chemical energy and splitting of water molecules into hydrogen and oxygen.
  - Reduction of carbon dioxide to carbohydrates.

**Heterotrophic Nutrition:** Heterotrophs depend on other organisms for their nutrition.
- **Saprophytes:** They break-down the food material outside the body and then absorb it, also termed as extra-cellular digestion. E.g. fungi like bread moulds, yeast, mushrooms etc.
- **Parasites:** Derive nutrition from plants or animals without killing them. E.g. cuscuta (amar-bel), ticks, lice, leeches, tape-worms etc.
- **Holozoic nutrition :** These organisms take in whole material & break it down inside their bodies. E.g. cow, deer, lion, tiger, humans etc. What can be taken in and broken down depends on the body design and functioning.

### Respiration

It is the process by which organism uses the food materi... produce energy. Diverse organisms do this in different ways:

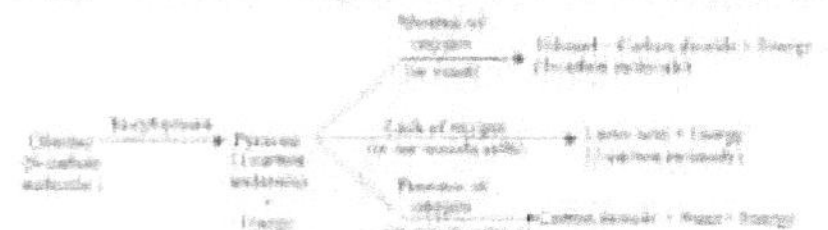

Energy released during cellular respiration is immediately use... synthesise ATP which is used to fuel all other activities in the... Aerobic organisms need to ensure that there is sufficient intak... oxygen:
- **Plants:** Exchange of gases takes place through stomat... simple diffusion. Large inter-cellular spaces ensure tha... cells are in contact with air. Direction of diffusion dep... upon the environmental conditions and the requirements o... plant. For e.g. $CO_2$ elimination majorly takes place at r... while oxygen release is the major event of the day time.
- **Aquatic animals** such as fishes take in water through... mouths & force it past the gills where the dissolved oxyg... taken up by blood.
- **In human beings,** passage of air can be written as nos... trachea→ bronchi→ bronchioles→ alveolar sac. The al... provide a surface where the exchange of gases can take p... Blood releases the dissolved $CO_2$ into the alveoli & carrie... from alveolar air. Haemoglobin in RBC of blood transpo... from lungs to various tissues of the body.

### LIFE PROCESS

The processes which maintain the body functions and are required for the survival of living being are called life processes. Some of the important life processes are nutrition, respiration, transportation, excretion etc.

### Nutrition In Human Beings

The alimentary canal is a long tube extending from the mouth to the anus. The nutrition in human being is divided into ... steps:
- **Ingestion:** Intake of food from outside source. Teeth & saliva crush the food to generate the particles of same size... texture. The food is then passed to stomach via oesophagus. The peristaltic movements occur all along the gut which he... in pushing the food forward.
- **Digestion:** In mouth, salivary amylase helps in carbohydrates digestion. In stomach, pepsin helps in protein digesti... However, small intestine is the main site of complete digestion of carbohydrates, proteins & fats. It receives pancreas ... liver secretions. Bile juice emulsifies fats and pancreatic enzymes, trypsin & lipases digest proteins & emulsified fats ... finally converts proteins to amino acids, complex carbohydrates into glucose & fats into fatty acids & glycerol.
- **Absorption:** The digested food is taken up by the walls of the intestine. The inner lining of the small intestine ... numerous finger-like projections called villi which increase the surface area for absorption. Large intestine absorbs wa... from the unabsorbed food.
- **Assimilation:** The villi are richly supplied with blood vessels which take the absorbed food to each & every cell of ... body, where it is required either for energy, build up or repair.
- **Excretion:** The waste material is removed from the body via anus which is regulated by anal sphincter.

# MAP-6

## Transportation
### Transportation in Human Beings

- **Blood** consists of fluid medium called plasma in which the cells are suspended. Plasma transports food, CO, & nitrogenous wastes in dissolved form. Oxygen is carried by RBC.
- **Heart:** Heart is the muscular organ made up of cardiac muscles and is as big as our fist. It is composed of four chambers (2 atria & 2 ventricles) to prevent the mixing of oxygenated & deoxygenated blood.
  - Ventricles are thick walled as they have to pump the blood to various organs of the body. In addition, valves are also present in heart and veins to prevent the backflow of the blood.
- **Circulation of blood:** Oxygenated blood is carried out from lungs to the left atrium with the help of pulmonary veins.
  - Left atrium contracts to release blood into the left ventricle which relaxes while collecting it. It then pumped out the blood to whole body via aorta.
  - Deoxygenated blood from whole body then enters the right atrium via vena cava vein.
  - Right atrium contracts to pump the blood in right ventricle. It then pumps the blood towards lungs via pulmonary artery for oxygenation.
- **Oxygenation of blood:** In vertebrates such as birds, mammals etc which constantly use energy to maintain their body temperature, blood goes through heart twice during each cycle which is known as **double circulation**.
  - In contrast, animals like amphibians or many reptiles have **three-chambered hearts** as they can tolerate some mixing of the oxygenated & de-oxygenated blood streams. They do not use energy for thermoregulation and body temperature depends on the temperature in the environment.
  - Fishes, on other hand, have only two chambered heart. Blood is pumped to the gills for oxygenation and passes directly to the rest of the body.

## Transportation In Plants

There are two main pathways present in plants: xylem pathway- moves water & minerals from the soil & phloem transports products of photosynthesis from leaves (where they are synthesized) to other parts of the plant.

**Transport of Water**

- In xylem tissue, vessels and tracheids of roots, stems & leaves are interconnected to form a continuous system of water-conducting channels reaching all parts of the plant.
- At root site, cells actively take up ions from soil which creates concentration gradient. Water then **diffuses** into the root cells in order to eliminate this gradient.
- It provides steady movement of water into root xylem, creating a column of water that is steadily pushed upwards.
- However, it is not efficient enough to push water over the heights of tall plants.
- So, plants use other method which is known as **transpiration** to push water upwards. The loss of water in the form of vapour from aerial parts of plant is known as transpiration.
- Evaporation of water molecules from the cells of a leaf creates a suction which pulls water from the xylem cells of roots. It also aids in **thermoregulation**.

- **Transport of food and other substances**
- Transport of soluble products of photosynthesis is called **translocation**.
- The translocation takes place in sieve tubes with the help of adjacent companion cells both in upward & downward directions.
- It utilizes energy (ATP) in contrast to xylem transport.
- Material like sucrose is transferred into phloem tissue using energy from ATP.
- It increases osmotic pressure of tissue causing water to move into it.
- This pressure moves the material in phloem to tissues which have less pressure.
- It allows phloem to move material according to plant's needs.

## Excretion

The biological process involved in removal of harmful metabolic wastes from body is called excretion.
Many unicellular organisms remove these wastes by simple diffusion from body surface into surrounding water. However, complex multi-cellular organisms use specialised organs to perform this function.
**Excretion in Human Beings:** The excretory system includes pair of kidneys, pair of ureters, urinary bladder & urethra.
- **Nephrons** are the functional units of kidneys. They are the clusters of thin-walled capillaries. Each cluster is associated with cup-shaped end (Bowmans capsule) of a tube that collects the filtered urine.
- Substance such as glucose, amino acids, salts & a major amount of water are selectively re-absorbed as the urine flows along the tube. The amount of water depends up on amount of excess water & dissolved waste in the body.
- The urine formed in each kidney is carried to urinary bladder by ureter. Urine is stored in urinary bladder until the pressure of the expanded bladder leads to the urge to pass it out through the urethra.
- **Excretion in Plants:** They get rid of excess water by transpiration.
- Many plant waste products are stored in cellular vacuoles.
- Waste products may be stored in leaves that fall off.
- In addition, some waste products are stored as resins & gums, especially in old xylem.
- Lastly, plants excrete some waste substances into the soil around them.

## CONTROL AND COORDINATION

Coordination is the process through which two or more organs interact and complement the functions of one another. The neural system & endocrine system jointly coordinate & regulate the physiological functions in the body. The neural system provides an organised network of point-to-point connections for a quick coordination. The endocrine system provides chemical integration through hormones.

### • Structure and Function of Neuron

- It is a structural & functional unit of neural system and is composed of three major parts:
- **Cell body** contains cytoplasm with typical cell organelles like nucleus etc.
- **Dendrites**: Short fibres which branch repeatedly & project out of the cell body. These fibres transmit impulses towards the cell body.
- **Axon** is a long fibre, the distal end of which is branched and forms nerve ending. Nerve endings possess synaptic vesicles containing chemicals called **neurotransmitters**.

### Transmission of impulses:

- **Stimulus** or information from the environment is detected by specialized tips of some nerve cells called as **receptors**.
- Dendritic tip acquire all these information and sets off a chemical reaction.
- This chemical reaction then creates an electric impulse that travels from the dendrite to the cell body, and then along the axon to its end.
- At the end of the axon, the electrical impulse sets off the release of some chemicals (**neurotransmitters**). These chemicals cross the gap, or **synapse**, and start a similar electrical impulse in a dendrite of the next neuron.
- A similar synapse finally allows delivery of such impulses from neurons to other cells, such as muscles cells or gland.

### Reflex Action

- The entire process of response to a peripheral nervous stimulation that occurs involuntarily (without conscious effort or thought) and requires involvement of a part of central nervous system is called a reflex action.
- Reflex action decreases the duration of action by bypassing the thinking and processing step.
- It does so by linking the nerves carrying the signal (say sensation of heat) directly to the nerves that move the muscle. These types of linkage or connection between input and output nerves are formed in the spinal cord.
- These connections are called as reflex arc (sensory/input nerve→ Spinal cord → motor/ output nerve)

### Animal Nervous System

The neural system of all animals is composed of hi specialized cells called neurons which can detect, recei transmit different kinds of stimuli. They are specialize conducting information via electrical impulses from one of the body to another.

**The human neural system is divided into two part**

- **Central neural system** (CNS) includes the brai spinal cord and is the site of information processin control.
- **Peripheral neural system** (PNS) comprises of nerves of body associated with CNS (brain and sp cord). The nerve fibres of PNS are of two types: **cra nerves** (arising from the brain) and **spinal ne** (arising from the spinal cord).

### Brain

- It is the **main coordinating centre** of the body. The b and spinal cord constitute the **CNS**. They rec information from all parts of the body and integrate it
- The brain is located in bony box called as **craniu** skull which protects the brain. Spinal cord is prote with the help of **vertebral column**. In addit **cerebrospinal fluid** also covers the brain and the s cord which provide the function of shock absorption.
- The brain has three such major parts or regions, na the fore-brain, mid-brain and hind-brain.
- **Fore-brain**: It is the main thinking part of the brai consists of cerebrum, hypothalamus etc.
  - **Function**: interpret information received f sensory receptors.
  - Control the movement of voluntary muscles.
  - It also contains centre associated with hunger w gives us the sensation of feeling full.
- **Midbrain**: It serves important function in involuntary movements, movements of the eye, audi and visual processing.
- **Hindbrain**: It consists of pons, medulla, and cerebel
  - **Function**: Medulla controls involuntary actions as blood pressure, salivation and vomiting.
  - Cerebellum is responsible for precision of volur actions and maintaining the posture and balance o body.

# MAP-7

## Coordination In Plants

Plants have neither nervous system nor muscles. Their movements or responses are either growth dependent or growth independent.

## Hormones In Animals

Hormones are non-nutrient chemicals which act as intercellular messengers & are produced in trace amounts. The timing and amount of hormone released are regulated by feedback mechanisms Examples:
- **Adrenaline**: Secreted from adrenal gland which prepare the body for fight or flight situation.
- **Thyroxin**: Secreted from thyroid gland and regulates carbohydrate, protein and fat metabolism so as to provide the best balance for growth.
  Deficiency of iodine in diet may cause hypo-secretion of thyroxin which results in goiter.
- **Growth hormones** which regulate growth and development of the body are secreted from pituitary gland.
  Hyper-secretion may cause gigantism and hypo-secretion may cause dwarfism.
- **Testosterone** in males and **oestrogen** in females lead to changes take place during puberty.
- **Insulin** produced by pancreas regulates the blood sugar level in the body.

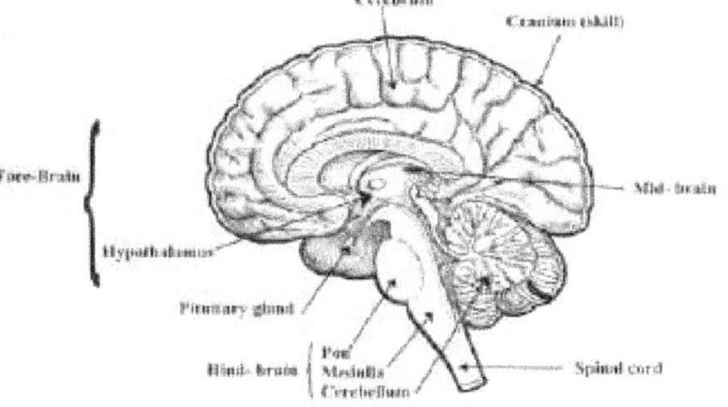


## Immediate Response To Stimulus Or Growth Independent

- The plants also use electrical-chemical means to convey information from cell to cell, but unlike in animals, there is no specialised tissue in plants for the conduction of information.
- Secondly, plant cells change shape by changing the amount of water in them, resulting in swelling or shrinking. In contrast, animal muscle cells have special proteins that change both their shape and their arrangement in the cell in response to nervous electrical impulses.
- Example: folding up and drooping of leaves of *chhui-mui* (the 'sensitive' or 'touch-me-not' plant of the Mimosa family) in response to touch.

## Movement Due To Growth

- The movement of a plant in response to the stimulus is called as **tropism**. The movement in the direction of the response is called as positive tropism and movement away from the stimulus is termed as negative tropism.
- **Types:**
  - **Phototropism**: Bending of plant in response to the light e.g. movement of sunflowers in response to day or night.
  - **Geotropism**: Movement of plant in response to gravity. Shoots show negative geotropism and roots show positive geotropism.
  - **Chemotropism**: Movement of plant in response to chemical as observed in case of growth of pollen tube.
  - **Hydrotropism**: e.g. roots beneath the Earth's surface bend in the direction of underground water.
- Other example may include the climbing of tendrils in response to touch. When they come in contact with any support, the part of the tendril in contact with the object does not grow as rapidly as the part of the tendril away from the object. This causes the tendril to circle around the object and thus cling to it.

## Plant Hormones

There are five main types of plant hormones or growth regulators:
- **Auxins**: Helps in cell elongation and thus phototropism, geotropism, and other plant responses.
- **Gibberellins**: Stimulate growth of the stem and flowering.
- **Cytokinins**: They cause cell division, enlargement, and organ formation. They are present in greater concentration in areas of rapid cell division, such as in fruits and seeds.
- **Ethylene**: Promotes ripening of fruits.
- **Abscisic acid**: Inhibits growth and causes wilting of leaves and fruits.

# MIND

## HOW DO ORGANISMS REPRODUCE?

- Reproduction is a biological process in which an organism gives rise to young ones similar to themselves.
- Basic event in reproduction is the creation of a DNA copy.
- Cells use chemical reactions to build two copies of the DNA in a reproducing cell.
- In addition, DNA copying is accompanied by the creation of an additional cellular apparatus.
- Then each DNA copy is separated with its own cellular apparatus.
- Effectively, a cell divides to give rise to two cells.

### Fission

- Organisms divide mitotically into two halves, each behaves like independent individual. It is termed as binary fission and is mostly shown by bacteria and protozoa.
- **Binary fission** can take place in any plane as observed in *Amoeba*, or it can occur in a definite orientation for e.g. *Leishmania* (causes kala-azar), *Euglena* (longitudinal), *Paramecium* (transverse) etc.
- In few organisms parent cell divides into many daughter cells simultaneously which is termed as **multiple fission**. It is observed in *Plasmodium*.

### Budding

- Formation of daughter organism takes place from a small projection called as **bud.** For e.g. *Hydra*, Yeast etc
- Organisms such as *Hydra* use regenerative cells for reproduction in the process of budding.
- Repeated cell division at one specific site leads to the formation of an outgrowth called as bud.
- These buds develop into tiny individuals and detach form parent body once they become fully mature.
- Detached organism acts as an independent organism.

### Vegetative Propagation

- It refers to the formation of new plants from parts of parent plants such as root, stem, leave etc. These parts are termed as vegetative units or vegetative propagules. For e.g. buds produced in the notches along the leaf margin of *Bryophyllum* fall on the soil and develop into new plants
- **Advantages of vegetative propagation:**
  - Vegetative propagation is used in methods such as layering, cutting, grafting to grow many plants like sugarcane, roses, or grapes for agricultural purposes.
  - Plants raised by vegetative propagation can bear flowers and fruits earlier than those produced from seeds.
  - It makes it possible to propagate plants that have lost the capacity to produce seeds such as banana, orange, rose and jasmine.
  - Plants produced are genetically similar enough to the parent plant to have all its characteristics.

### Asexual Reproduction

When offspring is produced by single parent with or without the involvement of gamete formation

### Fragmentation

- Parent organism breaks into smaller fragment upon maturation, each fragment grows into new individual.
- It is shown by multi-cellular organisms with simple body organization for e.g. *Spirogyra*

### Regeneration

- It is an ability of simple organisms to re-grow their lost body parts.
- In asexual reproduction, this ability is used by many organisms to give rise to new individual from their body parts. That is, if the individual is somehow cut or broken up into many pieces, many of these pieces grow into separate individuals.
- For e.g. *Hydra* and *Planaria*
- It is carried out by specialised cells which proliferate & differentiate to make various cell types & tissues.
- These changes take place in an organized sequence referred to as development.
- However, regeneration is not the same as reproduction, since most organisms would not normally depend on being cut up to be able to reproduce.

### Spore Formation

- An individual divides into no. of small spores each spore giving rise to new individual.
- Spores are covered by thick walls that protect them until they come into contact with moist surface or suitable environment and can begin to grow. E.g. Spore formation in *Rhizopus*

### Menstruation

Menstrual cycle is a cyclic event that place roughly every month in females after puberty. Unfertilized egg lives for 1 day after which it degenerates. Consequently, uterus lining slowly breaks & comes out through the vagina as blood & mucous. This discharge is known as menstruation which lasts for about 2-8 days.

# MAP-8

## Sexual Reproduction

involves the formation and fusion of the gametes. leads to formation of variations in individuals. variations form the basis of evolution of the species and ensure the survival of the species.

## Reproduction in Human Beings

**Puberty**: The period during which adolescents reach sexual maturity and become capable of reproduction.

**Changes in girls during puberty:** breast size begins to increase, darkening of skin of nipples, & girls begin to menstruate.

**Changes in boy during puberty:** hair growth on face, voices begin to crack & occasional erection & enlargement of penis

**Changes common to both boys & girls:** hair growth in various parts such as armpits, genital area, thin hairs on arms & legs and skin may become oily.

## Female Reproductive System

It consists of a pair of ovaries, pair of oviduct (fallopian tube), uterus, cervix, & vagina.

One egg is produced every month by one of the ovaries after reaching the age of puberty. The egg is carried from the ovary to the womb through a thin oviduct or fallopian tube.

Uterus serves as womb and is richly supplied with blood vessels to nurture the developing embryo.

Vagina serves as the site of entry of sperm during sexual intercourse.

## Events of Reproduction

The sperms after entering the vaginal passage travel upwards and reach the oviduct where they may fertilize the egg.

Post-fertilization, the zygote gets implanted in the lining of the uterus, and starts dividing.

Special tissue called placenta is developed to provide nutrition to the developing embryo as well as for removing waste from it.

The development of a child takes up approx. nine months.

The child is born as a result of rhythmic contractions of the muscles in the uterus.

## Sexual Reproduction in Flowering Plants

- **Stamens** and **carpels** are the reproductive parts of a flower which contain the germ-cells. Stamen is the male reproductive part and it produces pollen grains. Carpel is the female reproductive part made up of three parts: ovary, style and stigma.
- The ovary contains ovules and each ovule has an egg cell.
- The flower may be unisexual i.e. contains either stamens or carpels e.g. papaya, watermelon or **bisexual** i.e. contains both stamens and carpels e.g. *Hibiscus*, mustard.
- Transfer of pollen grains (shed from the anther) to the stigma of a pistil is termed **pollination**. Two types: self-pollination and cross pollination. Pollinating agents are air, water, insects, & animals.
- Compatible pollen grain germinates on stigma to produce **pollen tube**. Pollen tube grows through tissues of stigma, style & reaches ovary.
- Fertilization results in the formation of **zygote** which develops into an **embryo**.
- The ovule develops a tough coat and is gradually converted into a **seed**. The ovary grows rapidly and ripens to form a **fruit**.
- The petals, sepals, stamens, style and stigma may shrivel and fall off.
- The seed develops into a seedling under appropriate conditions which is known as **germination**.

## Male Reproductive System

- It consists of a pair of **testes** located outside the body in a pouch called **scrotum**. It helps in maintaining lower temperature which favors the perm formation. Testes are responsible for synthesizing **sperms** and **testosterone**.
- Sperms are tiny bodies consists of mainly genetic material and a tail that helps them to move towards the female germ-cell.
- Sperms are then delivered through **vas deferens** which unites with urethra to form a common passage for sperm and urine.
- **Accessory glands** like seminal vesicles, prostate, and bulbourethral add their secretion to sperm. It makes the sperm fluid in nature that not only eases the transportation of sperm but also provide the nutrition to it.

## Reproductive Health

- Sexually transmitted diseases include bacterial infections (gonorrhea, syphilis etc) & viral infections (warts, AIDS etc).
- Contraception refers to the act of preventing the unwanted pregnancies. Contraceptive methods may fall in following categories:
  - **Mechanical barrier**: e.g. condom, diaphragms. They also prevent STDs.
  - **Oral contraceptives**: they change hormonal balance, inhibits ovulation & thus fertilization e.g. saheli, iPill, etc.
  - **Intra uterine device**: plastic or metal devices placed in the uterus for e.g. loop, copper-T etc.
  - **Surgical methods** such as vasectomy & tubectomey.

# MIND

## HEREDITY AND EVOLUTION

### Accumulation Of Variation During Reproduction

- Characters or features or traits are inherited from one generation to the next during reproduction.
- This inheritance provides both a common basic body design & subtle changes in it for next generation.
- When this generation reproduces, the offspring would have differences they inherit from previous generation as well as newly created differences.
- Accumulation of these differences generation after generation leads to the development of variations in a population.
- Different variations provide different advantages to the population and the variation which provide best survival advantages are inherited to the next generation.
- For e.g. bacteria having variation to tolerate heat will survive and multiply better in heat wave.

**Experiment 2:** He crossed the plant with two different characteristics such as tall plant with round seed and short plant with wrinkled seed. Other example may include round & green seeds (RRyy) and wrinkled & yellow seeds (rrYY).
**Observation:** $F_1$ generation; all were tall & round i.e. tall & round are dominant.
$F_2$ generation; tall plants with round seeds, tall with wrinkled seeds, short with round seeds, and short plants with wrinkled seeds in 9:3:3:1.
Similarly, round & yellow, round & green, wrinkled & yellow, and wrinkled & green in 9:3:3:1.
**Inference:** The tall/short trait and the round seed/wrinkled seed trait are independently inherited.
**Conclusion:** It formulated the law of independent assortment which states that genes of different characters located in different pairs of chromosomes are independent of one another in their segregation during gamete formation.

### Sex Determination

Different species use different strategies for this:
- Environment: for e.g. the temperature at which fertilised eggs are kept determines the sex of developing animals in the eggs. It is observed in animals like crocodile, turtle etc.
- Snails can change sex, indicating that sex is not genetically determined.
- Sex of an individual is genetically determined for e.g. humans.
  - Humans have 22 autosomal & 1 sex chromosome pairs. Females have XX & males have XY. Hence, sex of a child is determined by what he/she has inherited (X or Y) from the father since, child will always inherit X from the mother. If X is inherited from father then child will be a girl & if Y is inherited then a child will be a boy.

### Heredity

Heredity refers to the transmission of characteristi from parent to offspring by means of genes in th chromosomes.

**Mendel's Contributions**
- Mendel was the first scientist whose studies lea to the formulation of laws of inheritance.
- He conducted cross hybridization experimen of garden pea plant (Pisum sativum) and studi the transmission of characters that had tw contrasting traits such as round/wrinkled seed tall/short plants, white/violet flowers etc.

**Experiment 1:** He cross pollinate pure breeds of ta (TT) & dwarf (tt) pea plant and calculated t percentages of tall & dwarf progeny.
**Observation:** $F_1$ generation was tall (Tt) with halfway characteristics.
$F_2$ generation produced by self pollination of included tall and short plants in 3:1. (Genotypic ra 1:2:1 for TT:Tt:tt)
**Inference:** This indicates that both the tallness shortness traits were inherited in the $F_1$ plants, b only the tallness trait was expressed.
Thus, two copies of the trait are inherited in ea sexually reproducing organism. These two may identical (TT or tt), or may be different (T depending on the parentage.
**Conclusion:** This study leaded to the formulatic of two laws:
Law of dominance: states that only or character expresses itself in $F_1$ generation.
Law of segregation: states that the two alleles a character in an individual get separated segregated during gamete formation ar distributed randomly in gametes.

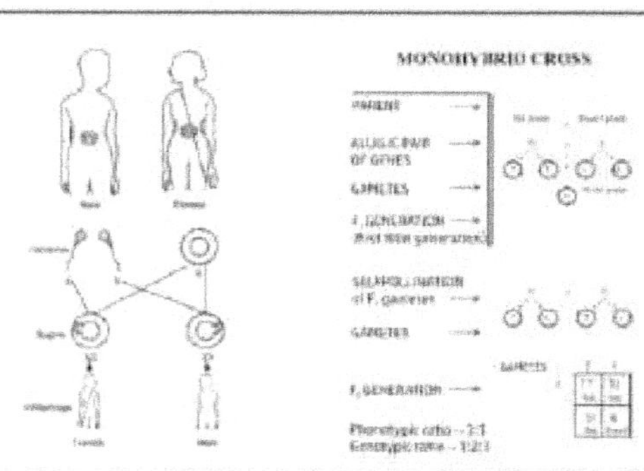

# MAP-9

## Evolution

- It refers to gradual change in the characteristics of the population (plants & animals) over successive generations.
- Errors in DNA copying during reproduction, mutations, & natural selection account for the evolution.
- Evolution gives rise to such a biodiversity at each level of biological organization such as at species level, among individuals, molecules etc.

## Evolution And Classification

- Classification is the process by which organisms are grouped into convenient categories based on some easily observable characters.
- Characters such as cell type (prokaryote or eukaryote), single cell or multi cellular, presence or absence of nucleus, autotrophic (such as photosynthesis) or heterotrophic, sexual or asexual reproduction etc. are used to classify different organisms in different groups.
- The more characteristics two species will have in common, the more closely they are related. And the more closely they are related, the more recently they will have had a common ancestor. For e.g. brother & sister are more closely related than a girl & her first cousin. Therefore, classification of species gives a reflection of their evolutionary relationship.

## Tracing Evolutionary Relationships

Few evidences which help us to trace evolutionary relationships among different organisms or species:
- **Comparative anatomy and morphology**: study of similarities & differences among organisms to understand the common ancestry.
  - **Homologous**: Similar structure different functions. It indicates common ancestry for e.g. bones of forelimbs in frog, lizard, bird & human.
  - **Analogous**: Similar functions but different structure. Different structures evolved for same function & hence having similarity. For e.g. wings of bats & birds, eye of octopus & mammals, etc.
- **Fossils**: Remains of hard parts of life-forms found in rocks. They represent extinct organisms (e.g.. Dinosaurs).
  - The age of the fossils can be estimated by two ways; relative depth of the fossils, dating fossils i.e. detection of ratios of different isotopes of the same element in the fossil material

## Speciation

- It refers to a gradual evolutionary process by which populations evolve to become different species.
- Reproductive and geographical isolation play an important role in the process of speciation. They result in change in the frequency of an existing gene variant in a population i.e. genetic drift.
- Over generations, genetic drift along with natural selection results in the formation of new species.
- Other factors that may result in speciation are sudden severe DNA changes (mutation) such as change in chromosomal no., variation such as female green beetle will not mate with red males. Her behavior ensures the reproductive isolation between them and thus results in generation of new species.

## Evolution Should Not Be Equated With 'progress'

- Evolution is simply the generation of diversity & shaping of diversity by environmental selection.
- The only progressive trend in evolution seems to be the emergence of more and more complex body designs over time. However, that doesn't mean that the older designs are inefficient.
- For e.g. simplest life forms; bacteria inhabits the most inhospitable habitats like hot springs, deep-sea thermal vents & ice in Antarctica.

## Human Evolution

- Tolls like excavating, time-dating and studying fossils, determining DNA sequences etc have been used for studying human evolution.
- All humans are a single species regardless of skin color or human races.
- The earliest members of the human species, *Homo sapiens*, can be traced back to Africa i.e. we all come from Africa.
- A couple of hundred thousand years ago, some of our ancestors left Africa while others stayed on.
- The migrants slowly spread across the planet; from Africa to West Asia, then to Central Asia, Eurasia, South Asia, & East Asia.
- They travelled down the islands of Indonesia and the Philippines to Australia, and they crossed the Bering land bridge to the Americas.

# MIND

**Snell's law** $\mu = \dfrac{sin\, i}{sin\, r}$

For two media

$$_1\mu_2 = \dfrac{\mu_2}{\mu_1} = \dfrac{sin\, i}{sin\, r}$$

---

**Necessary conditions for TIR**
(i) Ray of light must travel from denser to rarer medium

(ii) $\angle i > \angle c$ for two media

**Critical angle (c)** Angle $i$ in denser medium for which angle of refraction in rarer medium is 90°   $\mu = \dfrac{1}{sin\, C}$

---

### Laws of Reflection

• The incident ray the normal and the reflected ray all lie in the same plane

• The angle of incidence (i) is always equal to angle of reflection (r) i.e., $\angle i = \angle r$

---

**Mirror formula** $\dfrac{1}{f} = \dfrac{1}{u} + \dfrac{1}{v}$

When two plane mirrors are held at an angle $\theta$ with their reflecting surfaces facing each other and an object is placed between them, images are formed by successive reflections.

$f_{concave}$ = negative

$f_{convex}$ = positive

and $f_{plane} = \infty$

---

**Relation between focal length (f) and radius of curvature, R**

$$f = \dfrac{R}{2}$$

---

### Magnification

$$m = \dfrac{v}{u} = \dfrac{\text{height of image}}{\text{height of object}}$$

$$m = \dfrac{f}{f-u} = \dfrac{f-v}{f}$$

---

The incident ray, the normal and the refracted ray all lie in the same plane

---

Refractive index,

$$\mu = \dfrac{c}{v} = \dfrac{\text{real depth}}{\text{apparent depth}}$$

---

**Total internal Reflection :** Ray totally reflected back to denser medium

**Phenomena based on TIR**
• Mirage - optical illusion in deserts
• Looming - optical illusion in cold countries
• Optical fibre
• Brilliance of diamond

---

**Reflection of light :** Turning back of light in the same medium after striking the reflecting surface or mirror
• After reflection, velocity, frequency and wavelength of light remains same but intensity decreases
• If reflection takes place from denser medium then phase change '$\pi$'

---

### Laws of Refraction

**Refraction of light :** Bending of light ray while passing from one medium to another medium
• A ray of light bends towards the normal, while going from rarer to denser medium
• And bends away from the normal while going from denser to rarer medium
• Refraction of light takes place because the speed of light is different in the two media

---

## LIGHT
### REFLECTION & REFRACTION

Form of energy produces the sensation of vision in eyes. Light (EM waves wave-length 400 nm to 750 nm). The path of light (always travel in straight line) is ray of light

---

**Regular Reflection**
Reflection on smooth surface.

**Diffuse Reflection**
Reflection on rough surface.

---

### Characteristics of Light

---

**Plane Mirror**
Is a looking glass, highly polished on one surface.

→ Forms virtual and erect image

→ Distance of object from mirror = distance of image from mirror.

→ The size of the image is same as object.

→ Image is laterally inverted.

→ Used in kaleidoscope periscope, etc.

---

**Concave Mirror**
Spherical glass polished on the outside. It is also known as converging mirror.

→ Images produced are always real, inverted, can be enlarged based on the position except when object is placed between pole and focus.

→ Uses: Make-up and shaving mirrors, dentist mirror, in floodlight etc.

---

**Convex Mirror**
Spherical glass polished inside. It is also known as diverging mirror.

→ It forms virtual, upright and small images.

→ Uses: for security purposes, in vehicles as rear-view mirror and street lighting.

# MAP-10

### Atmospheric Refraction

Earth's atmosphere is thin at the top and dense at the bottom, thus leads to refraction of light.
$$\mu = c/v$$

- Twinking of stars
- Rainbow
- Advanced sunrise and delayed sunset

### Refraction Through a Glass Slab

$$x = \frac{t \sin(i-r)}{\cos r}$$
$$\therefore \quad x \propto \mu.$$

Lens formula $\dfrac{1}{f} = \dfrac{1}{v} - \dfrac{1}{u}$

$f_{concave}$ = negative
$f_{convex}$ = positive
and $f_{plane} = \infty$

### Power of a lens

$$P = \frac{1}{f(\text{in metre})}$$

Unit of power of lens is diopter (D)

$P_{convex} \rightarrow$ Positve
$P_{concave} \rightarrow$ Negative
and $P_{plane} \rightarrow$ Zero

### Concave Lens

Cental portion of lens is thinner than marginal. It as also known as diverging lens.

### Convex Lens

Central portion of lens is thicker than marginal. It is also known us converging lens.

### Lens

Piece of transparent material with two refracting surfaces, at least one is curved and refractive index should different as that of the surrounding.

### Magnification

Ratio of distance of image to the distance of object from the optical centre. Also equal to height of image to the height of object

$$m = \frac{1}{o} = \frac{v}{u} = \frac{h_1}{h_o}$$

### Nature, position and relative size of the image formed by a convex lens for various positions of the object

| Position of the object | Position of the image | Relative size of the image | Nature of the image |
|---|---|---|---|
| At infinity | At focus $F_2$ | Highly -diminished, point-sized | Real and inverted |
| Beyond $2F_1$ | Between $F_2$ and $2F_2$ | Diminished | Real and inverted |
| At $2F_1$ | At $2F_2$ | Same size | Real and inverted |
| Between $F_1$ and $2F_1$ | Beyond $2F_2$ | Enlarged | Real and inverted |
| At Focus $F_1$ | At infinity | Infinitely large or highly enlarged | Real and inverted |
| Between $F_1$ and Optical centre O | On the same side of the lens as the object | Enlarged | Virtual and erect |

### Nature, position and relative size of the image formed by a concave lens for various position of the object

| Position of the object | Position of the image | Relative size of the image | Nature of the |
|---|---|---|---|
| At infinity | At focus $F_1$ | Highly -diminished, point-sized | Virtual and erect |
| Between infinity and Optical centre O of the lens | Between $F_1$ and Optical centre O | Diminished | Virtual and erect |

- Rectilinear propagation of light
- Light travels with a speed of $3 \times 10^8$ m/s in air/vacuum.
- Speed of light depends on the medium.
- Light shows behaviour such as reflection, refraction, interference, diffraction, polarisation etc.

### Image formation by a convex mirror for different positions of the object

| "Position of the object" | "Position of the image" | "Size of the image" | "Nature of the image" |
|---|---|---|---|
| Anywhere between pole (P) and infinity ($\infty$) | Between P and F back of the mirror | Small | Virtual and erect |
| At infinity | At F | Very small in size | Virtual and erect |

### Image formation by a concave mirror for different positions of the object

| "Position of the object" | "Position of the image" | "Size of the image" | "Nature of the image" |
|---|---|---|---|
| At infinity | At the focus F | Highly -diminished, point-sized | Real and inverted |
| Beyond C | Between F and C | Diminished | Real and inverted |
| At C | At C | Same size | Real and inverted |
| B/W C and F | Beyond C | Enlarged | Real and inverted |
| At F | At infinity | Highly enlarged | Real and inverted |
| B/W P and F | Behind the mirror | Enlarged | Virtual and erect |

**MIND**

## THE HUMAN EYE AND THE COLOURFUL WORLD

### Human Eye

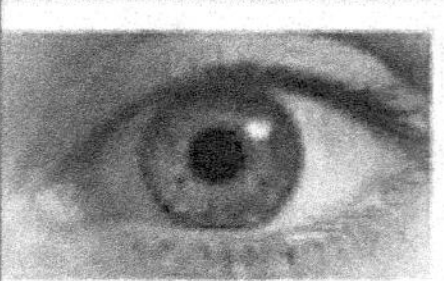

The organ which gives us the sense of light or enables us to see. It interprets the shapes, colours and dimensions of the object

### Power of Accomodation

The ability of the eye lens to adjust its focal length so as to see the objects clearly located anywhere. Near point of the human eye is 25 cm and far point of the human eye is infinity.

| Object | Ciliary muscles | Suspensory ligaments | Muscle tension on lens | Lens shape |
|---|---|---|---|---|
| Near | Contract | Slackened | Low | Thick |
| Distant | Relax | Stretched | High | Thin |

---

### Parts of the Human Eye

### Defects of Human Eye

---

**Retina** : It is a light sensitive screen on which image is formed.
It contains rods sensitive to intensity of light and cones sensitive to colour.

**Cornea** : Thin membrane acts like a lens which allow light to enter the eye.

**Sclera** : Outer part of the eye, protects interior of the eye.

**Eye Lens** : Convex lens made of transparent, crystalline and flexible jelly like material.
Refractive index of eye lens is 1.437

**Ciliary Muscles :**
Modify the shape of eye lens.

**Pupil** : Hole in the middle of iris through which light enters.

**Iris :** Controls the amount of light entering the eye by changing the size of pupil.

**Optical Nerve** : Nerves take the image to the brain in the form of electrical signals.

---

**Myopia or Short Sightedness:** can see nearby objects but cannot see far off objects distinctly. Corrected by using concave lens.

**Hypermetropia or Long Sightedness :** can see far off objects clearly but cannot see nearby objects clearly. Corrected by convex lens

**Presbyopia:** It is due to lessening of flexibility of the crystalline lens and weakening of ciliary muscles. Corrected by using bifocal lenses.

**Astigmatism:** Refractive problem responsible for blurry vision. Corrected by using cylindrical lenses.

**Cataract:** It is a clouding of the lens in the eye. Corrected using cataract surgery

---

### Persistence of Vision
Image of any object seen persists on the retina for 1/16 second even after the removal of the object. This property is used in cinematography

### Reason for Myopia
- Excessive curvature of cornea
- Elongation of eye-ball

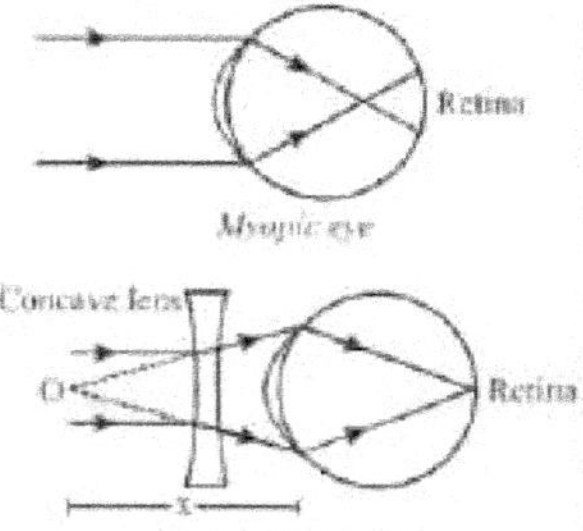


### Reason for Hypermetropia
- Increase in focal length of eye lens
- Shortening of eye-ball

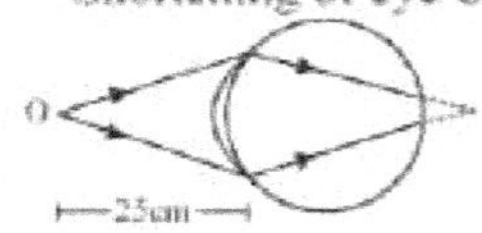


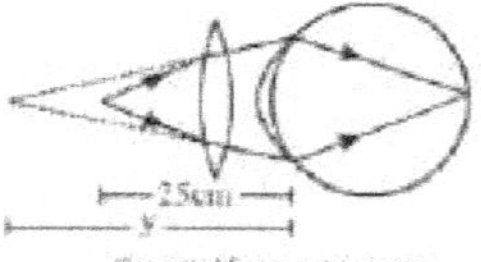

# MAP-11

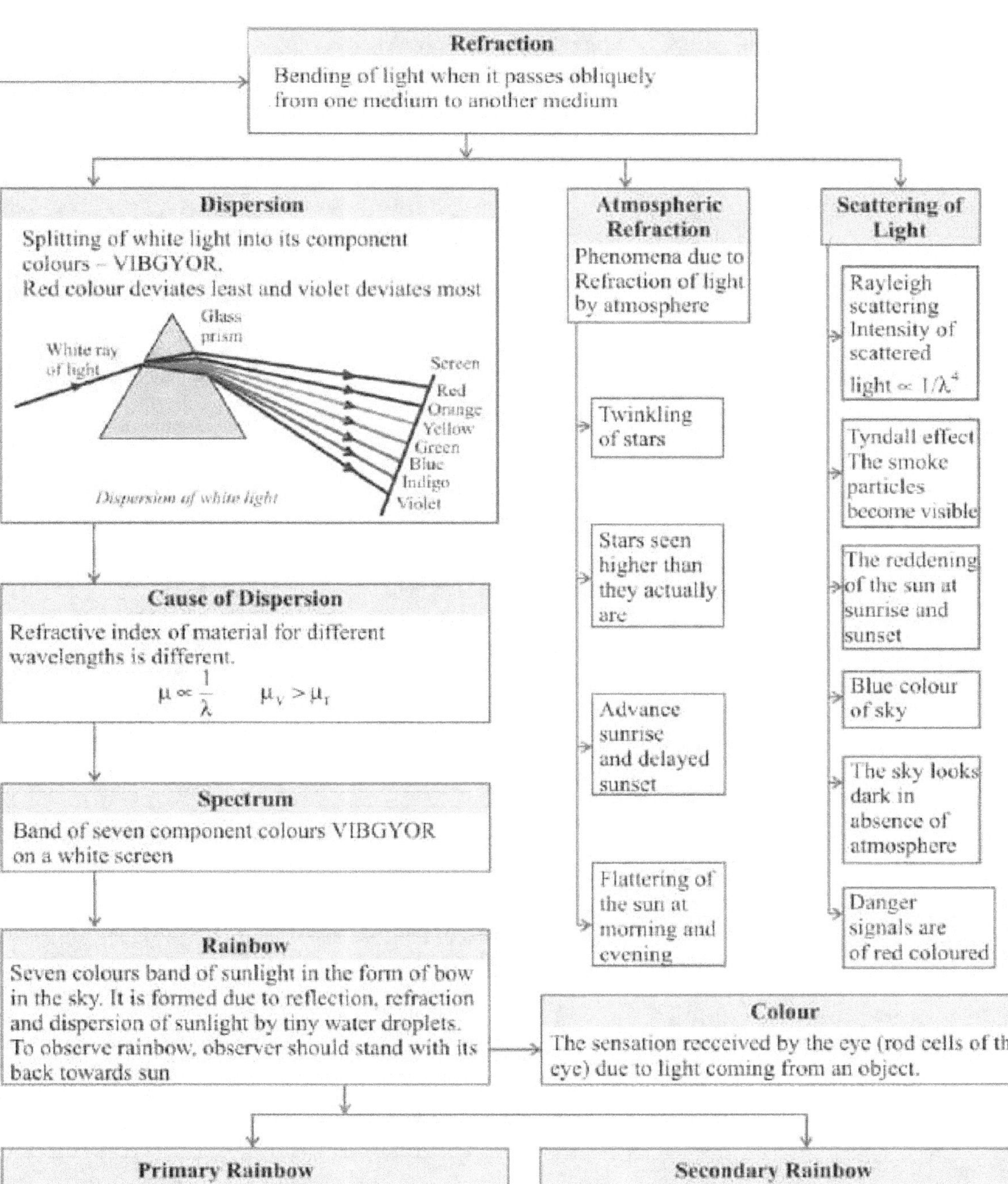

Refraction
Bending of light when it passes obliquely from one medium to another medium

Dispersion
Splitting of white light into its component colours – VIBGYOR.
Red colour deviates least and violet deviates most
Glass prism
White ray of light
Screen
Red
Orange
Yellow
Green
Blue
Indigo
Violet
Dispersion of white light

Atmospheric Refraction
Phenomena due to Refraction of light by atmosphere
Twinkling of stars
Stars seen higher than they actually are
Advance sunrise and delayed sunset
Flattering of the sun at morning and evening

Scattering of Light
Rayleigh scattering Intensity of scattered light $\propto 1/\lambda^4$
Tyndall effect The smoke particles become visible
The reddening of the sun at sunrise and sunset
Blue colour of sky
The sky looks dark in absence of atmosphere
Danger signals are of red coloured

Cause of Dispersion
Refractive index of material for different wavelengths is different.
$\mu \propto \dfrac{1}{\lambda}$     $\mu_v > \mu_r$

Spectrum
Band of seven component colours VIBGYOR on a white screen

Rainbow
Seven colours band of sunlight in the form of bow in the sky. It is formed due to reflection, refraction and dispersion of sunlight by tiny water droplets. To observe rainbow, observer should stand with its back towards sun

Colour
The sensation recceived by the eye (rod cells of the eye) due to light coming from an object.

Primary Rainbow
• Two refraction and one total internal reflection
• Subtends an angle of 42° at the eye of the observer
• Innermost arc is violet and outermost is red
• More bright

Secondary Rainbow
• Two refraction and two total internal reflection
• Subtends an angle of 52.5° at the eye
• Innermost arc is red and outermost is violet
• Less bright in comparison to primary rainbow

**MIND** [MAP]

## ELECTRICITY
**Study of Electric Charges at Rest and in Motion**

### Series Grouping of Resistances
Equivalent resistance, $R_s = R_1 + R_2 + ... + R_n$
In this case same current flows through each resistance but potential difference distributes in the ratio of resistance

### Parallel Grouping of Resistances
Equivalent resistance,
$$\frac{1}{R_P} = \frac{1}{R_1} + \frac{1}{R_2} + ... + \frac{1}{R_n}$$
In this case same potential across each resistance but current distributes in the reverse ratio of their resistances

After stretching, if length increases by $n$ times then resistance will increase by $n^2$ times i.e., $R = n^2 R_1$. Similarly if radius be reduced to $\frac{1}{n}$ times then area of cross-section decreases $\frac{1}{n^2}$ times so the resistance becomes $n^4$ times i.e., $R_2 = n^4 R_1$.
After stretching, if length of a conductor increases by $x\%$, then resistance will increase by $2x\%$ (valid only if $x < 10\%$).

### On length ($\ell$) and area of cross-section (A)
$$\left.\begin{array}{c} R \propto l \\ \propto \frac{1}{A} \end{array}\right\} R = \rho\frac{l}{A}$$
$\rho$ = resistivity
Resistivity depends on the material of the conductor only.

### Grouping of Resistances

### Resistance (R) : Obstruction offered to flow of electrons. SI unit ohm

Resistance, $R \propto \frac{\ell^2}{m}$
$\ell$ = length and
$m$ = mass of conducting wire

### Dependence of Resistance

### Ohm's law : If the physical conditions remain same, current $I \propto V \Rightarrow V = IR$
R-electric resistance
Substances which obey ohm's law called ohmic and that do not obey called non-ohmic substances.

### Electric Potential
Work done per unit charge
$$V = \frac{W}{Q}$$
S.I. unit volt

### On Temperature
$R_t = R_0(1 + \alpha t)$
$\alpha$ = temperature coefficient of resistance

### Charge
Something associated with matter due to which it produces and experiences electric and magnetic effects. Resides on the outer surface of conductor.
$Q = ne$　　S.I. unit coulomb (C)

### Electric Current (I)
The time rate of flow of charge (Q) through any cross-section
$$I = \frac{Q}{t}$$　　S.I. unit ampere (A)

### Types of Current

### Direct Current
Current whose magnitude and direction does not vary with time.

### Alternating Current
Current whose magnitude and direction periodically changes with time.

- Using $n$ conductors of equal resistance, the number of possible combinations is $2^{n-1}$.
- If the resistances of $n$ conductors are totally different, then the number of possible combinations will be $2^n$.
- If $n$ identical resistances are first connected in series and then in parallel, the ratio of the equivalent resistance is given by
$$\frac{R_s}{R_p} = \frac{n^2}{1}.$$
- If a wire of resistance $R$ is cut in $n$ equal parts and then these parts are collected to form a bundle, then equivalent resistance of combination will be $\frac{R}{n^2}$.
- If equivalent resistance of $R_1$ and $R_2$ in series and parallel be $R_s$ and $R_p$ respectively, then $R_1 = \frac{1}{2}\left[R_s + \sqrt{R_s^2 - 4R_s R_p}\right]$
and $R_2 = \frac{1}{2}\left[R_s - \sqrt{R_s^2 - 4R_s R_p}\right]$.

# MAP-12

## Electric Circuit

The arrangement of various electrical components along which electric current flow

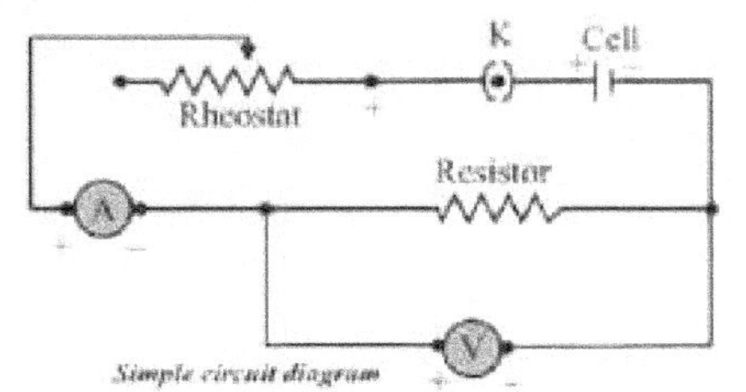


## Elements of Circuit

### Cell

Direct current source of electromotive force. Combination of two or more cells is called battery.

## Heating Effect of Electric Current

As current flows through a conductor, the free electrons lose energy which is converted into heat.

Joule's heating law

$$H \propto I^2$$
$$H \propto R$$
$$H \propto t$$
$$H = I^2Rt = VIt$$

### Rheostat

Wire of special type of alloy like manganin, eureka, nichrome etc. is wound on a hollow cylinder of china clay. It controls the current in the electric circuit.

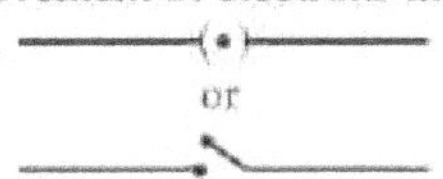

or

### Switch

It is used to close or open the electric circuit, controls the movement of electrons in a circuit.

or

## Practical Applications

Electric heater, electric iron and water heater, etc. work on the principle of heating effect of current

Electric bulb glows when electric current flows through the filament of the bulb

### Voltmeter

Measures the potential difference between two points in the circuit. Its resistance is high and it is used in parallel with the resistance wire.

### Fuse

It is a safety device having very thin wire which is made up of either tin or alloy of tin and lead. This wire has low melting point so it melts and breaks the circuit easily if the current in the circuit exceeds.

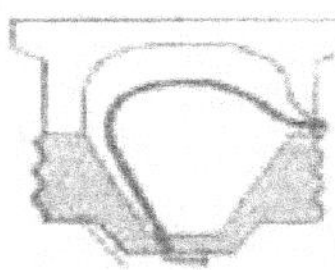

A plug fuse

## Electric Power

Rate at which electric energy is dissipated or consumed in a circuit,

$$P = VI$$
$$\text{or } P = I^2R = \frac{V^2}{R}$$

Watt is a smaller unit of power, its other bigger units are kilowatt (KW), Megawatt (MW) and Horsepower (HP)

$$1 \, Kw = 10^3 \, W \qquad 1 \, Mw = 10^6 \, W$$
$$1 \, hp = 746 \, W$$

The commercial unit of electrical energy is 1 Kwh.

$$1 \, Kwh = 3.6 \times 10^6 \, J$$

### Ammeter

Measures the value of current flowing in the circuit. The resistance of ammeter is small and it is used in series with the circuit.

### LED

It is a device which glows even if a weak electric current is allowed to flow through it

# MIND

## MAGNETIC EFFECTS OF ELECTRIC CURRENT
An electric current flowing in a conductor produces magnetism

### Properties of Magnets

**Attractive property** Magnets attract magnetic materials like – iron, cobalt, nickel, etc.

**Directive property** A freely suspended magnet always aligns in north-south direction

**Opposite poles** attract and like poles repel.

**Poles exist in pairs** North and South

**Repulsion is a sure test of magnet**

### Magnetic Field
Space around a magnet in which magnetic effect is experienced

**Magnetic Field Lines**
A line such that the tangent at any point on it gives the direction of the magnetic field at that point.

**Properties of Magnetic Field Lines**

All field lines are closed curves.

Field lines are close together near the poles.

Two field lines never intersect each other.

### Magnetic Field Due to a Current Carrying Conductor

The magnetic field around a straight conductor carrying current is in the form of closed circular loops, in a plane perpendicular to the conductor.

Direction of magnetic field can be determined by using Right hand thumb rule



### Solenoid
A solenoid is a long cylindrical helix, which produces a magnetic field when an electric current is passed through it

The magnetic field within the solenoid is uniform and parallel to the axis of solenoid.

### Magnetic Field Due to a Circular Current Carrying Loop

At every point of a current carrying loop, the concentric circles representing the magnetic field around it would become larger as we move away.



Direction of magnetic field can be determined by using right hand rule

### Force on a Current Carrying Conductor
The force experienced by the conductor
$$\vec{F} = I\vec{L} \times \vec{B}$$

Direction of force can be determined by Fleming's left hand rule, right hand palm or screw rule.



Anti clockwise North-pole



Clockwise South-pole

The magnetic field due to solenoid depends upon
(a) number of turns i.e., $B \propto n$
(b) strength of current i.e, $B \propto I$
(c) Nature of material inside solenoid i.e., $B \propto \mu$

# MAP-13

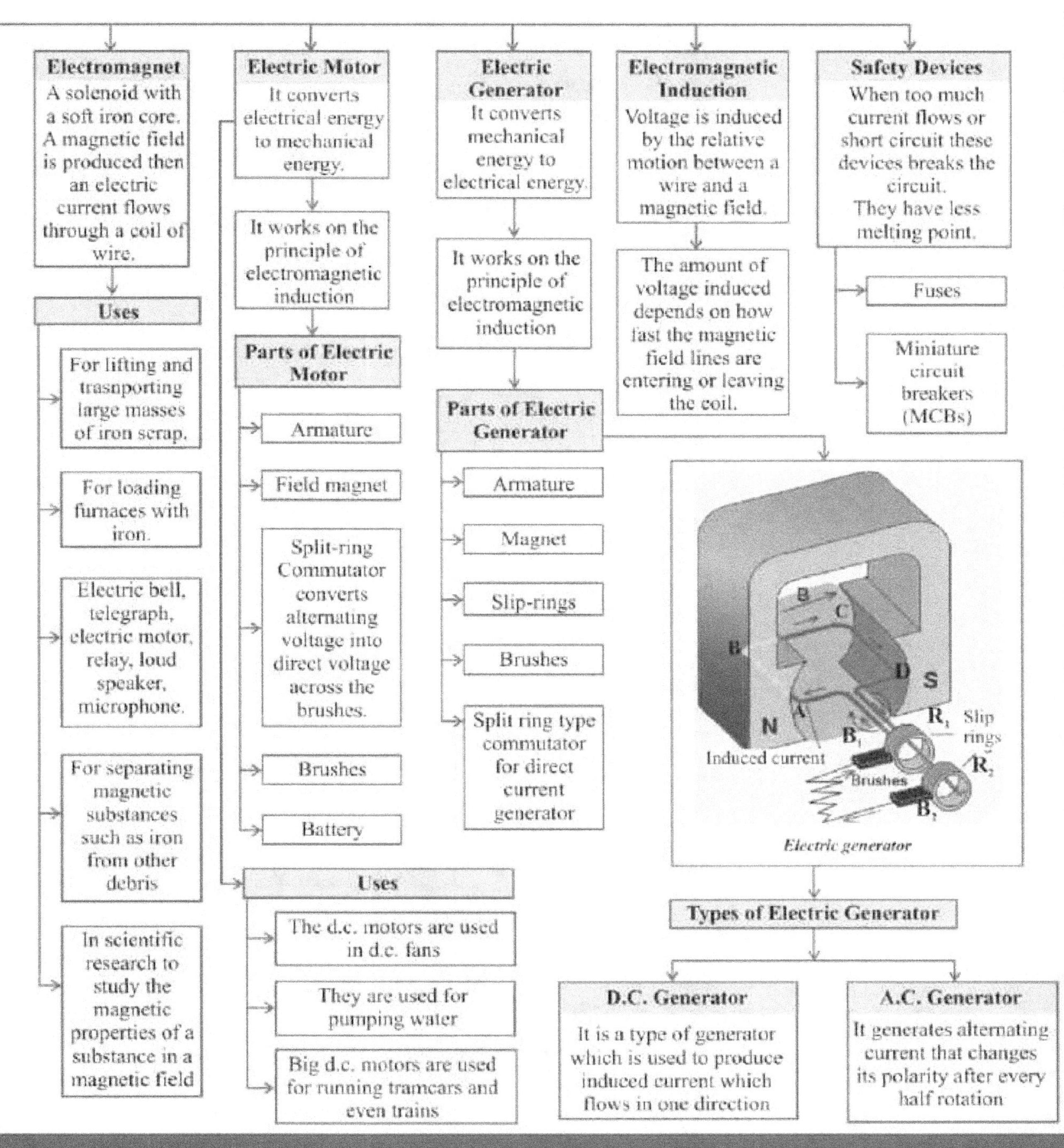

Electromagnet
A solenoid with a soft iron core. A magnetic field is produced then an electric current flows through a coil of wire.

Uses

For lifting and trasnporting large masses of iron scrap.

For loading furnaces with iron.

Electric bell, telegraph, electric motor, relay, loud speaker, microphone.

For separating magnetic substances such as iron from other debris

In scientific research to study the magnetic properties of a substance in a magnetic field

Electric Motor
It converts electrical energy to mechanical energy.

It works on the principle of electromagnetic induction

Parts of Electric Motor

Armature

Field magnet

Split-ring Commutator converts alternating voltage into direct voltage across the brushes.

Brushes

Battery

Uses

The d.c. motors are used in d.c. fans

They are used for pumping water

Big d.c. motors are used for running tramcars and even trains

Electric Generator
It converts mechanical energy to electrical energy.

It works on the principle of electromagnetic induction

Parts of Electric Generator

Armature

Magnet

Slip-rings

Brushes

Split ring type commutator for direct current generator

Electromagnetic Induction
Voltage is induced by the relative motion between a wire and a magnetic field.

The amount of voltage induced depends on how fast the magnetic field lines are entering or leaving the coil.

Safety Devices
When too much current flows or short circuit these devices breaks the circuit.
They have less melting point.

Fuses

Miniature circuit breakers (MCBs)

B
C
B
D
S
N
A
B₁
R₁
Slip rings
Induced current
Brushes
B₂
R₂
Electric generator

Types of Electric Generator

D.C. Generator
It is a type of generator which is used to produce induced current which flows in one direction

A.C. Generator
It generates alternating current that changes its polarity after every half rotation

# MIND

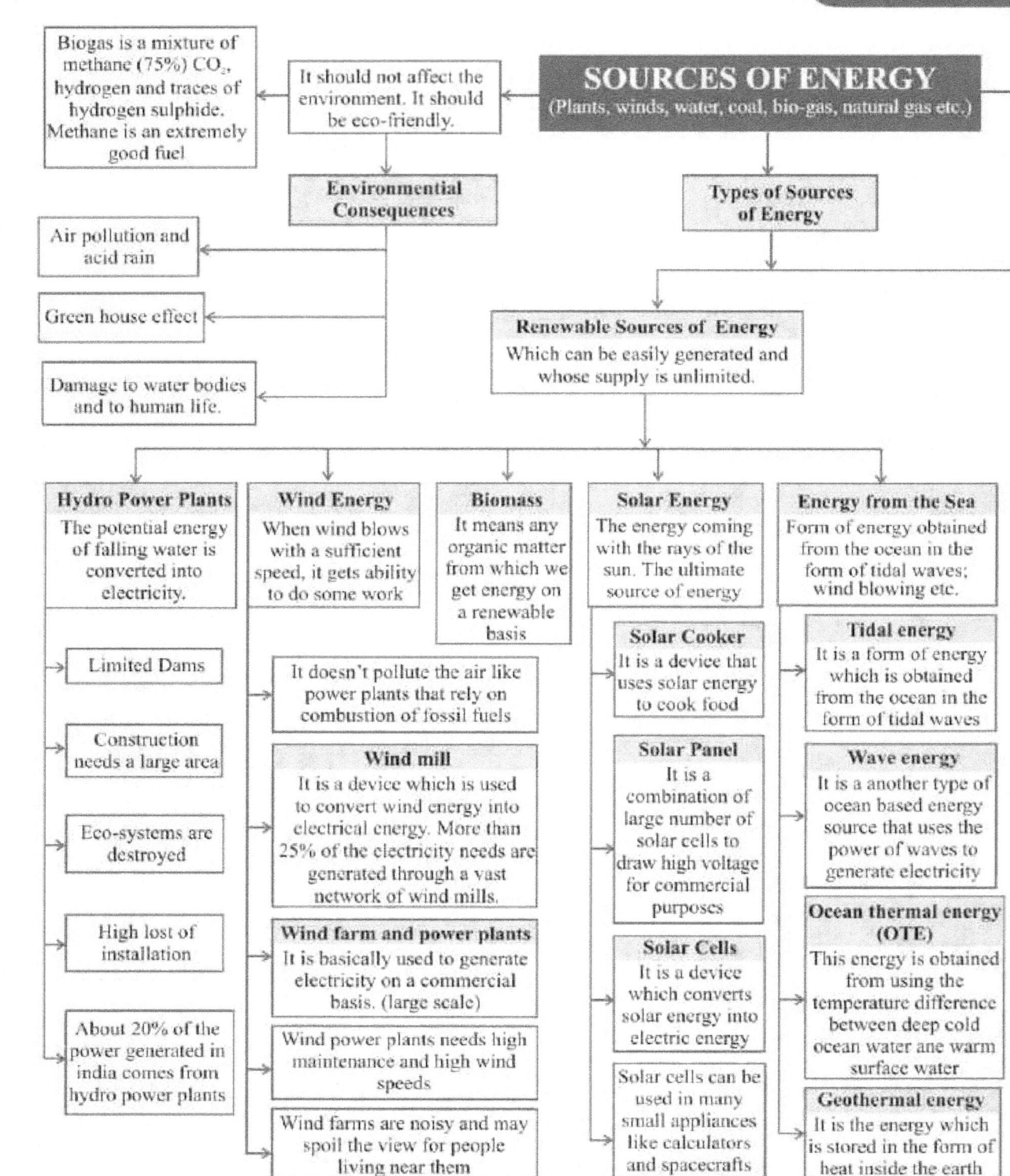

Biogas is a mixture of methane (75%) CO₂, hydrogen and traces of hydrogen sulphide. Methane is an extremely good fuel

It should not affect the environment. It should be eco-friendly.

SOURCES OF ENERGY
(Plants, winds, water, coal, bio-gas, natural gas etc.)

Environmential Consequences

Types of Sources of Energy

Air pollution and acid rain

Green house effect

Damage to water bodies and to human life.

Renewable Sources of Energy
Which can be easily generated and whose supply is unlimited.

Hydro Power Plants
The potential energy of falling water is converted into electricity.

Wind Energy
When wind blows with a sufficient speed, it gets ability to do some work

Biomass
It means any organic matter from which we get energy on a renewable basis

Solar Energy
The energy coming with the rays of the sun. The ultimate source of energy

Energy from the Sea
Form of energy obtained from the ocean in the form of tidal waves; wind blowing etc.

Limited Dams

Construction needs a large area

Eco-systems are destroyed

High lost of installation

About 20% of the power generated in india comes from hydro power plants

It doesn't pollute the air like power plants that rely on combustion of fossil fuels

Wind mill
It is a device which is used to convert wind energy into electrical energy. More than 25% of the electricity needs are generated through a vast network of wind mills.

Wind farm and power plants
It is basically used to generate electricity on a commercial basis. (large scale)

Wind power plants needs high maintenance and high wind speeds

Wind farms are noisy and may spoil the view for people living near them

Solar Cooker
It is a device that uses solar energy to cook food

Solar Panel
It is a combination of large number of solar cells to draw high voltage for commercial purposes

Solar Cells
It is a device which converts solar energy into electric energy

Solar cells can be used in many small appliances like calculators and spacecrafts

Tidal energy
It is a form of energy which is obtained from the ocean in the form of tidal waves

Wave energy
It is a another type of ocean based energy source that uses the power of waves to generate electricity

Ocean thermal energy (OTE)
This energy is obtained from using the temperature difference between deep cold ocean water ane warm surface water

Geothermal energy
It is the energy which is stored in the form of heat inside the earth

# MAP-14

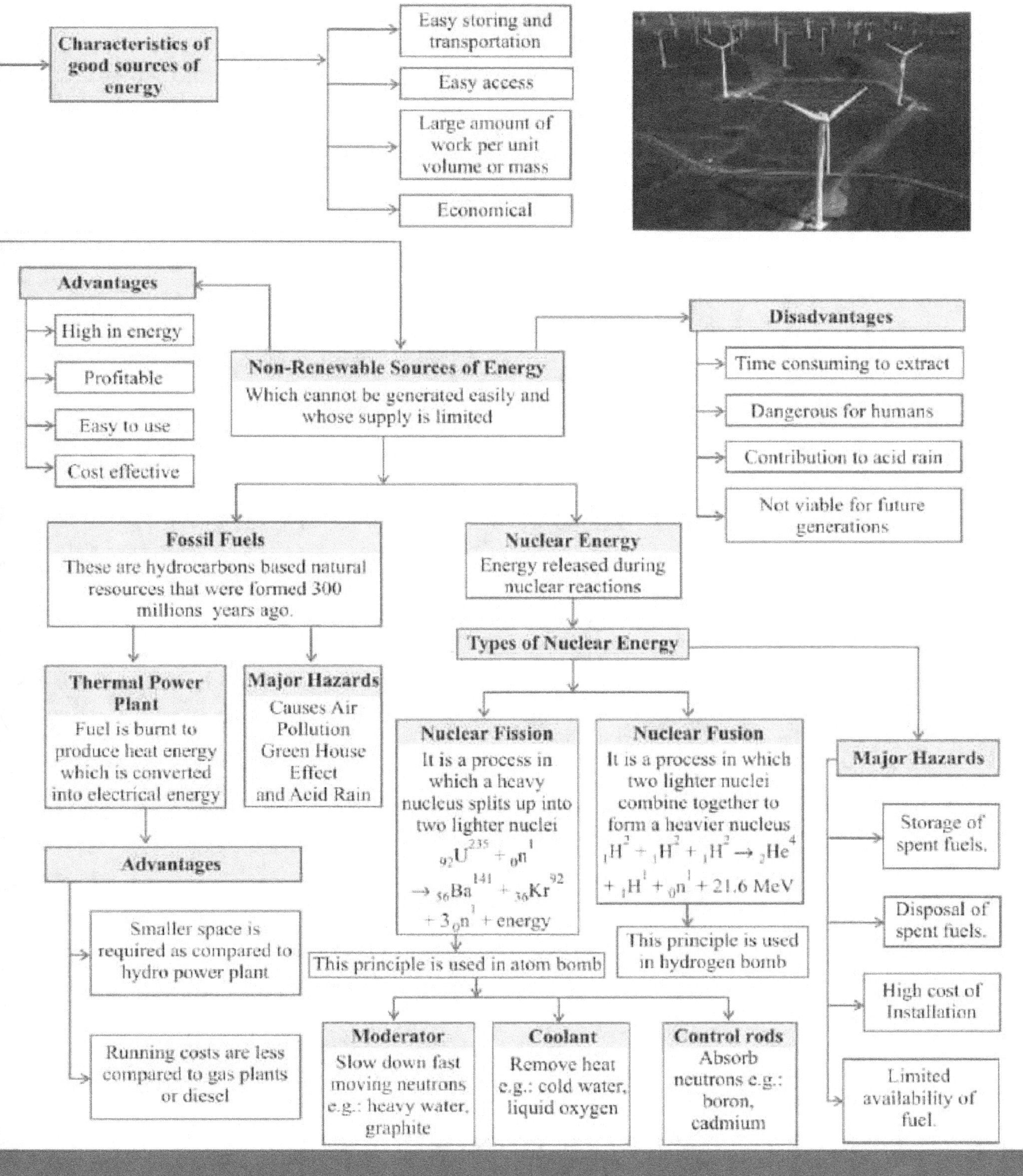


$$_{92}U^{235} + _{0}n^{1} \rightarrow _{56}Ba^{141} + _{36}Kr^{92} + 3\,_{0}n^{1} + energy$$

$$_{1}H^{2} + _{1}H^{2} + _{1}H^{2} \rightarrow _{2}He^{4} + _{1}H^{1} + _{0}n^{1} + 21.6\ MeV$$

# MIND

## OUR ENVIRONMENT

## Eco-system

It is defined as functional unit of nature, where living organisms interact among themselves and also with the surrounding physical environment.
Hence, there are two main components of the ecosystem:
**Biotic**: Living organisms such as plants, animals, microorganisms and humans.
**Abiotic**: It includes physical factors such as temperature, rainfall, wind, soil and minerals.
Examples of natural ecosystem: forests, ponds, lakes, etc, and human made or artificial ecosystems are gardens, crop-fields, aquarium etc.

Ecosystem consists of various organisms which can be classified as **producers** and **consumers**.

**Producers** are the organisms which make organic compounds like sugar, starch, etc from inorganic substances with the help of sunlight and chlorophyll.

**Consumers** are the organisms which are dependent on producers for their nutrition. They can be grouped as herbivores, carnivores, omnivores, parasites, and decomposers.

**Decomposers** are the microorganisms (bacteria & fungi) which break down complex organic substances (dead remains & waste material of living organisms) into simpler inorganic substances that go back into the soil and are used up again by the plants.
Thus, they help in proper cycling of the nutrients in an ecosystem.

**Have you ever wondered why we need to clean aquarium but not lakes or ponds?**

It is because aquarium is an artificial and incomplete system which lacks producers, food chains, and decomposers.
Hence, it lacks natural nutrients recycling and self-cleaning abilities. In contrast lake or ponds are natural and complete ecosystem where there is perfect recycling of nutrients and thus does not need to be cleaned very often.

## Waste Material

Waste material can be broadly classified into categories depending on their degradation:

### Biodegradable Waste

- These are the wastes that can be broken down simpler compounds by the action of bacteri other saprophytes.
- In addition, physical processes such as temperature and pressure also act on them howe under ambient conditions these substances p in our environment for a very long time.
- Some examples of such wastes are food mater kitchen wastes, and other natural wastes.
### Non-biodegradable Waste
- These are the substances that are not broken d into simpler compounds by the action microorganisms.
- These substances may be inert and simply pers the environment for a long time or may harm various members of the eco-system.
- They are the main causes of air, water and pollution and diseases like cancer.
- Some examples of such waste are plastic, metals, and chemicals for agricultural and indus purposes.

## Food Chains And Webs

In an ecosystem, there exists a series of organi feeding on one another. This series or organisms ta part at various biotic levels form a food chain.
Alternatively, food chain can be defined as a li network of food or energy flow starting from prod and ending at apex predator.

## Trophic Level

Based on the source of their nutrition or food, organ occupy a specific place in food chain that is know their **trophic level.** There are usually four tro levels:
- **I trophic level**: It includes producers or autotr for e.g. phytoplanktons, grass, trees etc.
- **II trophic level**: It includes primary consume herbivores for e.g. zooplanktons, grasshoppers, co
- **III trophic level**: It includes secondary consum small carnivore for e.g. birds, fishes, wolf etc.
- **IV trophic level**: It includes tertiary consume larger carnivores for e.g. level lion, tiger, man et

# MAP-15

## Environmental Problems

**Depletion of the ozone layer:** Ozone ($O_3$) is a molecule formed by three atoms of oxygen. It is located in upper part of the atmosphere called stratosphere and it acts as shield absorbing UV radiation from sun.

- At higher levels of atmosphere, high energy UV radiations split apart some moleculer oxygen ($O_2$) into free oxygen (O) atoms. These atoms then combine with the molecular oxygen to form ozone.
- Ozone depletion permits entry of harmful UV radiations which lead to diseases like skin aging, irritation & cancer, snow-blindness, cataract, etc.
- Ozone-depleting substances: CFCs, HCFCs, hydrobromofluorocarbons, etc.

**Waste disposal:** Improvements in our life-style have resulted in greater amounts of waste material generation. For e.g. increased use of disposable items, plastic bags, packing materials etc have resulted in much of our waste becoming non-biodegradable.

Following methods can be helpful in managing the garbage we produce: categorization of waste materials into biodegradable, recyclable & non-biodegradable, reduction in use of non-biodegradable substances such as plastics, thermocol etc, burning & proper dumping of waste.

## It is interesting note that how unknowingly some harmful chemicals enter our bodies through the food chain.

It happens by two ways:

**Overuse of several pesticides:** These chemicals are either washed down into the soil or into the water bodies.

From the soil, these are absorbed by the plants along with water and minerals, and from the water bodies these are taken up by aquatic plants and animals

**Biological magnification:** It is defines as an increase in concentration of the toxicant at successive trophie levels.

These chemicals are not degradable and organism can neither metabolise nor excrete them and thus they get accumulated progressively at each trophic level.

In addition, human beings occupy top level in any food chain and thus maximum concentration of these chemicals gets accumulated in our bodies.

## Energy Flow

- The flow of energy is unidirectional.
- The green plants in a terrestrial ecosystem capture about 1% of the energy of sunlight that falls on their leaves and convert it into food energy.
- On an average only 10% organic matter is present at each step and reaches the next level of consumers. It is because a great deal of energy is lost as heat to the environment and rest goes into digestion, in doing work and in growth & reproduction.
- In addition, the loss of energy at each step is so great that very little usable energy remains after four trophic levels and this is the reason that a food chain usually contain maximum of four trophic levels.
- Generally, there are greater number of individuals at lower trophic levels of an ecosystem (the greatest number is of the producers).
- The length and complexity of food chains vary greatly.
  - Each organism is generally eaten by two or more other kinds of organisms which in turn are eaten by several other organisms.
  - So instead of a straight line food chain, the relationship can be shown as a series of branching lines called a food web.

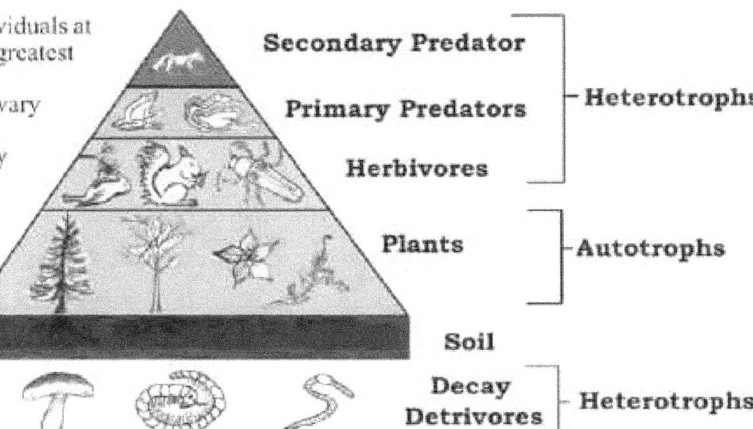

# MIND

## MANAGEMENT OF NATURAL RESOURCES

Natural resources are resources that exist without actions of humankind. They can be abiotic (such as air, water, land, mineral ores, etc) or biotic (such as plants, animals, fossil fuels as they are obtained from decaying organic matter).

Natural resource management is an interdisciplinary field of study that considers the physical, biological, economic and social aspects of handling natural resources. It involves putting resources to their best use for human purposes in addition to preserving natural systems.

### Why Do We Need To Manage Our Resources?

- All the things we use or consume such as food, clothes, books, toys, furniture, tools and vehicles are obtained from resources on this earth.
- A majority of natural resources is **limited**.
- Human population is increasing at a tremendous rate.
- Utilization of natural resources is increasing at an exponential rate.
- Need to conserve resources for future generations.
- Equal distribution of resources for equal benefit.
- Need to reduce the damage caused to the environment while these resources are either extracted or used.

### Forests And Wild Life

Forests are 'biodiversity hot spots'. Biodiversity hotspots are the regions with very high levels of species richness & high degree of endemism. It is very important to preserve biodiversity we have inherited as loss of diversity may lead to a loss of ecological stability.

**Stakeholders**

Stakeholders are:

- The people who live in or around forests are dependent on forest produce for various aspects of their life.
- The Forest Department of the Government which owns the land and controls the resources from forests.
- The industrialists who use various forests' produce, but are not dependent on the forests in any one area.
- The wild life and nature enthusiasts who want to conserve nature in its pristine form.

### Pollution Of The Ganga

Ganga Action Plan, a multi-cro project came about in 1985 becaus the quality of the water in th Ganga was very poor. Sever factors responsible for this poo condition of the river are:

- Hundred of towns & cities po their garbage and excreta into
- Large amount of untreate sewage is dumped into th Ganges every day.
- In addition, human activities li bathing, washing of clothes immersion of ashes or un-bur corpses also lead to the hug amount of pollution in the river
- Lastly, industries contribu chemical effluents to the Gang pollution load which kills fish large sections of the river.

### When we consider the conservation of forests, we need to look at the stakeholders.

Let us look at an example for this:

- The local people depend on forests for their firewood, timber, thatch, food, fruits, nuts, as well as medicine. In addition, their cattle also graze in forest areas or feed on other fodder which is collected from forests.
- However, when vast tracts of forests have been converted to monocultures of pine, teak or eucalyptus for industrial use, a large amount of biodiversity in the area was destroyed. In addition, the varied needs of the local people (fodder, herbs, fruits & nuts for food) can no longer be met from such forests.
- Hence, conservation of forests resources must be done at the broader level and should consider each and every group of stakeholder associated with forests resources.
- In other words, while the environment is preserved, the benefits of the controlled exploitation should go to the local people, a process in which decentralised economic growth and ecological conservation go hand in hand.

### Example of People's Participation in the Management of Forests

- Amrita Devi Bishnoi, in 1731 sacrificed her lif along with 363 others for the protection of 'khejri trees in Khejrali village near Jodhpur i Rajasthan.
- The Chipko Andolan, result of a grass-root leve effort to end the alienation of people from thei forests. The movement was originated in a remote village called Reni in Garhwal during the earl 1970s.
- In 1972, the West Bengal Forest Departmen failed in reviving the degraded Sal forests in th southwestern districts of the state.
  - With the active and willing participation o the local community, the sal forests o Arabari underwent a remarkable recovery by 1983, a previously worthless forest wa valued Rs 12.5 crores.

# MAP-16

## Three R's

**Reduce**: This means that you use less. For e.g. saving electricity by switching off unnecessary lights & fans, save water by repairing leaky taps etc.

**Recycle**: This means that you collect plastic, paper, glass & metal items & recycle these materials to make required things instead of synthesising or extracting fresh material. It requires proper segregation of wastes to prevent the dumping of recyclable materials along with other wastes.

**Reuse**: In this strategy, one simply use things again & again for e.g. plastic or glass bottles used for packaging of food can be used for storing things in the kitchen.

## Coal And Petroleum

Coal and petroleum were formed from the degradation of bio-mass millions of years ago & hence they will be exhausted in the future no matter how carefully we use them i.e. they are **exhaustible resources**.

The management of these resources includes sustainable use of these resources, finding the alternative in forms of renewable energy such as solar energy, wind energy, geothermal energy etc, and increasing the efficiency of our machines or automobiles.

## Water Conservation

**Dams:** Large dams can ensure the storage of adequate water for irrigation as well as for generating electricity.

Canal systems leading from these dams can transfer large amounts of water to greater distances. For e.g. Indira Gandhi Canal has brought greenery to considerable areas of Rajasthan.

However, constructions of large dams address three problems in particular:

- Social problems as they displace large no. of peasants & tribals without adequate compensation or rehabilitation.
- Economic problems, they invest huge amounts of public money without the generation of proportionate benefits.
- Environmental problems, they contribute enormously to deforestation & loss of biological diversity.

- **Water Harvesting:** Watershed management emphasises scientific soil and water conservation in order to increase the biomass production.
- Various organisations have been working on rejuvenating ancient systems of water harvesting as an alternative to the 'mega-projects' like dams.
- These communities have used hundreds of indigenous water saving methods such as dug small pits & lakes, put in place simple watershed systems, built small earthen dams, constructed dykes, sand & limestone reservoirs, and set up rooftop water-collecting units. This has recharged groundwater levels & even brought rivers back to life.
- Water harvesting is an age-old concept in India for e.g. khadins, tanks & nadis in Rajasthan, bandharas & tals in Maharashtra, bundhis in Madhya Pradesh & Uttar Pradesh, ahars & pynes in Bihar, kulhs in Himachal Pradesh, ponds in the Kandi belt of Jammu region, eris (tanks) in Tamil Nadu, surangams in Kerala, and kattas in Karnataka.
- Their main purpose of water harvesting is not to hold surface water but to recharge the ground water beneath. The advantages of storing ground water are:
  - It does not evaporate, but spreads out to recharge wells & provides moisture for vegetation over a wide area.
  - It does not provide breeding grounds for mosquitoes.
  - Ground-water is also relatively protected from contamination by

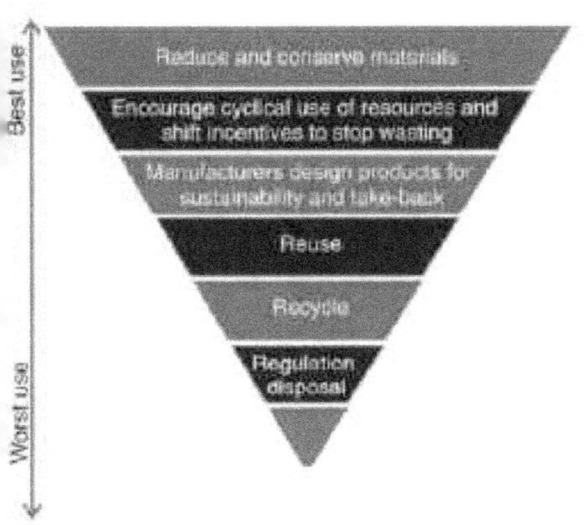


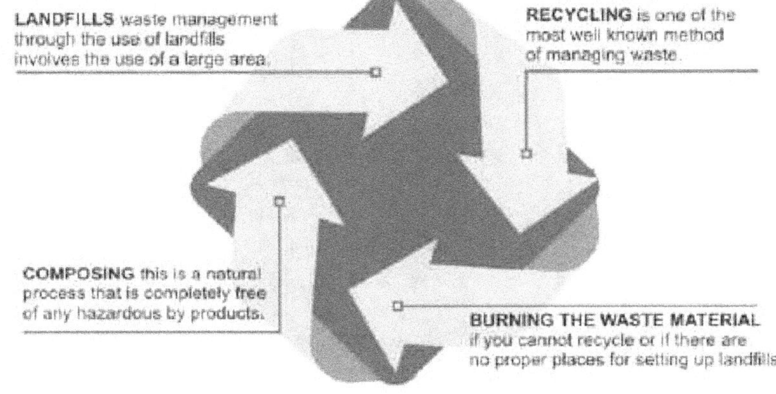

# CHAPTERWISE
# MIND MAPS
# ENGLISH

# FIRST FLIGHT

## *PROSE*

## SUMMARY OF THE STORY

The story, "A Letter to God" by G.L. Fuentes, depicts the power of unwavering faith in God. Lencho, as its central character, is a farmer who is hoping for a rain shower to nourish his field of corn. To his utmost excitement, rainfall did happen but soon, it turned into a hailstorm destroying his entire crop fields. He became apprehensive about how he and his family would manage to survive.

However, even in such a difficult phase ,the help from God was his only hope.

Therefore, he wrote a letter to God expressing his concern and a simple request, 'A hundred pesos in order to sow his field again and to live until the crop ripes'.

He confidently dropped the letter at the post box which becomes a source of amusement when read by the post office employees. The postmaster too laughed uncontrollably but almost immediately he turned sombre, deeply touched by the faith that Lencho possessed in God.

He decided to do whatever was possible to ensure that Lencho's faith in God was not shaken. He along with other post office employees and with the help of few other acquaintances collected seventy pesos and put the same and a letter in an envelope and sent it to Lencho. The postmaster signed the letter as 'God' so that Lencho would be convinced that it was God Himself who had helped him.

The irony in the story appears when Lencho writes another letter to God complaining that he had received only seventy pesos instead of hundred. In this letter, Lencho requests God to send him the remaining amount directly and not via mail as the post office employees are a bunch of crooks.

## A LETTER TO GOD

### *by* **G.L. Fuentes**

### Character Sketch: LENCHO

Lencho is the central character of the story A Letter to God. He is a poor farmer who works day in and day out and leaves no stone unturned in his profession as a farmer. He is not highly educated but knows his corn fields intimately. He is a family oriented man and possesses unwavering faith in God. Though devastated, Lencho continued to have faith in God and was convinced that it is only God who could help him in this situation.

In a nutshell, Lencho can be called an innocent man who firmly believes in God and feels that any prayer attached with strings of faith is definitely answered.

### Character Sketch: POSTMASTER

The postmaster was a fat and amiable fellow. He possessed a sense of humour, but never intended to mock anyone in the name of hilarity. He is empathetic towards people around him.

He decided to help Lencho in a manner that would sustain Lencho's faith in God.

He along with his employees collects an amount of seventy pesos. He himself contributes a part of his salary into it. Thereafter, he puts the money in an envelope addressing to Lencho and with it, a letter containing only a single word as a signature: God.

This shows that he was a kind and empathetic person as well. He loved to help others.

## SUMMARY OF THE STORY

'Long Walk to Freedom' is an autobiography of former and first black president of South Africa. Excerpts from "Long Walk to Freedom" include description of the inauguration ceremony, citations from his speech and his journey to being a freedom fighter along with a tribute to many others who worked untiringly for the establishment of a society that shall be free from any form of discrimination.

Mandela portrays two contradictory pictures of his country. One is of his early life and upbringing in South Africa. He has described what freedom meant to him during his childhood days. He was an enthusiastic boy then; staying away from home was freedom for him. Later, he wanted to marry a person of his choice but then he realized that it was not so easy for the people belonging to his race. Freedom was only illusion for them. Black people used to suffer a lot at the hands of the White people. He mentions that there were two separate national anthems for the Blacks and the Whites.

In the second picture, Mandela focuses on the political and social aspects of apartheid in South Africa, and holds the politicians responsible for its prevalence. As he faced oppression along with the others who suffered, he was determined to fight against what he called 'an extraordinary human disaster'. He goes on to describe the methods that he and other freedom fighters employed to sabotage the government. He has also talked about his arrest in1961 and how he was convicted for inciting people to strike. Although he was facing the death penalty, Justice Dr. Quartos de Wet sentenced him to life imprisonment. Mandela marks the tenth of May, 'the inauguration' day, as a bright new dawn in South Africa as its first democratic, non-racial government, headed by him was to take oath of office.

## NELSON MANDELA- LONG WALK TO FREEDOM
### by Nelson Rolihlahla Mandela

## Character Sketch: NELSON MANDELA

Nelson Rolihlahla Mandela was born on the 18th of July, 1918. He was a South African political leader, a revolutionary, and a philanthropist who played a vital role in ending the apartheid regime of the 20th century. During the year 1962, Nelson Mandela spent around 27 years in part of the political offences.

He served as the country's first black President from 1994 to 1999, and is considered one of the most noteworthy figures of the 20th century. He was the winner of the 1993 Nobel Peace Prize for his role in bringing the apartheid regime to a peaceful end and laying the foundations for a truly democratic South Africa. He is honoured around the world and regarded as 'The Father of Modern South Africa'.

Mandela strongly believed that every individual has 'twin obligation' or two types of obligations— first of these is towards one's family, while the second is towards one's country. According to him, 'to love', rather than 'to hate', is natural because man is not born to loathe. He inspires every individual to inculcate the moral values of sympathy, love, honesty and living in harmony.

### /// Character Sketch: SEAGULL ///

The young seagull is wilful as he does not listen to repeated requests from his parents. His parents request him to make an effort to fly but the young seagull is conquered by aviophobia.

He can be further described as comfort loving because he is dependent on his parents for satisfying his hunger. He also seems stubborn at one point in the story.

Though the young seagull does not listen to repeated requests from his parents, he is not really disrespectful towards them. Even after being mocked by his younger siblings, he does not answer back nor does he show any hatred or jealousy.

His fear of failing keeps him away from hard work and determination at the beginning of the story, but when he is given stimulus, he learns to fly and soon overcomes his fears.

### /// Character Sketch: MOTHER SEAGULL ///

The mother seagull is portrayed as a tough but a motivating parent. She understood that her little one needed motivation to achieve the goal of flying. Initially, she tried threatening the young seagull in many ways but all in vain. The mother seagull then realised that only a dire need would spur the frightened seagull to soar into the sky. Taking advantage of the fact that the seagull was in desperate need of food, she flies towards him with a piece of fish. The young seagull dives at the fish and experiences his first flight.

Thus, the mother motivated the young one to do what was expected of him, even if it meant that the latter had to fall down a few times.

*by* **Liam O' Flaherty**

## /// I. SUMMARY OF THE STORY, HIS FIRST FLIGHT ///

The story "His First Flight" by 'Liam O' Flaherty' is about a young seagull that is frightened to fly. All his younger siblings despite their much shorter wings had learnt to fly fearlessly while he (young seagull) could not muster up the courage to trust his own wings. His parents tell him repeatedly to make an effort to fly but he refuses to do so. He is mocked by his sibling seagulls and is called a coward by his parents.

At one point of time, his family leaves him in isolation. The seagull makes several efforts to grab his parents' attention, but all in vain. By the end of the day, the seagull starts feeling puny due to long hours of starvation.

However, his mother observed him keenly. She in order to feed herself and the other seagulls tore a piece of fish that lay at her feet and then scrapped each side of her beak on the rock. The seagull, maddened out of starvation, looked at his mother with hopeful eyes. His mother then picked up a piece of fish and started flying towards him. The young seagull became excited to see this and dived at the fish, completely forgetting that he was afraid to fly. Finally, he took his first flight. All the family members celebrated the young seagull's victory by cheering and dancing around him.

The story, thus, explains the importance of independence, self esteem and confidence. It also highlights the need of a stimulus to reach our goals.

## TWO STORIES ABOUT FLYING

*by* **Frederick Forsyth**

## /// 2. SUMMARY OF THE STORY, THE BLACK AEROPLANE ///

The black aeroplane, written by Frederick Forsyth is a mysterious and interesting story about a pilot who gets helped by another pilot. The story begins with the narrator expressing his happiness as he is on his way to England hoping to have a good English breakfast with his family. While he is busy weaving thoughts about spending time with his family, he encounters thick black clouds. He is suddenly in an anxious state of mind. The necessary instruments like the radio, etc. had started to malfunctioning. The narrator finds himself in a fix and begins to panic. At this point, he notices another plane next to him. The other plane was black in colour with no lights on its wings and the narrator could only see the pilot's face. The pilot of the other plane waves at the narrator and gesticulates at him to follow. The narrator, left with only this as a hope, follows the other pilot. To his amazement and relief, the narrator soon finds himself out of the thick black clouds, safe and sound.

After the narrator is rescued, he looks around for the other pilot but surprisingly could not see anyone. He, then, enquires the control station on the whereabouts of the other pilot. To his surprise, he is informed that there was no other plane on the radar apart from his!

This leaves the narrator perplexed but he is overjoyed to be able to land safely and meet his family.

### /// Character Sketch: THE PILOT ///

The pilot in the story 'The Black Aeroplane' can be described as a family loving man. This is understood by the fact that the pilot during his flight dreams about spending time with his family.

He takes a calculated risk. Even after knowing that he is going to encounter storm clouds, he heads into them. This is mainly because he did not have enough fuel to fly back to Paris and at the same time after passing through the passage of storm clouds, he would land back home.

He is alert enough to employ his skills as a pilot in case of an emergency situation. On seeing that the storm is overpowering, he immediately looks into the equipments that could help him in a safe landing.

Even on learning that all the equipments are out of order, he is still hopeful to get help. This hope is manifested in the form of a black aeroplane that seems to come out of nowhere to help the pilot reach safely at the airport. The pilot can, therefore, be described as a person who doesn't lose hope in adverse circumstances.

## SUMMARY OF THE STORY

This lesson is an excerpt from "The Diary of Anne Frank". It is an autobiography that was first published in 1947. Anne Frank was a young Jewish girl. She was born on 12th of June 1929. She lived with her parents in Germany. But Hitler's Nazi Party was against the Jews. The Nazis were killing the Jews or forcing them to work in the concentration camps. The Frank family fled from Germany in 1933 and took shelters in the Netherlands. But in 1940, Germany attacked the Netherlands and captured it. Her family went into hiding.

In this' Anne expresses her thoughts in a diary which was gifted to her on her thirteenth birthday. She names the diary "Kitty" which she considers as her only true friend. In this diary, Anne mentions about her childhood, her family, her school life and emotional developments. Anne considers writing as more productive and helpful as she feels that 'paper has more patience than people'.

The excerpt describes particularly about Anne's school life. Anne relates how she got scolded by the teachers due to her talkative behaviour. She goes on to describe about the manner in which she took the writing task given by her teacher, Mr. Keesing. Anne in this writing task, made a set of arguments about the importance of establishing a conversation. Her arguments were appealing enough and Mr. Keesing no longer scolded her for being a chatter box. In fact, he read the poem in other classes also. He appreciated the writing style of Anne frank.

## FROM THE DIARY OF ANNE FRANK

### by Anne Frank

### Character Sketch: ANNE FRANK

Anne was an enthusiastic writer who shared her thoughts and emotions more with her diary than people around her. She is respectful towards her teachers and has keen interest in academics. She employs her writing skill in a task given by her teacher, Mr. Keesing and earns appreciation for the same.

### Character Sketch: MR. KEESING

Mr. Keesing was an aged teacher at Anne's school. He taught Mathematics and was very strict. He never tolerated any misbehavior or talking in the class. Naturally, he remained annoyed with Anne who was a chatterbox. He would punish her by giving her extra homework. Anne would stuff her assigned homework with such funny contents that not only the class but even Mr. Keesing felt greatly delighted. With wewthe intention of making a mockery of Anne, he gave her an essay on a topic and then on another topic. Her style of writing was very interesting and funny with character pointing towards Mr. Keesing. Luckily, Mr. Keesing took the joke in the right way. He enjoyed this poem and read it to several classes. Thus, Mr. Keesing can be described as a teacher who acknowledged Anne's talent and took humour in the right sense.

## SUMMARY OF THE STORY

The Hundred Dresses is a story about a girl named Wanda Petronski who is a polish immigrant. She attended a school where maximum students were of American origin. Wanda belonged to the economically weaker section of the society and was mocked by the other students as they thought that the name 'Wanda Petronski' was amusing.

Wanda was also a laughing stock for the girls student as she claimed to possess a hundred dresses. Peggy and Maddie generally led this group who made fun of Wanda.

Wanda's classmates discovered her talent when she won the first prize in the drawing competition as she had made hundred unique designs. The students were amazed to see a hundred dresses that were drawn by Wanda.

A letter from Wanda's father to Miss Mason- a teacher at Wanda's school acts as a turning point in the story. Mr. Petronski in his letter informed that Wanda won't be attending the school anymore as the family had shifted to another region. Mr. Petronski in his letter also pointed out that there won't be any more funny names to be laughed at.

Miss Mason was left shocked and conveyed her disappointment to the class. Maddie and Peggy were deeply affected by this letter and developed an ardent desire to apologies to Wanda. The moment the school got over, they rushed to Wanda's place .But to their dismay, there was no sign of life in and around the house.

That weekend Peggy and Maddie wrote a letter to Wanda asking her how did she like the new place. On a day near Christmas, Miss Mason announced that she has heard from Wanda. In that letter, Wanda wrote she missed everyone and conveyed her intention of gifting one dress each to Maddie and Peggy because she possessed a whole new lot of hundred dresses lined up in her new house. Both of them were happy to receive it and later realised that it was their faces she had drawn along with the dresses.

The story in a nutshell, throws light on the prejudice that people carry based on their appearances and status. It also explains the power of compassion and forgiveness that can earn us lifelong friends.

## THE HUNDRED DRESSES - I & II

### by El Bsor Ester

### Character Sketch: WANDA PETRONSKI

Wanda is the owner of the hundred dresses mentioned in the book's title. She is of Polish heritage and has a name that most people struggle to pronounce. She belongs to a poor family and lives in the poor area of town. She is a gifted artist as her work was always a treat for eyes.

Wanda is teased, not because she wears the same dress to school every day, but because she claims to have one hundred dresses at home. At first the other children believe her, assuming that she means party dresses that would be inappropriate at school, but when she tells them she has all kind of dresses, the teasing begins. She never retaliates when other children bully her. Wanda has an incredible capacity for forgiveness.

### Character Sketch: PEGGY

Peggy is the most popular girl in school and is confident and talented. Although she is the one who initiates teasing Wanda, she is not really a mean girl. She protected small children from bullies and would cry for hours if she encountered any animal that was mistreated.

In Peggy's perspective she is just calling Wanda out for her obviously silly lie about possessing one hundred dresses at home. However, Peggy along with her inseparable friend Maddie is amazed to see the drawing of a hundred dresses made by Wanda. Peggy feels rather guilty about Wanda leaving and is worried that her witty behaviour has driven Wanda away. She is not bad at heart as she realises her misconduct and is willing to apologies for her behaviour. She believes in the importance of possessing friends.

### Character Sketch: MADDIE

Maddie is Peggy's best friend and also teases Wanda. However, deep down she is well aware that this is an undesirable act .She and Wanda share one thing in common- the fact that both of them belong to a poor family. Maddie is not as popular as Peggy. She too wears Peggy's discarded clothes which her mother alters or embellishes with braid and ribbons to make sure nobody at school remembers seeing them before. It is this fact that makes her reluctant to stick up for Wanda

In the concluding part of the story, Maddie is portrayed as a strong person who promises herself not to encourage bullying at all under any given circumstances.

by **Lucio Rodrigues**

## 1. SUMMARY OF THE STORY, A BAKER FROM GOA

The lesson 'A Baker from Goa' is a description of a traditional Goan village baker that still has an important place in Goa.

At the very outset, the narrator describes how the elders often recall the time when Goa was under the rule of the Portuguese. They talk of how the importance of bakers is still maintained in their villages even after the Portuguese left. One can still find the tradition of bakery inherited from Portuguese bakers alive in the Goan baker's unique way of baking and selling their creations.

The Bakers are popularly known as 'Paders' in Goa. The mixers, moulders and their time-tested furnaces continue to serve the people of Goa. The narrator recalls his childhood days when he and his friends sorted out the bread bangles for themselves. The arrival of a baker was full of entertainment and created joyful moments for everyone in Goa. The baker's entry was marked with a jingling thud of his bamboo. The narrator remarks that bakers had an important role in society and their presence was an important part of any function or festivals. He has further observed that bakery products have a place of importance in the culture and traditions of Goa. 'Bol' or sweet bread is a part of marriage gifts, cakes and 'Bolinhas' or coconut cookies are eaten at every festival; and the lady of the house prepares sandwiches on the occasion of her daughter's engagement. Bakery was a profitable business at that time, specially, in Goa.

### Character Sketch: BAKER

The baker or the 'Pader' is portrayed as an essential part of the Goan's life. The baker or bread seller had a peculiar dress during the Portuguese days known as the Kabai. It was a single piece long frock reaching down the knees. Their plump physique made them look like a jack fruit. This was also a proof of their prosperity. The baker was punctual and taught the lesson of punctuality, honesty and cooperation to the children of Goa. He made a jingling sound with the bamboo which was music to the ears of the people giving them a pleasant feeling. The narrator mentions that the baker was a happy and satisfied person. He used to visit the village at least twice a day and his emptied huge basket was proof of great demand for his bread . With the passage of time, the baker's wardrobe changed from 'Kabai' to a shirt and trousers which were shorter than full-length ones and longer than half pants. The people of Goa and even the small children looked forward to meet the Baker every morning to relish his bread.

The baker was good at keeping track of his daily sales. He collected the bills at the month end after maintaining a record of his sales on the walls, in pencil.

The baker and his family always looked happy and prosperous in the olden days. His sweet bread till date occupies a special position in festivals and functions in Goan families.

by **Lokesh Abrol**

## 2. SUMMARY OF THE STORY, COORG

The hill station of Coorg, known in the present time as Kodagu, is the smallest district of Karnataka. It is located midway between Mysore and the coastal town of Mangalore. It is famous for coffee plantations and spices, which lend a sweet aroma to the entire region. There are many hills here; so, this place is also called 'the place of rolling hills'. Abundant rainforests cover 30 percent of the area. The suitable time to visit Coorg is from September to March.

The narrator points out that Coorgis are possibly of Greek or Arabic descent. Different sets of stories are narrated regarding the origin of Coorgis. The Coorgi men are brave warriors who are permitted to keep firearms without a license due to their trustworthiness. The women of Coorg are pretty. One of the Coorgi communities, Kodavus, though Hindus by religion, stray from mainstream Hindus in marrying within their community. Their ethnic dress, Kuppia, too is similar to the Arab garment Kuffia; therefore, they are supposed to be the descendants of Arabs.

The river Kaveri originates from Coorg. The river serves as a habitat for various fishes and animals. Tourists here enjoy adventure sports like river rafting, canoeing, rappelling, mountain biking, rock climbing and trekking. The major tourist attractions are Brahmagiri hills, Nisargadhama Island and Bylakuppe. Coorg provides the tourists a glimpse of India's diverse culture.

### Character Sketch: PEOPLE OF COORG

The people of Coorg are independent and brave. They are of Greek or Arabic descent. According to a story, a part of Alexander's army did not return and settled here. They married the locals that led to the intermingling of two different races. This is very much evident in their marriage and other religious customs. Another theory says that these people originated from the Arabs. This story holds ground looking at the wardrobe that resembles 'kuffia' worn by the Arabs.

Coorgi homes have a tradition of hospitality. Coorgis are brave people. The Coorg regiment is one of the most decorated in the Indian Army. The first Chief of the Indian Army, General Cariappa, was a Coorgi. Even today, the Kodavus are the only people in India who are allowed to carry firearms without a licence. Kodavus are nature loving people . They have been protecting their culture and environment since they inhabited this place. They worship the nature as they are well aware of the impact of interfering with nature. We should learn from them to save and respect the nature.

## GLIMPSES OF INDIA

by **Arun Kumar Datta**

## 3. SUMMARY OF THE STORY, TEA FROM ASSAM

The story 'Tea from Assam' gives an insight about the origin of tea and tea gardens of Assam. The story elaborates the train journey of two friends- Pranjol and Rajvir. Pranjol, a youngster from Assam, is Rajvir's classmate in school in Delhi. Pranjol's father is the manager of Dhekiabari tea garden in Upper Assam. Pranjol has invited Rajvir to visit his home during the summer vacation. Rajvir takes pleasure in the sight during the journey.

He looks keenly on the tea gardens and workers in plastic apron looking like dolls. He calls them 'doll like figures'. He had never seen such a magnificent sight ever. He noticed that all the tea plants were pruned to the same height. The magnificent sight of tea gardens adds to Rajvir's excitement. Pranjol informs Rajvir that Assam has the largest concentration of plantations in the world.

Rajvir, at this point, discloses the knowledge that he possesses about the origin of tea. He tells Pranjol two stories: one, of a Chinese emperor who always boiled water before drinking it; and one day, a few leaves of the twigs burning under the pot fell into the water giving it a delicious flavour. The second story was about Bodhidharma, an ancient Buddhist ascetic who cut off his eyelids because he felt sleepy during meditations. Ten tea plants grew out of the eyelids. When the leaves of these plants were put in hot water and this water was consumed, it banished sleep. He further described the origin of the words 'Chai' and 'Chini' from China.

When they arrived at Mariani junction and then at the tea garden, Rajvir elaborated his knowledge about tea. Pranjol's father was impressed on listening to the details pertaining to tea plantation that Rajvir possessed.

### Character Sketch: RAJVIR

Rajvir was a friend of Pranjol . Pranjol and Rajvir were classmates in a school in Delhi. Rajvir goes to visit Pranjol' s home in Assam situated amidst the tea garden. This shows Rajvir loves travelling . He is curious to know about new things and new places. He readily shares whatever he knows about any place .

## SUMMARY OF THE STORY

Gavin Maxwell was fond of keeping pets.  While travelling with his friend to Basra, he expressed his desire to own a pet, as he had recently lost his pet dog. The need for the pet was due to loneliness that had dawned upon the narrator.

His friend suggested him to domesticate an otter, particularly one of those that are from the marshes along river Tigris in Iraq. They left for Basra to the Consulate-General to collect and answer their mail from Europe. When they reached the destination, they found that only the friend's mail had arrived. After a few days, the friend left while the narrator was still waiting to receive his mail. Upon receiving it, he went to his room only to find an otter (brought to him in a sack), accompanied by two Arabs with a note. It was a gift from his friend. He named the otter Mijbil, or Mij, in short.

Initially, Mijbil took time to get acquainted with his surroundings. The narrator describes Mijbil as so water loving that he learnt to open the tap on his own.

While everything seemed to be going fine, the narrator had to fly to London. The trouble in this scenario was that the British airlines did not allow animals, so he had to book another flight that allowed Mij with a condition that he had to be carried in a box. Mijbil, however, during the flight created havoc for other passengers until he was put back into the box and handed over to the narrator.

London, being unfamiliar with otters, made wild guesses about what animal Mij was. Some thought it to be a baby seal, others, squirrel, or even a hippo.

## MIJBIL THE OTTER

### by Gavin Maxwell

## Character Sketch: GAVIN MAXWELL

Maxwell was a naturalist and author, best known for his work with otters. Maxwell's famous book Ring of Bright Water (1960) describes how in 1956,he brought up an otter in scotland.  He has fondness for animals .

He takes tremendous care of animals and particularly the otter gifted to him by his friend. He can also be described to be considerate towards people around. This is authenticated by the fact that he on his plane journey to London was not just concerned about Mijbil but other passengers too. He also expresses appreciation towards the Air Hostess, who helped him find Mijbil.

## Character Sketch: MIJBIL

Mijbil,the otter was in fact, of a species previously unknown to science. At last, it was christened Lutrogale perspicillata maxwelli or Maxwell's otter by a Zoologist.

He resembled a small imaginary dragon of the middle Ages. Initially, Mijbil did not seem interactive but once he is acquainted by his surroundings.  Mijbil wanted to derive pleasure from every drop of water.

Mijbil favourite game was juggling with small objects with his paws lying on his back.

Mijbil did not like to stay within any boundaries. This can be seen in the part of the story when Mijbil created chaos on the flight to London because he was being put in a box.

In a nutshell, Mijbil can be described a mischievous, fun loving creature.

## SUMMARY OF THE STORY

This story is about an eight year old girl named 'Valli' who lives near a bus stop in a village. She enjoys playing with her friends and standing in her doorway looking at the bus stop.

The reason for which Valli looked at the bus stop was a deep desire that she had; the desire to ride the bus. The bus travelled between her village and the nearest town. It passed through her street each hour, once going to the town and next, coming back. The sight of the bus, filled each time with a new set of passengers, was a source of unending joy for Valli.

Valli, in order to fulfil this desire, curtailed her expenses to manage the fare for the bus ride. In addition, she also picked up every minute detail of the bus ride to enjoy it thoroughly.

One day, she is able to realise her desire to ride the bus. She does not like being called a child; therefore, the bus conductor addresses her as 'Madam'. She looks at everything  keenly during her bus ride. Valli's bus ride is full of entertainment. She comes across a funny scene on the road. She sees that a cow is running on the road with her tail high in the air. She enjoys her ride except for one spoiler— on her return journey, she encounters a cow lying lifeless on the road. This dampens Valli's enthusiasm. She doesn't want to look out of the window any more, revealing her sensitive side.

However, by the end of the journey, Valli gathers back her happy frame of mind and wishes good bye to the conductor.

## MADAM RIDES THE BUS

### by Vallikkannan

### Character Sketch: VALLI

Valli is an eight year old cheerful girl. She is full of curiosity about things surrounding her. The idea of visiting a town fascinates her. Valli is a person of strong determination. She believes in making every effort to fulfil her desires.

It is only her determination to have a bus ride that makes her find every minute detail about it. She collects important details like time required for the entire bus journey and the bus fare.

She is wise enough not to trust the strangers as she refuses an offer of free cold drink from the conductor.

She doesn't like being addressed as a child and believes in being self reliant. She is fond of nature and its various elements. She is a sensitive girl. She does not like animals dying due to careless activities of human.  Subjects like death seem to disturb her.

She realises that in a short span of time, people/ creatures around us are snatched away by death; because the cow she had seen running on the road during her onward bus ride, she finds lying dead on her return journey. At the end, however, she recollects herself and calls her journey a good one.

### Character Sketch: BUS CONDUCTOR

The conductor is a good natured man. He is patient and does not gets offended by Valli's resenting attitude towards him.

He tries to make his passengers comfortable and help them in every possible way. He is considerate towards the elderly as well as the children. He takes special care for handicapped persons. He creates an atmosphere of good temper and kindness.

He is ready to offer help to the passengers. He is of a jovial nature and admires the confidence that Valli possesses.

## SUMMARY OF THE STORY

This story is about Gautama Buddha who gave up life full of material prosperity so as to gain true knowledge about life .He left his house even though he was a married person . He had a son named Rahul.

During one of his lectures in Benares, a woman named Kisa Gotami came to him carrying her dead child with the hope that Gautam Buddha would bring her son back to life. Gautam Buddha told her that in order to bring her son back to life, he required a handful of mustard seeds. However, Gautam Buddha put one condition before her. He asked her to get seeds from only that house where no one had lost a child, husband, parent or a friend.

Kisa Gotami visited every house, but was unable to find even a single house where no one had suffered loss of a family member or a friend. In a tired and devastated state of mind, Kisa Gotami sat down at the wayside watching the lights of the city, as they flickered up and were extinguished again. At last, the darkness of the night reigned everywhere. At this point of time, Kisa Gotami understood that a human life is similar to that. Each person born on this planet has to undergo ups and downs in life and finally at one point has to submit himself to death. She further understood that death is a universal phenomenon and therefore cannot be avoided. Gautam Buddha laid the foundation of Buddhism . King Ashoka was great follower of this path. He sent his son and daughter to far countries to propagate the ideals of Buddhism.

# THE SERMON AT BENARES

### by **Betty Renshaw**

## Character Sketch: GAUTAM BUDDHA

Gautama Buddha gave up life full of material prosperity in order to attain enlightenment. In the wake of seeing the sufferings of the world, he chose to surrender every single common delight and sought enlightenment. He at long last achieved enlightenment under a tree that came to be called as Bodhi tree. He delivered his first sermon in Benares close to the bank of the Ganges.

Gautama Buddha is the founder of the religion called Buddhism after him. He was born in Northern India as a prince named Siddhartha Gautama. When he was 12 years old, he was sent for schooling in the Hindu Sacred Scriptures. He returned four years later to get married to a princess who soon bore him a son. Prince Siddhartha lived a royal life for ten years before something changed his life. While out hunting one day, he encountered a sick man, then an aged man, then a funeral procession, and finally a monk begging for alms. These sights moved him and made him gloomy. He renounced his life of luxury and left to seek enlightenment concerning human suffering that he had witnessed. In order to find the true purpose of life, he started living the life of an ascetic. His teachings have been a great source of knowledge and inspiration.

## Character Sketch: KISA GOTAMI

Kisa Gotami is a humble woman in Benares where Gautam Buddha delivered his first sermon after enlightenment. When her only son dies, she, hysterical with overpowering grief, carries her son's corpse to every door pleading for a magic potion that could bring her son back to life. She exudes her intense love for her son.

She is led to Sakyamuni, the Buddha, who asks her to bring mustard seeds from a household where no one had died. She finds no such house; and, the exercise opens Kisa Gotami's mind. It reveals her ability to grasp the lesson of life Buddha wanted her to learn. Sitting in despair, she observes the flickering citylights and reflects that human life is just the same — taking birth and meeting death, alternately. She understands Buddha's teaching that death is inevitable and man is mortal; so, grieving for death only takes away one's peace of mind.

## SUMMARY OF THE STORY

The play 'The Proposal' is a depiction of the tendency of wealthy families to seek ties with other wealthy families, to increase their estates by encouraging marriages that make good economic sense.

The play begins with Lomov entering his neighbour Chubukov's house fully dressed up in his evening attire. Chubukov is surprised to see him well-dressed and asks him the occasion. Lomov reveals that he had come with the proposal to marry Chubukov's daughter Natalya.

Chubukov is overwhelmed about this proposal for his daughter.

When Natalya arrives, Lomov begins the conversation about how grateful and glad he is that both their families are on good terms since the very beginning. While continuing to talk about his land, he somehow mentions about Oxen Meadows which earlier was a disputed property but is now his. Natalya, at this point of time, picks up an argument with Lomov because she believes that Oxen Meadows belong to her family. The argument reaches a stage when Lomov is asked to leave the house.

While speaking ill of him, Chubukov reveals that Lomov had come with a marriage proposal for Natalya and she regrets sending him out. She tells her father to bring him back immediately.

When Lomov returns, Natalya and Lomov get into another heated argument. This argument is on a silly topic about whose dog is better.

Everyone is agitated and Lomov finally falls due to his palpitations. Even then, the cursing continues when suddenly Natalya notices that Lomov is unconscious. They try to get water down his throat but are unsuccessful and declare him dead. It is only when Lomov moves a little, they make him drink some water and Chubukov forcefully gives over Natalya's hands into his, showers his blessings and asks them to marry before another argument begins.

# THE PROPOSAL

## by **Anton Chekov**

## Character Sketch: LOMOV

Lomov was an unmarried bachelor of thirty five. He was eager to get married as he had already reached a critical age.

Lomov was a funny character who suffered from palpitations in situations of heated arguments. He behaved like an eccentric. He was silly to quarrel on topics like Oxen Meadows and dogs.

He is a simple person rather than someone bearing grudges as he readily agrees to marry Natalya.

## Character Sketch: NATALYA

Natalaya was a young unmarried girl of twenty five years. She lived in the neighbourhood of Lomov, a bachelor aged thirty five.

She was an excellent housekeeper and was in desperate search for love. Though she was well educated, it did not reflect in her behavior. She was very quarrelsome and abusive by nature. She began a bitter quarrel with Lomov over a piece of land and soon turned it into a intense one.

When Lomov faints out of palpitation, she is scared and makes every effort to bring back Lomov to his consciousness. This shows she was caring . She was successful in doing so and takes her father's blessings to marry Lomov.

# FIRST FLIGHT

### Poetry

## SUMMARY OF THE POEM

We all go through days when we want to curl up inside the warmth of the blanket in our room and not face the outside world. There could be umpteen causes for such a feeling—bad grades at school; scolding by a loved one; missing a dear friend immensely, etc. The short poem 'Dust of Snow' by Robert Frost echoes the same sentiment wherein the poet is in a gloomy mood and is regretting the happenings of the day.

The poem is split in two stanzas of four lines each:

In the first stanza, the poet describes what once happened to him, on one of his not-so-bright days. He was, perhaps, standing beneath or walking by a hemlock tree when a crow slid down a speck of snow on him. The incident though insignificant and trivial, had a lasting impact on the poet. The aforementioned impact is described in the next stanza.

In the second stanza, the poet describes how the touch of snow brings about a change in his mood—from sad to happy. He also describes how he was disliking and regretting the day, but the crow's incidental act saved him from the despair.

A light read, the poem reminds us how small things which we mostly overlook, hold supreme value like the big, hyped things. Had the snow speck not fallen on Frost, he would have remained cheerless. The poem owes Frost's subsequently achieved cheerfulness to the crow's accidental action.

## DUST OF SNOW

## ABOUT THE POET

**Robert Frost** (26 March 1874–29 January 1963) was the most famous American poet of the 20th century. He was greatly lauded for his:

- accurate description of rural New England.
- realistic and relatable verse centering around ordinary people in ordinary, everyday situations.
- great grasp of American colloquial speech.

He was the Poet Laureate, a title granted in England in the 17th century for poetic excellence, from 1958–1959. He was also a proud recipient of Bollingen Prize (award for achievement in American poetry) and Pulitzer Prize (award for achievement in American journalism, letters and music).

His notable works include poems such as "The Road Not Taken", "Stopping by Woods on a Snow Evening", "Mending Wall", "After Apple-Picking", "A Boy's Will", "New Hampshire", and "The Death of the Hired Man". He wrote the poem "The Road Not Taken" as a joke about his friend.

## POETIC DEVICES/FIGURES OF SPEECH IN THE POEM

### 1. Alliteration

"And saved some part"

The repeated "s" sound in "saved some" make the poem fun to read aloud as the repeated consonant sound of "s" allows the words to appear perhaps playful and enjoyable.

### 2. Symbolism

Symbolism is the use of symbols to represent ideas. In the poem, 'hemlock tree' symbolises sorrow and 'snow' symbolises joy.

### 3. Assonance

The effect of assonance is created in the poem when words—such as 'way' and 'day'; 'change' and 'saved'—that are close together have the same vowel sound but different consonants.

## SUMMARY OF THE POEM

All living beings are mortal and would cease to exist one day. Like humans, sooner or later the world too would reach the perish line and meet its expiry date. The perishable property of the world forms the undercurrent of Frost's poem 'Fire and Ice'.

In the first stanza of the poem, Frost expresses that the end of the world would be caused by either of the two natural elements—fire or ice. He adds that a section of world's inhabitants believe that there would be a day when the Earth's surface will get furnace-like hot that it would eventually result in fire destroying everything. The other section of people is of the view that the catastrophic effect of destruction would be caused by a significant dip in the level of Earth's temperature. Frost then relates the natural phenomenon of fire and ice with the man-made emotions of desire and hatred respectively. He continues saying that his experience of desire, compels him to side with the section that believes the end would be caused by fire. By this, he essentially means that limitless longing and allowing emotions to take control, leads to a state of utter chaos.

In the second stanza, Frost adds that if by any chance the world had two expiry dates, then ice would have been equally competitive in destructing it. By doing so, he brings to light a subtle contrast between 'ice' and 'hatred'. The twin capabilities of humans of hatred and insensitivity have the power of inner destruction.  Though a slow and steady killer, hatred has the same consequences as desire. So, if Frost were given an option between fire and ice, both would be equally good to bring about an end to the world.

## FIRE AND ICE

### ABOUT THE POET

**Robert Frost** (26 March 1874–29 January 1963) was the most famous American poet of the 20th century.  He was greatly lauded for his:

- accurate description of rural New England.
- realistic and relatable verse centering around ordinary people in ordinary, everyday situations.
- great grasp of American colloquial speech.

He was the Poet Laureate, a title granted in England in the 17th century for poetic excellence, from 1958–1959. He was also a proud recipient of Bollingen Prize (award for achievement in American poetry) and Pulitzer Prize (award for achievement in American journalism, letters and music).

His notable works include poems such as "The Road Not Taken", "Stopping by Woods on a Snow Evening", "Mending Wall", "After Apple-Picking", "A Boy's Will", "New Hampshire", and "The Death of the Hired Man". He wrote the poem "The Road Not Taken" as a joke about his friend.

### POETIC DEVICES/FIGURES OF SPEECH IN THE POEM

**1. Assonance**

The effect of assonance is created in the poem when long 'o' sound words—such as 'hold' and 'those'—that are close together have the same vowel sound but different consonants.

**2. Alliteration**

The repeated "f" sound in "favour fire" and "w" sound in "world will" make the poem fun to read aloud as the repeated consonant sounds allow the words to appear both playful and enjoyable.

**3. Anaphora**

The group of words "Some say" is repeated at the start of Lines 1 and 2 of the poem. This repetition of a word or a group of words at the start of two or more consecutive lines is termed anaphora.

## SUMMARY OF THE POEM

Imagine a day you did something wrong and were locked up in a room for the whole day. How did you feel? Suffocated, bored and irritated to sum the least. Now picture the plight of animals caged in zoos for human infotainment. Don't they feel suffocated, bored and irritated? Yes, they do.

In the poem, 'A Tiger in the Zoo' the poet 'Leslie Norris' records a contrast between a tiger stuck in the zoo and a tiger fearlessly prancing in its vast natural habitat, the jungle.

The tiger, covered in vivid stripes, walks about in the small space offered by his enclosure at the zoo. The loneliness that accompanies his life in the cage has muted his rage. He, like others of his family, should ideally have been walking through the tall and long blades of the grass in the jungle; hiding behind the blades near a water body where he would hunt plump, thirsty deer. He should be making his way from the jungle to the houses near it to frighten the villagers with his white fangs and sharp claws.

Unfortunately, the tiger is deprived of all that he should be doing freely. He is locked in a cage in the zoo where he gets no chance to hunt, to frighten or to display his mighty strength. He is looked upon by visitors as if he is a showpiece and he prefers to ignore their countless numbers passing by his cage every day.

Every night, the last sound his ears hear is that of the patrolling cars. At this time of the day, he is mostly staring at the night sky and the countless stars in it, as if conversing and requesting the universe to let him free at the earliest.

## A TIGER IN THE ZOO

### ABOUT THE POET

**Leslie Norris** (1921–2006) was a Welsh poet and short-story writer. Until 1974, he made his living by donning the hats of a college lecturer, teacher and headmaster. From 1974, he took up writing as a full-time career with residencies at academic institutions in the United States and Britain. Contemporarily, he is remembered as one of the most significant Welsh writers of the post-war period. His collections—Collected Stories of Leslie Norris and Collected Poems—have won many rewards namely the Cholmondeley Poetry Prize, the Katherine Mansfield Memorial Award, the David Higham Memorial Prize, the AML Award and the Welsh Arts Council Senior Fiction Award. They were both published in 1996 by Seren, a Welsh publisher.

### POETIC DEVICES/FIGURES OF SPEECH IN THE POEM

**1. Oxymoron**

"quiet rage"

An oxymoron is a phrase that combines two words that seem to be the opposite of each other. 'Rage' is loud and full of anger but the helpless tiger caged in a zoo has a quiet, muted rage.

**2. Personification**

The tiger deprived of the simple pleasures of prancing fearlessly and hunting at will, has been addressed by the poet with the pronoun used for human males, 'he'.

**3. Metaphor**

The paws of the tiger in captivity are compared to pads of velvet. He can no longer use his noise-free velvety paws to hunt on plump deer as he is stuck in a cage where he can only hope for a free life.

## SUMMARY OF THE POEM

We differentiate between different humans on the basis of their physical attributes and nature. Similarly, we differentiate between different animals on the basis of their differentiating physical and temperamental characteristics. In the poem 'How to Tell Wild Animals' the poet 'Carolyn Wells' has talked about the traits that can help man recognise a few wild animals. Her tone is not terse and serious like a zoologist's but is funny and humorous like a comedienne's.

She begins by describing the Asian lion—an animal with tawny skin who inhabits the jungles of the east and whose thunderous roar can lead to fear-caused death. She describes the Bengal tiger as a noble animal, that attacks and kills swiftly, saving pain. She remarks in humour, that if ever a black-striped, beautiful-looking animal attacks, kills and eats you, be certain that you have met a Bengal tiger! Next, she acquaints the reader with another ferocious feline—the black-spotted leopard who leaps; adding, that if the leopard's victim cries with fear, it only instigated the animal to leap again. Next, she describes the bear, who is fond of hugging and has given us the bear-hug. Its extremely tight hug can even result in death.

The poet explains how hyenas and crocodiles behave while killing their prey—the former smile merrily while the latter let out fake tears. The last in her list is a lizard-like creature called chameleon. She points out that unlike a lizard, a chameleon does not have ears and wings. But it has a unique quality of camouflaging by changing its colour to merge with the surface on which it sits. She enlightens her readers, that if they cannot see anything on the tree, they have seen the chameleon who has camouflaged well with the tree.

## HOW TO TELL WILD ANIMALS

## ABOUT THE POET

**Carolyn Wells** (1862–1942) was a prolific American writer who is fondly remembered for her popular children's books, mysteries and humorous verse. She complemented her formal education with her love for voracious reading. She worked as a librarian, after completing her schooling, for some years. She loved puzzles and her love took the form of her first book of charades, At the Sign of the Sphinx. She followed with The Jingle Book, The Story of Betty and Idle Idyls. Over the years, she wrote nearly 170 titles that fell into a wide array of genres: mystery stories, detective stories, children's stories, anthologies, humorous and nonsense writings. Wells gained popularity mainly because of her nonsense verse and whimsical pieces.

## POETIC DEVICES/FIGURES OF SPEECH IN THE POEM

**1. Poetic license**

As soon as he has lept on you

The poet has taken poetic license, or the freedom to depart from the fact or convention in order to create an effect, in changing the spelling of the word 'leapt' to 'lept'.

**2. Alliteration**

A novice might nonplus; roaming round; If when you're walking round your yard

The effect of alliteration is created by the repetition of sound 'n' in the words 'novice' and 'nonplus';

sound 'r' in 'roaming round' and 'round your yard'; sound 'y' in 'you're…your yard'; and sound 'w' in 'when…walking'; etc.

**3. Inversion**

The Bengal Tiger to discern

The poet has changed the standard format of a sentence by applying the inversion literary technique.

**4. Assonance:**

or if some time when roaming round

The effect of assonance is created by the repetition of the vowel sound 'o'.

## SUMMARY OF THE POEM

We all get upset and disappointed when something we love or value a lot, goes far from us. It could be a material possession or a familial relation. In the poem 'The Ball Poem', the poet 'John Berryman' describes the importance of letting go and moving on, by giving the example of a boy who has lost his ball.

A young boy was playing with a ball when it bounced down the street and accidentally made its way in the water. The incident leaves the boy unhappy and teary. He wants his very same ball back in his hands. The adults around him would recommend him to get another ball to play with, but the boy wants the ball in water as he associates it with the wonderful memories of his childhood.

The boy stares at his ball rested in the harbour, stiff and trembling. The poet does not want to intrude his feelings nor does he want to suggest him to buy another ball as he wants the boy to learn about the meaning of loss and experience the momentary pain associated with moving on.

According to the poet, the loss of the ball will help the child realise that in the world full of possessions, there will be times when people will snatch away an opportunity from him; times when his  belonging(s) would get lost and times when no one would offer to get him something he lost and misses a lot. So as part of growing up, the child needs to learn some lessons in pain.

The poet further adds that the incident involving the loss of the ball will help the child understand the true meaning of loss and the way to bear and put on a brave front, in testing times.

## THE BALL POEM

## ABOUT THE POET

**John Berryman** (1914–1972) was a scholar, professor and poet. He shot to fame with his intensely personal sequence of 385 poems called Dream Songs (1969), which made him the proud recipient of the Pulitzer Prize and National Book Award. The sequence became a worldwide hit because of its varied form and style that encapsulated a vast range of material and expressed Berryman's turbulent emotions. The frankness and the depth in his works influenced his friend Robert Lowell and many other Confessional poets like Anne Saxton. He struggled with depression and alcoholism throughout his life. The struggle ended in 1972 when in the dead of winter, Berryman jumped off a Minneapolis Bridge. Some of his notable works include The Dispossessed and Homage to Mistress Bradstreet.

## POETIC DEVICES/FIGURES OF SPEECH IN THE POEM

### 1. Symbolism

The ball in the poem is symbolic of the child's wonderful childhood. It could be a plaything for most of us, but for the child it held more value as he associated his beautiful past with it.

### 2. Imagery

"bouncing down the street"

The poet's words help us create a vivid picture of a ball bouncing down the street.

### 3. Anaphora

The use of anaphora is noticeable in a few sentences beginning with the same word 'What'.

What is the boy now, who has lost his ball,

What, what is he to do? I saw it go

## SUMMARY OF THE POEM

Our parents constantly remind us to refrain from doing a zillion things: watching television, eating chocolates, playing in the mud, cycling on the footpath, etc. Do your parents' reminders bother you? They sure do. In the poem 'Amanda!', the poet 'Robin Klein', gives voice to a young girl named Amanda's feelings when she is controlled and repeatedly instructed by her parents.

Amanda's parents remind her not to bite her nails, not to bend her shoulders, not to slouch and to sit up straight. The poor girl, Amanda gets so bothered by the constant scoldings that she wishes to be a mermaid in a sea that is relaxed, and which has no inhabitants, the sole inhabitant being she herself. That way, there would be no one to watch over and scold her, and she would get to live a free life.

Amanda's parents ask her if she has finished her homework, has tidied her room and cleaned her shoes. Little Amanda wishes to be an orphan, a child without parents. She wants to roam the streets freely and taste the sweet flavour of freedom.

Amanda is asked to not eat chocolates, to remember her acne and to look at her parents when they speak to her. Amanda wishes to lead a tranquil life in a tower like that of a Rapunzel with absolutely nobody to disturb her. She is certain to not let her hair down as then someone might climb the tower.

Through the poem, the poet brings to light the negative effects of parents' constant jabber on young minds.

## AMANDA

### ABOUT THE POET

**Robin Klein** (1936–present) is an Australian author for children's books. She worked as a tea lady, nurse, bookshop assistant, before becoming an established writer. She suffered an aneurysm rupture and is living in a nursing home since 2005. Because of her illness, she no longer writes or publicises her books. She is well-known for Hating Alison Ashley, Halfway Across the Galaxy and Turn Left, Came Back to Show You I Could Fly and Boss of the Pool. In her brief writing career, she has been the proud recipient of Human Rights Literature and Awards (1989) and Dromkeen Medal (1991).

### POETIC DEVICES/FIGURES OF SPEECH IN THE POEM

**1. Anaphora:** Repeated use of a word at start of two or more lines

don't bite… don't hunch

**2. Metaphor**

A metaphor is used when a covert comparison is struck by the poet between two different things. In the poem, it is used when Amanda compares herself to mermaid, orphan and Rapunzel in stanzas 2, 4 and 6 respectively.

**3. Alliteration:** Repetition of a consonant sound

Stop that slouching and sit up straight

's' sound is being repeated at the start of closely placed words.

## SUMMARY OF THE POEM

Do you feel animals are better than humans, or are they as corrupt and selfish as humans? In the poem 'Animals', the poet 'Walt Whitman' applauds animals for displaying qualities that humans lack.

The poet wishes to turn into an animal and live with animals as they are calm and their mind is pure. Unlike the human race, animals are satisfied with their lives and cheerful in their natural surroundings. The simplicity of life helps animals practice self-control and stay rational. The poet stares at them adoringly for a long time.

The poet feels that animals neither complain nor whine about their conditions. They eat and sleep in peace as they have nothing to worry about. In contrast, human mind keeps racing even at the odd hours of night due to which they can't sleep cosily. Humans commit sins and then talk about God and rightness whereas animals are simple creatures who do not have to put the false front of praying to God. The poet implies that animals are so pure that they don't need to pray to God asking for forgiveness.

Unlike humans, animals are not proud owners of material belongings so they don't have any desires. They also do not have any ancestors whom they should pay respect to as all of them are equal.

The poet further adds that animals and humans are related in one way: Animals possess what humans once had—virtues of kindness, innocence and contentment. He believes that civlisation corrupted human race and taught it greed and stole away all positive values from it. He believes that in the race of competition, humans dropped and forgot all the values.

## ANIMALS

### ABOUT THE POET

**Walt Whitman** (1819–1891) was an American poet, journalist and essayist. He is a latter-day successor to Homer, Virgil, Shakespeare and Dante. His collection of verse titled Leaves of Grass, published in 1855, is a landmark in the history of American Literature. The collection celebrates democracy, nature, friendship and love. It praises both body and soul and echoed beauty and reassurance in death. Some of his other notable works include "Drum-Taps", 'Democratic Vistas', "Crossing Brooklyn Ferry", "O Captain! My Captain!", "I Sing the Body Electric" and "Specimen Days and Collect". These works influenced later poets like Ezra pound, William Carlos Williams, Simon Ortiz and Allen Ginsberg.

### POETIC DEVICES/FIGURES OF SPEECH IN THE POEM

#### 1. Repetition

They do not sweat and whine about their condition,

They do not lie awake in the dark and weep for their sins,

They do not make me sick discussing their duty to God

In each of these lines, the group of words 'They do not' is repeated. The poet has done this to show the contrast between animals and humans.

#### 2. Alliteration

They do not make me sick

I wonder where they get these tokens

The effect of alliteration is created by the repetition of the sounds 'm' and 'w' in 'make and me' and 'wonder and where' respectively.

#### 3. Free Verse

Whitman was instrumental in breaking the classic rhythmic or metred poetry. He became famous for writing a revolutionary new kind of poetry which was in free verse—poetry without a regular rhythm or rhyme.

## SUMMARY OF THE POEM

To meet the demands of the ever-growing population, trees are being cut down in large numbers. The forests are deprived of trees, however they adorn human houses. Have you ever felt how trees feel inside your house and away from their natural surroundings? The poem 'The Trees' by Adrienne Rich echoes the sentiments of a population of trees trying to free themselves from the confinement of a greenhouse or a container of nature.

According to the poet, the treeless forests didn't seem inviting to birds, insects or the sun. And now that the trees are moving into the forest, it would be full of them by morning.

The poet describes the struggles undertaken by the trees to reach the forest: the roots burnt the midnight oil to disjoint themselves from the floor of the veranda; the tiny stems put in a lot of strength to free themselves; and the big branches also pulled out themselves from the roof of the room. The efforts of different parts to pull and run away is compared to a patient who has just been discharged and is confused as he/she is under the influence of some sleep-inducing drug.

The poet further adds that she is sitting in her veranda and writing long letters which have no mention of the departure of the trees from her house. She says that the night is clear with full moon visibility. The smell of leaves and lichens is expressing and shouting a desire for freedom.

The poet's head is full of the slow sounds made by the trees desperate to move into the forest. She is certain there sounds will not be heard the following morning. She asks her reader to pay attention to the change that is going to take place.

## THE TREES

## ABOUT THE POET

**Adrienne Rich** (1929–2012) was born in Baltimore, Maryland, USA. She was a famous poet, scholar, teacher, critic, essayist and feminist. She has published nineteen volumes of poetry, three collections of essays and other writings. Her volumes of poetry trace a stylistic transformation from formal, well-crafted but imitative poetry to a more personal and powerful style. She was the proud recipient of Bollingen Prize (2003), National Book Critics' Circle Award (2004) and Wallace Stevens Award (1996). Her works reflect her mastery of the formal elements of poetry and her considerable restraint. Rich addressed many problems plaguing humanity, as well as the role of her art form in addressing them. Some of her notable works include A Change of World, The Diamond Cutters and Other Poems, Telephone Ringing in the Labyrinth, Tonight No Poetry Will Serve and What Is Found There: Notebooks on Poetry and Politics.

## POETIC DEVICES/FIGURES OF SPEECH IN THE POEM

**1. Personification**

No sun bury its feet in shadow

Sun has been personified here, i.e. given a human characteristic. Since the forest is treeless, Sunlight cannot form any shadows.

**2. Imagery**

The trees inside are moving out into the forest,

This line helps to draw an image in mind, of the trees walking out from inside the houses and entering inside treeless forests.

**3. Anaphora**

No insect hide

No sun bury its feet in shadow

Both of the above lines begin with the same word 'no'. This helps to pay emphasis to what the treeless forests lacked.

## SUMMARY OF THE POEM

During winter mornings, we see a thick cloud of tiny water droplets in the atmosphere around us. These droplets are called fog and they visit uninvited. In the poem 'Fog', the poet 'Carl Sandburg' compares fog to another common uninvited visitor, cat.

The poet describes the arrival of fog towards the city and the harbour. He says like the little feet of cat, fog also visits the city on its little feet. By this, he essentially means that the fog is advancing towards the city slowly and calmly in a hushed manner like a cat. We never know when fog would visit us just as we don't know when cat, an unpredictable visitor, would visit us.

He further adds that the cloud of fog sits over the city in a manner similar to that of a cat folding its legs behind itself and looking around nearby places and things. Similarly, it seems that the fog is sitting over the harbour and the city and is looking at the nearby happenings with keen eyes.

After sitting and observing the city for a while, the fog leaves silently. (The fog is a natural phenomenon that does not stay at a place for a long time and generally leaves after a few hours.) Just like a cat, the fog arrives and leaves without being noticed by anyone.

The poem is an extended metaphor and it fills the reader's mind with the twin images of fog and cat. The comparison helps the poet to accord the status of a living entity to fog.

## FOG

## ABOUT THE POET

**Carl Sandburg** (1878–1967) was an American poet, historian, novelist and folklorist. His autobiography, Always the Young Strangers (1953) describes the other occupations he tried his hands on including a barbershop porter, a milk truck driver, a brickyard hand and a harvester. Sandburg's poetry became popular as it made an instant and favourable impression on the reader's minds. He was the proud recipient of Grammy Award and Pulitzer Prize. Some of his notable works include Abraham Lincoln: The War Years, , Remembrance Rock, The People, Yes and Chicago. He wrote four books for children: Rootabaga Stories (1922), Rootabaga Pigeons (1923), Rootabaga Country (1929) and Potato Face (1930).

## POETIC DEVICES/FIGURES OF SPEECH IN THE POEM

**1. Metaphor**

Fog has been compared to a cat which comes and leaves uninvited and unnoticed. Its arrival and departure are both very silent and calm.

**2. Personification**

Fog has been personified, i.e. given the human traits of coming, sitting, looking and moving on.

**3. Enjambment**

It sits looking

Over harbour and city

The line continues to the next line and then completes the thought conveyed by the poet.

## SUMMARY OF THE POEM

We all have that one friend who never really knows about his/her real talents. We also have a friend who loves boasting. The poem 'The Tale of Custard the Dragon' by the poet 'Ogden Nash' is a humorous account of a timid dragon and a few boastful pets around him.

A little girl named Belinda lives in a little house with her pets: a little black kitten named Ink; a little grey mouse named Blink; a little yellow dog named Mustard; and a little pet dragon named Custard. The dragon had sharp teeth, spikes, scales, fireplace-like mouth and chimney-like nose. Despite of such fierce physical traits, the dragon was timid and coward. Unlike the dragon, Belinda was bear-like brave, the kitten and the mouse could chase lions and the dog was tiger-like brave.

Belinda, kitten, mouse and the dog made fun of the dragon's timidity. Each time he cried for a nice safe cage, the other pets mocked at him.

One day, a pirate, with a pistol in each of his hand, came to Belinda's house. Belinda cried for help and the kitten, the mouse and the dog fled from the scene. Little Custard fought with the pirate and gobbled him down.

Belinda hugged Custard for saving their lives, but the kitten, the mouse and the dog confessed to having fought the lion more bravely if they hadn't got confused. Little Custard still believed that the other animals were braver than him.

To sum, Ogden Nash has tried to bring home the point that sometimes a timid person proves to be the real hero and the saviour in the toughest situations thrown at us in life.

## THE TALE OF CUSTARD THE DRAGON

## ABOUT THE POET

**Ogden Nash** (1902–1971) was an American writer of humorous poetry. He won a large fan-following for his audacious verse. Certain Nash lines like 'If called by a panther, don't anther' have become important bits of American folklore. He remarked that in the turbulence of the modern world, there was a dire need of the whimsy offered by his verses: 'In chaos sublunary/What remains constant but buffoonery?' His peculiar variety of poetic buffoonery combines imagination and wit with eminently memorable rhymes. Some of his well-known poems are: A Caution to Everybody, Adventures of Isabel, A Word to Husbands, A Lady Who Thinks She is Thirty, A Drink with Something In It, and Always Marry an April Girl.

## POETIC DEVICES/FIGURES OF SPEECH IN THE POEM

**1. Poetic License**
The spellings of the words 'real' and 'true' have been changed to 'realio' and 'trulio' to create a musical effect.

**2. Anaphora**
And the little grey mouse, she called him Blink,
And the little yellow dog was sharp as Mustard
The word 'and' has been used at the beginning of both the above lines.

**3. Simile**
Belinda was as brave as a barrel full of bears
Mustard was as brave as a tiger in a rage
Both Belinda and Mustard are portrayed to be brave. Their courage is compared to bears and an angry tiger respectively.

# SUMMARY OF THE POEM

Do you think physic appearance plays an important role in deciding whom we should love? Well, inner beauty certainly outweighs outer beauty in the long run.

In the first six lines of the poem, the poet is speaking to a young maiden named Anne Gregory. He tells her that her hair is honey-like and when they fall over her ear, he is reminded of the ramparts surrounding and protecting a castle from attack. The poet is certain that many young men fall in love with Anne because of her appearance and her yellow hair. He feel that these men have no knowledge of Anne's inner beauty as they have no knowledge of it.

In the next six lines, Anne is replying to the poet and telling him if her hair is the only thing that men like in him, then she can easily dye it using some other colours like brown, carrot or black. What Anne implies is that she can choose to look ugly to find out if it is possible for men to love her despite her ugliness.

In the last six lines, the poet tells Anne that the previous night, he met a religious-minded man who asserted that he had found a manuscript that stated that only God could love any if she turned ugly. In other words, the poet is trying to convey that most men cannot look beyond the physical beauty of a woman.

## FOR ANNE GREGORY

### ABOUT THE POET

**William Butler Yeats** (1865–1939) was an Irish poet, dramatist, and prose writer. One of the greatest English-language poets of the twentieth century, he received the Nobel Prize for Literature in 1923. Some of his notable works include The Wild Swans at Coole, Leda and the Swan, The Second Coming, The Countess Cathleen, Sailing to Byzantium, The Tower, At the Hawk's Well and The Green Helmet. Most of his poetry used symbols from ordinary life and from familiar traditions. He founded the Abbey theatre and was extremely active in its management. He wrote ten plays and the simple style of dialogue became an important consideration in his poems as well.

### POETIC DEVICES/FIGURES OF SPEECH IN THE POEM

#### 1. Apostrophe

The rhetorical device named Apostrophe is used when the poet addresses the poem to an absent audience. In 'For Anne Gregory', the poet is addressing himself to Anne Gregory, but the readers do not see him at any point in the poem.

#### 2. Metaphor

A metaphor is used when a covert comparison is made between two different things or ideas. In the poem, the comparison is made when the poet compares Anne's hair with the ramparts of a castle. Like the ramparts protect the castle, Anne's hair protect her face from being seen completely.

#### 3. Metonymy

A metonym is used to substitute an attribute or an adjunct for the thing meant. In the poem, while making suggestions about the colours Anne can dye her hair into, the poet uses 'carrot' to mean the colour 'orange'.

# FOOTPRINTS WITHOUT FEET

## THEME

Over indulgence and excessive display of love may often have negative effects. Self-discipline and physical well-being is important for a healthy existence. Love does not mean----smothering, it involves caring.

## SUMMARY OF THE STORY

This is the story of a dog name Tricki and his mistress Mrs Pumphrey. She loved her little dog excessively. Mrs Pumpfrey worried that her dog was mal-nourished and therefore fed him with all the wrong food which made him lazy, fat, and therefore inactive. This she misunderstood as ill-health and indulged in him even further. Overfeeding on one hand and lack of exercise on the other affected the poor canine's health. Mr. Herriot, the veterinary doctor was called upon to help handle the pathetic condition of the poor dog. He advised reducing the feed and increasing his exercise schedules, so as to burn the excess fat and thereby lower the immense pressure that was being put on his heart.

However within a few days a very distraught Mrs Humphrey makes a desperate call to the vet. Tricki health was failing further. Hospitalisation was now inevitable. Mr Herriot, refusing to be swayed by the emotions of the pet's mother, took the ailing dog to his hospital. At the hospital, along with the other dogs, Tricki managed to put in efforts to move his body, rush for meals, play with them, run around and thereby acquire the exercise he needed to reduce his weight. He began losing his weight and enjoying his life along with his friends. Within a short span of two weeks the obese Tricki was transformed into a lithe, muscular and agile dog.

Mr Herriot informed Mrs Humphrey that Tricki was now ready to be taken back home. When she saw her dog healthy and strong, she was overwhelmed and thanked the doctor profusely. She assumed that the transformation of the dog was the triumph of a surgery that was done on him.

## A TRIUMPH OF SURGERY

### *by* **James Herriot**

### Character Sketch: MRS HUMPHREY

Mrs Humphrey is a rich who led a very comfortable life in a huge mansion perhaps, with a number of maids and staff. The lady has perhaps not had the opportunity to understand or experience the hardships of life. As is commonly seen, Mrs Humphrey had a dog to be part of her extremely lavish life style. She is extremely fond of the animal and smothers him with her love. She treats him like a human child, and feeds him with food that caused more harm to the poor canine than good. His failing health made Mrs Humphrey very concerned, and the silly lady began feeding him more, as she assumed that his deteriorating health was due to mal-nutrition. This resulted in his condition failing even further. She had to then seek medical help, to revive the poor dog, which was on the verge of near death. It goes without saying that the lady had kept the dog to fill in the empty spaces in her lonely life. She had not been prepared to take care of the canine in a scientific manner. Thereby she comes across as an absolute failure as a dog parent.

### Character Sketch: MR HERRIOT

The narrator of the story, Mr James Herriot is a veterinarian by profession. He seems to be a person who has chosen to do the job out of his own volition and not by default. In the story we get to see the dignity and excellence with which he saves a dog from eminent death. Tricki is the dog in question. He is an excessively obese dog, that suffers a great deal because of the over indulgence of his human mother. Seeing him unable to eat his favourite food, immobile and panting with any slight movement, accompanied by bouts of vomiting, the vet. Decides to take him over to his hospital and keep him there for observation. The doctor just thought that it was important to keep hydrating the dog, keeping him off rich and unhealthy food and making him burn his excessive fat. This is exactly that he did. In a short span of three to four days, Tricki began taking his first steps forward towards regaining his lost health. Within a fortnight he was transformed into an agile, muscular dog, keeping pace with the other dogs at the doctor's place. His love for animals and his determination to keep them as healthy as possible comes across very profoundly in the narrative. Besides of this, Mr Herriot is also very sensitive and understanding towards the lonely Mrs Humphrey and does nothing to hurt her, or admonish her, in any way while trying to resolve the crisis, created by the poor handling of her pet.

## THEME

Love, care and sensitivity may sometimes help to change the course of an individual's life. Also the author wishes to establish the importance of education in a human-beings life.

## SUMMARY OF THE STORY

This is the story of a 15 year old petty thief, Hari Singh (his name in this story), and his interlude with Anil. Hari tries to charm his way into Anil's life and home. He requests Anil to allow him to work for him (Anil). Anil was a struggling writer, often seen with a little or no currency in his wallet. Hari was willing to do so in return for food and a roof over his head. Yielding to his request Anil decides to take him on as a cook. This proved to be a big mistake as the young teenager did not know the ABC of cooking. Thus Hari was told to leave.

Hari was in no mood to give up. Using his exceptional charm, he found his way back into his new found home. Along with give him a roof over his head, Anil decided to teach Hari cooking and also introduce him to the world of letters. The errand boy and helper Hari would not miss a chance of pocketing a coin or two while he shopped for the house-hold supplies.

The twist in the story occurred when Anil came home one day with a lot of money. This was as a result of his book being published. Seeing this the thief in Hari raised its head. At night he when Anil was asleep, he stole the money and planned to escape from the city to make a new beginning. However, his conscience perhaps, told him otherwise. He could not go. Stranded in a railway platform, nowhere to go on a cold winter night, accompanied by rain, Hari decides to return back to his mentor's home. Slipping in silently, he replaces the money from where he had taken.

Hari, the thief, had been reformed. The following morning, Anil promised him to make further progress with his studies, totally ignoring the happenings of the night while handing him a moist 50 rupee note.

## THE THIEF'S STORY

### by Ruskin Bond

### Character Sketch: HARI SINGH

The author Ruskin Bond, has portrayed a very typical character of an orphaned and wayward teenager, Hari Singh as his protagonist.

Hari singh is a young lad, left alone in the world apparently as the author makes no mention of a family while describing him. He moved from place to place taking a new name and a new identity after every theft. A true charmer, Hari knew the ways of the world and how to con his way to exist. In this part of his life however, we see a transformation that happened to him as a result of the treatment he received from his new victim—Anil, a writer. This association made Hari realise the importance of education and trust. He realised that being literate could change the course of his life. Hari a petty thief was taken away from the world of crime and introduced into the mainstream of society.

### Character Sketch: ANIL

Anil is a writer by profession and a struggling one at that. This 25 year old man, has be described as easy-going, kind and simple by the author Ruskin Bond. Being vulnerable may also be considered as one of his characteristics, as he falls prey to the charms of a petty thief very easily.

Anil was conned into being sympathetic to the plight of a poor teenager who sought refuge in his home. Though penniless for most of the time, the young man did not refrain from providing succour to the vagabond and employed him as his cook. Along with teaching him to cook, he also very generously introduced him to the world of letters. Anil perhaps was able to understand the misery of the young lad, as he himself struggled for want of money. This made him magnanimous enough to overlook the fact, that his young cook tricked him of money, while running errands for household goods. This kind writer's attitude played a major role in transforming the life of a potential hard-core criminal and ensuring that he was allowed to lead a dignified life in the society.

# THEME

The importance of a keen presence of mind to keep one safe during adverse situations

# SUMMARY OF THE STORY

The midnight visitor, as the name suggests is a thriller, written by the author Robert Arthur. This short story has a comic streak to it. The protagonist Ausable, is a secret agent, portrayed as a very fat man, who spoke in an American accent. Ausable was meeting up with a writer, Fowler, who seemed disillusioned, as what he expected to get acquainted with was not anywhere close to his expectations. Ausable however, takes him to his small, dingy hotel room giving him the assurance that the drama Fowler was looking for was yet to come. He mentioned about a certain paper that he was expecting. He then told the young writer that the paper was the one that would change history.

A s they enter Ausable's little room, they were in for surprise, as they stood face to face who was wielding a gun. This was Max another secret agent, whom Ausable recognised. Max mentioned that he was there to take the paper before Ausable laid his hand on it. How did Max enter the room?

The smart Ausable did not lack a presence of mind. He changed the tone and tenor of the conversation that Max had resorted to, and expressed dismay with the management of the hotel for ignoring his concern regarding the access people had into his room through the erstwhile balcony by the window. He added that the room-break had happened earlier too.

A knock on the door was what changed the whole course of events. Was this pre-planned too? Perhaps! Ausable warned Max that the police were at the door. Repeated knocks agonised the rival secret agent. Max decided to temporarily step into the balcony. Lo and behold, what followed was a thud. Was there a balcony at all? And who was at the door?

Fowler the writer had perhaps found something worthy after all, in the personality, style and functioning of the ungainly and unimpressive secret agent Ausable.

## THE MIDNIGHT VISITOR

### by Robert Arthur

## Character Sketch: AUSABLE

The author Robert Arthur chose to portray an unconventional picture of a secret agent in his story "The Midnight visitor".

Ausable is described as being fat, with a peculiar accent, living in a gloomy down-market French hotel. In his preliminary interaction with Fowler, a writer of romantic adventure books, he came across as an absolute disappointment. Ausable did not meet the accepted personality norms required for thorough-bred secret agent.

Noticing the disillusioned look on the writer's face, Ausable advised him to be patient, and assured him that the perfect scene he wanted to visualise would soon unfold. He mentioned about a certain secret paper that he was expecting. As promised to Fowler, when they entered his meagre room in a humble French hotel, they had a gun-wielding intruder, a rival secret agent waiting for the same secret paper. What followed was a display of immaculate presence of mind on the part of the senior secret agent. Fowler sat open- mouthed, as the intruder, was effectively made to step out of the room into a balcony that did not exist by the very brilliant Ausable. The ungainly, secret agent Ausable comes across as a  person who relies on the strength of his brain to solve cases than the power of his physique.

## Character Sketch: FOWLER

Fowler was a young writer who had approached secret agent Ausable to help him provide the content required to write a perfect romantic adventure. He was initially far from impressed in what he saw of the man. The secret agent did not meet his expectations. His physical appearance and the place he stayed in did not appeal to Fowler, as they did not match the picture of a secret agent he had in his  mind.

Fowler, however, experienced his first authentic thrill when the two of them reached Ausable's room in the dingy hotel. As the drama promised by Ausable unfolded, he seemed to devour the magnificence on display and played his part as an innocent spectator. He did not for a second question or interrupt, the display of superior intellectual skills of Ausable.  He had defended both of them deftly from the gun-wielding rival secret agent Max.

Totally impressed now, Fowler was now adequately satisfied to write his new book. He probably must have realised that a smart head is better equipped that a styled body to handle adverse situations.

## THEME

The author is trying to decipher if there is "honour" or "deceit" , among thieves.

## SUMMARY OF THE STORY

Victor Canning has written a very interesting story on the question of trust among thieves. Is it a thief who enables catching a thief, or is there honour among thieves?

Horace Danby a 50 year old man loved to read and stock rear and expensive books. However, he was not gainfully employed to indulge in this expensive passion. Thus he robbed a safe every year to provide him with the resource to buy books and take care of his needs for the year. His modus operandi was very specific and well-planned. He would never break into a house without being adequately prepared. In this story we are introduced to his plan for robbing a house at Shotover Grange.

He entered the house when the servants had left, fully equipped with the necessary tools and gloves on his palms to avoid a trail for the cops to follow him. Greeted by a friendly canine Sherry, Horace was taken aback when he heard a female voice address him as he sneezed due to an allergic reaction. He felt ashamed and prepared to leave promising that he would never step into any house again. Unfortunately, the lady was too bold and commanding for his comfort. She refused to allow him to walk away and threatened to call in the cops. She finally gave in to his pleas, and put forth a condition that he had to fulfil. What could that be? Did it have anything to do with the family safe? Was the lady the person who she claimed to be?

The story concludes with the protagonist Horace, serving a sentence in the prison where he worked as the librarian. Now, How did this happen?

## A QUESTION OF TRUST

### by Victor Canning

### Character Sketch: HORACE

Horace the protagonist of , "A question of Trust", was a 50 old man who has been referred to as being a voracious reader. People in the neighbourhood he lived in, believed that Horace Danby was a good and honest citizen. Horace lived all by himself with a house-keeper who took care of his home for him. An otherwise healthy man, he had problems in summer because of the 'hay fever'. Horace was passionate about reading stocking rear and expensive books. To indulge in this hobby, he did not have resources. The solution he found to feed his urge to read was absolutely dishonest. Horace resorted to robbing safes of rich people, at the rate of one safe a year, to handle his need for the books and his personal needs for each year. This was done with absolute precision and care. He would never leave a clue for the cops to latch on to. In this episode at Shotover Grange, he was outsmarted by another of his own tribe, who had presented herself as the lady of the house. Despite all the caution he normally exercises, Horace foolishly succumbed to the pressure exercised on him by the "lady of the house". He broke the safe as he was ordered to do. Unfortunately he had not worn on his gloves. He paid heavily for this folly, and landed in prison for a crime he had not committed. Horace was disturbed by the fact that the concept of "honour among thieves", was a myth.

### Character Sketch: THE LADY OF THE HOUSE

The most interesting character in the lesson, "A question of Trust" is 'the lady of the house'. She addressed the intruder, Horace with a quiet, kind yet firm voice, thus unnerving him. Young and pretty, she held up with confidence against the burglar in the house. The young lady, displayed immense confidence, when she threatened to call the police and hand over the trespasser. She seemed to be deriving extraordinary pleasure while she pushed Horace into a state of absolute discomfiture. Eventually though, pretending to sympathise with him, she gives into the pleas of the burglar Horace. But he had a task to perform. She, the lady of the house, had forgotten the combination to open the safe, and Horace had to break it open for her. Effortlessly the lady got away with what she wanted by orchestrating a very crafty plan. She played the role of the lady of the house immaculately, proving to be a handful for the seasoned male counterpart.

## THEME

The author has tried to impress upon the reader that intelligence if misused can be lethal.

## SUMMARY OF THE STORY

"Footprints without feet", is an excerpt from H G Well's novel 'The Invisible Man'. It is the story of a scientist who discovered the art of making himself invisible. The excerpt begins with two little boys getting startled when they noticed fresh muddy footprints on the steps of a house, but there was no human being visible. Further, these footprints were seen descending the steps and moving down towards the street. What was happening? They were absolutely flabbergasted with what they saw.

The footsteps belonged to an invisible man –Griffin, a scientist. He had entered a store to get some clothes to get himself warm. In the process he felt fatigued and dropped asleep on a pile of quilts in the store. Griffin was woken up by the employees when they had come in to open the store. Taken aback, he threw away all his clothes. This made him invisible and he continued to roam the crowded streets of London, feeling extremely chill on the cold winter morning.

He began to realise that London was not suitable for him and decided to move over to a small village called Iping. He checks himself into an inn, paying an advance on the rent of the two rooms he had booked for himself. Here he begins unleashing his atrocities on the local people. Griffin does not hesitate to commit a theft at the house of the local clergy too.

The innkeeper's wife was attacked by flying chairs and furniture, when she questioned him about his weird ways. It was not possible for the constable Mr. Jaffer who was summoned for help by Mrs. Hall, the lady of the inn, to get hold of him. Griffin made himself invisible and escaped from the inn, perhaps to continue the saga of his dreaded social nuisance.

## FOOTPRINTS WITHOUT FEET

### by H G Wells

### Character Sketch: GRIFFIN

Griffin the protagonist of "Footprints without feet", was a scientist with great qualities and intelligence, but of a severely perverted character. He comes across as a callous, self-centred and lawless human being who was at war with mankind.

This brilliant scientist developed a potion to make himself invisible. Having succeeded in his experiment, he used this discovery for all the wrong reasons. He engaged in anti-social activities that included robbery and murder, which he did without a prick of his conscience. In this excerpt Griffin is seen stealing to keep himself warm, to find food sustenance, or to secure currency for his basic needs. City life was fairly dangerous and he therefore shifts to a small village to wreak havoc on the humble village folks. His victims ranged from the clergy to the ordinary citizen. The highlight of Griffin's intelligent discovery was that, he managed to escape imminent arrest at all times, because removing his clothes made him invisible, and this allowed him to go scot free. It is unfortunate that such a great intellectual chose the path of crime, to unleash the excellence of his discovery. He could have alternately used it to serve the society and protect it from negative influences.

### Character Sketch: MRS. HALL

Mrs Hall is a very important character in the lesson, "Footprints without feet". She was the owner of the inn at Iping which the scientist Griffin had checked into. Mrs Hass was an astute business woman, a dominating wife and a very practical person, who did the job of running the inn with great finesse.

It was the off-season and Griffin came in as a relief especially having booked two rooms and paid the rent in advance. This being the approach of the new tenant, Mrs Hall chose to ignore the strange and eccentric behaviour she had most definitely observed in him.

Mrs Hall managed her inn meticulously. Therefore, she did not hesitate to express her concern when she observed that Mr Griffin was not adhering to the basic rules and regulations that were in place at the inn. Unfortunately an aggrieved scientist, decided to react violently by hurling furniture at the Hall couple when confronted by them, while remaining invisible himself. The smart lady had called over the constable to help them with the man, who eventually escaped. Mrs Hall could never decipher how the man got in and out of a locked door. Now, perhaps, after witnessing his last vanishing act, she must have gathered what was actually happening.

## THEME

To rise when you fall and follow your passion despite the many hurdles you come across is the way to reach your goal. Hard work and diligence is the key to imminent success.

## SUMMARY OF THE STORY

Richard H Ebright, fondly called Richie by his mother was a very curious child from his early days. He was fascinated by butterflies by the time he reached the age of two, he had collected all the 25 species around his hometown. He assumed that he would not be able to get any more of these beautiful creatures. This was not to be. One day his mother bought him a book, "The Travels of Monarch X". He learned from this book about monarch butterflies that migrated to Central America. He started tagging butterflies which was a task given at the end of the book.

This proved to be a turning point in his life. Richard's interest in Science developed further. He decided to participate in the county science fair. His presentation of the frog tissue on a slide did not make a mark on the authorities. Though upset, Richard realised that he had to do something more real and relevant.

Richard followed up his zeal by communicating with Dr. Urquhart of the University of Toronto to help him with ideas for projects. The long list he thus received kept him busy through his high school. The following year Richard embarked on the project of looking at viral diseases that killed all the monarch caterpillars. Assuming that the beetles were responsible, he started breeding them together. Nothing ensued. However his experiment did fetch him a prize at the science fair.

His study of monarch and viceroy butterflies as bird food fetched him the first prize in the zoology division and the third in the overall county science fair.

An encouraged Richard along with his friend James R Wong, began working on deciphering the significance of the 12 golden spots on the back of a monarch pupa. They discovered that more than it being a design, the spots were responsible for releasing a growth hormone. Furthering this study in a more sophisticated lab, he was able to solve one of the greatest puzzles of life—how a cell blueprints its DNA. A scientist was born.

# THE MAKING OF A SCIENTIST

### by Robert W Peterson

### /// Character Sketch: RICHARD H EBRIGHT ///

Richard H Ebright the only son of his widowed mother, was grew up in the North of Reading in Pennsylvania. Richard was a multi-faceted genius. He embedded in himself a competent scientist, a lovable son, a star gazer, an eager astronomer and a brilliant student. His passion in collecting butterflies set in motion his climb towards being a great molecular biologist.

By the time he was in the second grade, Ebright collected all twenty-five species of butterflies found around in his hometown. A great learner, he learnt an important lesson at his first county science fair, to accept failure with grace. He learnt that winners do real experiments than making a neat display. The book, Travels of Monarch X opened the world of science to the eager young collector. One of his famous projects was based on the theory that viceroy butterflies copied monarch butterflies to escape being eaten by birds. This project was placed first in the zoology division. Later, Ebright showed that the spots on a monarch pupa produced a hormone necessary for the butterfly's development. He also proved that DNA controls heredity and is the blueprint for life.

Richard Ebright got all his encouragement, help and inspiration from his mother, Dr Urquhart who helped him with new suggestions and ideas and his Social Studies teacher, Richard A Weiherer.

This great scientist found time for other interests and hobbies. He was a champion debater and public speaker, a good canoeist and an expert photographer.

### /// Character Sketch: RICHARD'S MOTHER ///

Richard was the only son of his widowed mother. Her world therefore revolved around her little son, her only companion. In Richard Ebright's success as a scientist his mother had a major role to play. He was her only companion and they spent almost every evening at the dining table when Ebright's mother encouraged his interest in learning. To encourage his curiosity she took him on trips, bought him telescopes, microscopes, cameras, mounting materials and other equipment. She helped Ebright in every way possible as she recognised the potential in her son. She knew that her son had a passion for collecting things. By the time he was in the second grade, Ebright had collected all twenty-five species of butterflies found around his hometown. His interest in his butterfly collecting would have ended had she not got him a children's book called. 'The Travels of Monarch X'. While reading that book he learnt how monarch butterflies migrated to Central America. It opened the world of science to the eager collector. Perhaps the success Ebright achieved may have not have been possible without the love encouragement and acceptance from his mother.

## THEME

The author has based his lesson on a very important theme—live within your means. Trying to embrace another's life-style, or covet the possessions of another will lead one to situations from which escape is next to impossible.

## SUMMARY OF THE STORY

The Necklace is the story of Matilda who was a pretty young lady, born into a family of clerks by what the author says, " an error of destiny".  Her life did not give her an opportunity to be recognised, loved, or become rich and distinguished.  As was her social status, she married a clerk that left her unhappy and dissatisfied for her entire life.

This story tells us about the tragedies that followed because of Matilda's desire to climb the social ladder.  Having been invited to a grand social get together at the Minister's residence, she invests all her husband's savings in buying a dress. To make things worse she borrows a necklace to go with it, from her friend Mme Forestier.

The couple enjoyed the party, but the worst was yet to come.  When they got back home Matilda realised that her necklace had fallen off.  Her husband went back along the path they  had covered but all in vain.  The necklace was not to be seen anywhere. Dejected, the two of them decide to buy a new necklace.  It cost them thirty six thousand francs, eating into all their resources and inheritance, leaving them in debt.

Life became difficult for the unfortunate couple.  They aged ahead of time.

One day Matilda met Mme Forestier . What she heard from her friend left her in a state of absolute shock.  What did she learn from Mme Forestier?  Did the Loisel's make a mistake in concealing the fact that they had lost the necklace?

## THE NECKLACE

### by Guy De Maupassant

### Character Sketch: MADAME MATILDA LOISEL

The protagonist of the lesson The Necklace, is portrayed as a woman who feels that she was born for luxury. She is a beautiful woman and believes that she should be living an aristocratic life, draped in fine clothes, jewels and furs. She imagines herself to be living a life of luxury a distant dream, as she did not have the means to go beyond a humble existence

Madame Loisel chose to believe that life had cheated her justifying her reaction to the invitation to the fancy party. The party, Madame Loisel felt that if she were to attend the party she must look the part of a social elite.  Eventually, after squeezing out the last penny of her Mr. Loisel's earnings to buy herself a suitable dress and a borrowed necklace to go with it  she goes to the function.  Unfortunately she loses her friend's necklace. Replacing it cost them thirty six thousand francs. Misfortune hit back at  Matilda with a vengeance. Life became miserable. The couple had to give up on the basic amenities of life. Every day was a struggle.  But all this was in vain, when she discovered from her dear friend that the cost of the original necklace was only five hundred francs. All this, because, the couple chose to hide the truth.  Matilda and her unwarranted desire to slip into a different social stratum, destroyed the peace and happiness of the Loisel household.

### Character Sketch: MONSIEUR LOISEL

Monsieur Loisel was the husband of the damsel in distress, Matilda Loisel.  He was a hard-working man and worked as a clerk in the office of the Board of Education.  Loisel loved his wife and wanted to please her by catering to all her needs while sacrificing his own.  He was a simple man who had  no regrets about  his social standing in life. He had no aspirations to be among the aristocrats like his wife. He is content with his simple life. This humble man's life was rocked when they received an invitation to go to the Minister's house. Attempting to satisfy his wife's desire to dress like an aristocrat, he lost his savings, his inheritance, and his peace of mind.  He was in debt too, as he had to borrow money to buy a necklace his wife had lost.  Could he have avoided all this?  Yes.  It was necessary for Loisel to be firm and make his wife to understand their financial condition, before succumbing to all her vain fancies.  Their pathetic plight could have been reversed if he had the courage to say no, to her indiscriminate desires of being one she was not. Loisel had to suffer because of his wife's follies.  Though he played a major role in encouraging her dream big.

## THEME

The author has tried to base his story on the theme of trust. Blind trust in somebody, may lead us to embarrassing situations that could often cause extreme pain. To an innocent man, appearances and the general demeanour of a person, often prove to be deceptive and probably losing his faith in all of mankind.

## SUMMARY OF THE STORY

"The Hack Driver", written by Sinclair Lewis encapsulates the saga of a young lawyer who had been sent to a distant village to issue summons to an unresponsive witness. Though an honours graduate in law, in his capacity as a junior clerk with a law firm, he was entrusted with very insignificant duties as an errand boy.

As a part of his job, the young lawyer was sent to a small town New Mullion to serve summons to Oliver Lutkins, the witness in a law case that was up for hearing the following day.

New Mullion was not as appealing geographically as the narrator expected it to be. However he felt that the people here were humble and innocent. Well, this was the impression he gathered after his interaction with a hack driver who volunteered to take the lawyer around the village to search for Oliver. The hack driver said that his name was Bill was ready to help the visitor in fulfilling his job. The 'kind', Bill took him to and fro the streets of New Mullion, from the Fritz's to the Gustaff's and finally to the home of the witness Lutkins. All in vain. Disappointed at not being able to complete his job the young lawyer went back to the city.

The firm was angry and disapproved of his incompetence. They sent him back with another person who had seen Lutkins as his presence in the court was inevitable the following day. As they approached the station, the narrator pointed out Bill to his companion, and raved about the help he had provided him with. "He helped you hunt for Oliver Lutkins ?" was the response from the companion to the lawyer's claims. Why? Is anybody's guess.

## THE HACK DRIVER

### by Sinclair Lewis

### Character Sketch: OLIVER LUTKINS

Oliver Lutkins a resident of New Mullion was a key witness to a case that was up for hearing. He had refused to acknowledge the summons that was being repeatedly served to him. Though from a small town, this man cheats a lawyer who had come looking for him, with ease, while pretending to be Bill Magnuson, a hack driver. Bill volunteering to help him, takes the lawyer around town, never once allowing him to get off the hack, and coincidentally missing the wanted man at every place by split seconds. He projects himself to be very kind and helpful and charms his way into the good books of the unsuspecting lawyer. It was when the lawyer returned with his companion a while later that the man he was looking for was with him throughout the day. Bill was Oliver Lutkins. He came across as a very dishonest and untrustworthy man, who made a fool of an innocent man and derived excessive pleasure while doing so. He managed to shatter the faith that the lawyer had reposed in him and all the humble people of New Mullions.

### Character Sketch: THE LAWYER

The lawyer who is the narrator of this story was a graduate with honours in Law. He had taken up a job as a junior clerk in a reputed law firm. However the young man was extremely dissatisfied with his job profile, hated the city life and contemplated moving to a small town hoping to begin a more fruitful career.

The narrator has an extremely unpleasant experience, while on an assignment to a rural town by the name of New Mullion that required him to issue summons to a key witness. The lawyer was put to a lot of embarrassment, by a hack driver Bill, whom he trusted to be an aid in his assignment. The young lawyer proved to be at his incompetent best, when he returned to the city without completing the job at hand. His romantic ideas of rural life and its people catapulted into a feeling of despair and remorse, having been let down by one he trusted. The question that rises in the reader's mind would probably be, can a novice like the lawyer ever be able to graduate into a seasoned legal luminary?

# THEME

The author has most definitely based his story on two themes
1. Beauty is skin deep, and it lies in the eyes of the beholder.
2. Education is the only ladder that does not allow a person who uses it to climb face the fear of falling. Education gives one the confidence and will to move ahead. The book does not shy away from you if you do not look appealing enough for it.

# SUMMARY OF THE STORY

This is a story of a village numberdar Ramlal and his family that included seven children, three boys and four girls. Bholi or Sulekha, is the protagonist of K A Abbas's story. Inflicted by small-pox a deadly infectious disease at the tender age of two, and a severe fall on her head, Bholi had problems with her appearance and her speech. The child was treated like an outcaste in her own home, and more so by her biological parents. Shunned to a corner of the house, the poor child became a burden for the family. Who will marry this ugly girl?

Time was in the little girls favour. The opening of a primary school in her village proved to be a turning point in Bholi's life. Though her parents admitted her here to get rid of her from the house, it came as a blessing in the little girl's life. The icing on the cake was a very understanding and loving teacher who paved the way for this neglected soul to grow. Bholi had secured the basic education.

Years went by. The family now tried to get rid of her by making her tie the knot with a man as old as her father. However when the groom saw that his bride's face was disfigured, though he himself was a widower with a limp, refused to complete the marriage rituals without being handed over a huge sum as dowry. Bholi was now a force to reckon with. She stood her position strongly and refused to be sold. How will Bholi's decision affect her future? What did she propose to do with the rest of her life? Will she make her mentor proud?

## BHOLI

### by K A Abbas

## Character Sketch: BHOLI

Sulekha means a person who writes with a beautiful handwriting. Ironically, this Sulekha did not have anything that could be considered beautiful as she was intellectually and physically found wanting. She suffered a brain injury due to a fall and therefore stammered and was slow in understanding things. Along with this, she was inflicted with severe pock-marks all over her body and face that made her look ugly

The butt of everyone's rebuke, the little girl saw a glimmer of hope when she was admitted to the newly opened primary school in the village. Though she was admitted here by her parents to keep her away from home and she herself was initially vary of going to school, this was the turning point in Bholi's life. A caring teacher groomed the misfit into a competent and confident girl. She proved this when she vehemently refused to be sold to an old man to be his bride for a huge sum of 5000 rupees. The erstwhile ' Bholi' had transformed. In response to her father's concern regarding her future, she told him that she would dedicate the rest of her life to taking care of her parents and teaching at the school that had changed her life that was hitherto dismal.

## Character Sketch: RAMLAL

Ramlal was the revenue officer or numberedar of the village. He was a prosperous farmer and the father of seven children. An orthodox man, he did not believe in sending girls to school as he feared that educated girls would face problems in securing suitable grooms. Ramlal and his wife did whatever was possible as parents in the up-bringing of their six children, but that was not the case with their fourth daughter Bholi. All the parental emotions seemed to have eluded them when it came to Bholi. This physically and mentally challenged child proved to be a spoke in their wheel. As a father, he failed. He would listen to the mean instructions that was given to him by Bholi's mother and did things that parents usually never did. However the cruel decision of admitting her in school proved to be in the child's best interest, though the rationale behind it was not all too good. The final straw on the camel's back was when Ramlal decided to pack his little girl off with a man twice her age. He was even willing to hand over a huge sum as dowry, to get rid of his cursed child. Little did this man realise that the child they hated and disregarded would be the source of support to him in his old-age. Perhaps it was not too late for him to open his heart out and begin loving his unfortunate fourth child –Bholi.

## THEME

The author has based her story on the theme that partial knowledge is more harmful than no knowledge.  She also wishes to emphasise the need for interpreting data appropriately.

## SUMMARY OF THE STORY

The book that saved the earth is a science fantasy.  It is written in the form of a play that uncovers an imaginary story that is set in the 25th century. The author has chosen is a 20th century Museum of Ancient History as the location for the scene. There are six characters and one off-stage voice participating in the play.  It begins with an introduction by the historian, where she is projecting on a screen a historical event of how a book saved the earth from imminent invasion by Martians.  The book in question was an old book of rhymes , "Mother goose".

The great and mighty Think-Tank, the commander in chief and ruler of the Mars was a despicable despot.  None of his people dared to question or disobey him.  Captain Omega and the team to invade the earth had landed on earth, which turned out to be a library.  They begin to make wild guesses about the books they find here, and the Think-Tank identifies these as sandwiches. He instructs them to eat it.  Oops has a problem swallowing the 'sandwiches'.  Noodle, comes to the rescue by identifying these as communication devices.  The confusion in the identity and purpose of the books continues.  Noodle eventually states that the earthlings used these books to communicate with the eye, thus saving the situation again.

Finally, it was the time for decoding the content in the books, the curves and the dots that the Martians had difficulty in comprehending. It was Noodle who suggested taking vitamins to sharpen the brain.  Omega was now able to read.  The book was a collection of nursery rhymes. They misinterpreted each and every rhyme.  Humpty dumpty made the Martians evacuate to a place hundred million miles away called Alpha Centuari. This is how a kindergarten book saved the earth from the Martians.

## THE BOOK THAT SAVED THE EARTH

### by Claire Boiko

### Character Sketch: THINK TANK

The Think Tank who was the commander-in-chief and ruler of Mars, was described to he shaped like an egg. He wore a protracted gown embellished with stars and circles, and wished that his mirror always declared him as belonging to the most handsome race. He considered himself to be intellectually gifted and the most powerful creature in the universe. A vain character, the Think Tank expected his people to keep showering him with praises all the time.

He was leading the team that had embarked on a plan to invade the earth. Unfortunately for the rest of the team, the Think Tank was far from capable of handling an exercise of such great magnitude.  He was unable to make the right interpretations of things they perceived on the earth in the library that they had landed. This led to gross miscalculations and misunderstanding, leading to his decision to evacuate even the Mars and go far away to a place located millions of miles away. The ThinkTank is a typical example of how a wrong leader and his wrong decisions can create problems for everyone being led by him or her.

### Character Sketch: NOODLE

Noodle was a member of team Mars that was on a mission to invade the earth. He was an apprentice working under the mighty Think Tank.  However unlike his leader, Noodle was a smart and intelligent fellow. He was the one who saved the day for his team members who were forced to eat the dry sandwiches.  Even though he made all the appropriate decisions he did not make any attempt to steal the praises from his boss.  He was smart, humble and modest. The intelligent Noodle was wise and knew when to make the right moves. He was wise enough to understand the fact that the books were a means of communication.  His wisdom and logical reasoning skills were recognised eventually as the historian explains that Noodle had replaced the Think-tank as the leader of the Martians.

# CHAPTERWISE
# MIND MAPS
# HINDI

# पुनरावलोकन नोट्स

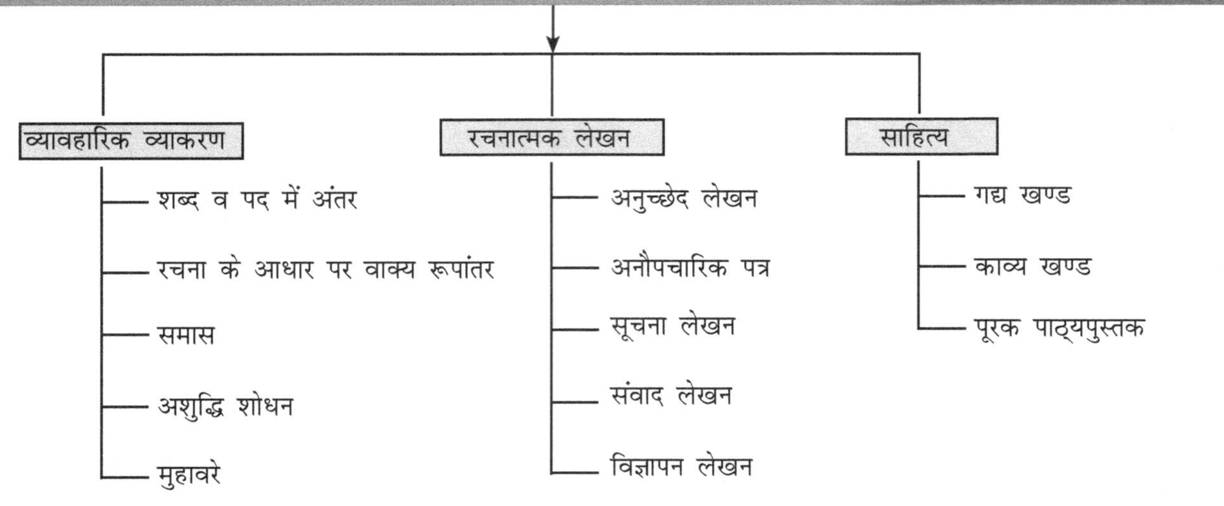



## व्यावहारिक व्याकरण

### शब्द व पद में अंतर

वर्णों के व्यवस्थित और सार्थक समूह को शब्द कहा जाता है। शब्द भाषा की आधार इकाई है। जब शब्द व्याकरणिक नियमों में बंधकर वाक्य में प्रयोग हो जाता है तो वह पद बन जाता है। वह वाक्य का अर्थ समझने में मदद करता है।

जैसे– कमल, पानी, तालाब आदि शब्द हैं।

तालाब के पानी में कमल खिले हैं। यहाँ तालाब संज्ञा का कार्य कर रहा है। कमल विधेय बन गया है। अत: वाक्य में प्रयोग के बाद शब्द कर्ता, संज्ञा अथवा सर्वनाम आदि बन जाता है।

### रचना के आधार पर वाक्य रूपांतर

रचना के आधार पर वाक्य के तीन भेद होते हैं–

1. सरल वाक्य     2. संयुक्त वाक्य     3. मिश्र वाक्य।

(1) **सरल वाक्य** में एक उद्देश्य और एक विधेय होता है। सरल वाक्य में एक ही क्रिया होती है। जैसे, राम आता है। यहाँ 'राम' उद्देश्य है तथा 'जाता है' विधेय है।

(2) **संयुक्त वाक्य** में एक से अधिक प्रधान उपवाक्य समुच्चय बोधक अव्यय द्वारा जुड़े होते हैं। ये उपवाक्य अपना स्वतंत्र अर्थ भी देते हैं और जुड़कर पूरा अर्थ प्रदान करते हैं। जैसे, राम मोहन का भाई है और वह दसवीं कक्षा में पढ़ता है। यहाँ 'राम मोहन का भाई है' वाक्य पूरा है तथा 'वह दसवीं कक्षा में पढ़ता है' भी पूरा है। दोनों जुड़कर राम के विषय में जानकारी को पूरा करते हैं।

(3) **मिश्र वाक्य** में दो या दो से अधिक उपवाक्य जुड़े होते हैं। इसमें एक प्रधान उपवाक्य होता है तथा अन्य आश्रित उपवाक्य होते हैं। ऐसे वाक्य में एक से अधिक समापिका क्रियाएँ होती हैं और एक-दूसरे के बिना पूर्ण अर्थ समझने में कठिनाई होती

है जैसे- (i) यदि अभिनव परिश्रम करता, तो पास हो जाता। (ii) मैं जानता हूँ कि तुमने उत्तीर्ण होने के लिए दिन-रात एक कर दिया। यहाँ प्रथम वाक्य में 'यदि अभिनव परिश्रम करता' प्रधान उपवाक्य है तथा 'पास हो जाता' आश्रित उपवाक्य है।

## समास

दो या दो से अधिक शब्दों से मिलकर जब कोई नया एवं सार्थक-संक्षिप्त शब्द बनता है तो उसे समास कहते हैं। संक्षिप्तीकरण ही इसकी विशेषता है। जैसे, राजपुत्र- राजा का पुत्र। देशभक्ति- देश की भक्ति या देश के लिए भक्ति।

समास के छह भेद होते हैं-

1. अव्ययीभाव 2. तत्पुरुष 3. द्वंद्व 4. द्विगु 5. बहुब्रीहि 6. कर्मधारय

1. **अव्ययीभाव समासः** अव्यय का अर्थ है अपरिवर्तनीय। इसमें समस्त पद अव्यय बन जाता है। इसमें पूर्वपद प्रधान होता है, उत्तरपद गौण। जैसे- रातोंरात = रात ही रात में। यथाविधि = विधि के अनुसार।

2. **तत्पुरुष समासः** इसमें उत्तरपद प्रधान होता है और पूर्वपद गौण। इसमें कारक विभक्तियों का लोप होता है। विग्रह करने पर विभक्ति प्रकट हो जाती है। जैसे, ग्रामगत = ग्राम को गत (गया), गंगाजल = गंगा का जल।

3. **द्वंद्व समासः** इस समास में दोनों पद प्रधान होते हैं तथा दोनों पद योजक चिह्न से जुड़े होते हैं। विग्रह करने पर 'और' 'या' लगता है। जैसे, माता-पिता = माता और पिता, आना-जाना = आना और जाना।

4. **द्विगु समासः** द्विगु समास विद्यार्थियों की समझ में जल्दी आ जाता है। इसकी पहचान यह होती है कि इसमें पहला पद (पूर्वपद) संख्यावाची होता है। जैसे, त्रिलोक = तीन लोक, नवरात्र = नौ रात्रियों का समूह।

5. **बहुब्रीहि समासः** इसमें कोई पद प्रधान नहीं होता अपितु समस्त पद के अर्थ के अतिरिक्त कोई अन्य अर्थ (सांकेतिक) प्रधान होता है। जैसे, नीलकंठ = नीला है कंठ जिसका अर्थात् शिव। गजानन = गज जैसा आनन है जिसका अर्थात् गणेश।

6. **कर्मधारय समासः** इसमें उत्तरपद प्रधान होता है तथा पूर्वपद और उत्तरपद में विशेषण-विशेष्य, उपमान-उपमेय का संबंध होता है। जैसे, सज्जन = सत् जन (अच्छा आदमी), पीतांबर = पीला अंबर।

**विशेषः** कुछ समस्त पदों में कर्मधारय और बहुब्रीहि दोनों समास बनते हैं। ऐसे में विग्रह के अनुसार ही समास की पहचान होती है।

## अशुद्धि शोधन

व्याकरण की दृष्टि से वर्तनी, वाक्य की शुद्धता, स्पष्टता और सार्थकता ही भाषा को परिष्कृत करती है। 'वाक्य' भाषा की महत्वपूर्ण इकाई है। अतः व्याकरणिक नियमों के अनुरूप शुद्ध करना ही अशुद्धि शोधन कहा जाता है। वाक्यों में लिंग, वचन, विभक्ति, संज्ञा, सर्वनाम, विशेषण तथा क्रिया आदि संबंधी अशुद्धियाँ पाई जाती हैं।

**जैसेः** राम और सीता वन को **गई**/ (गए)। उसने **अनेकों** ग्रंथ लिखे / (अनेक)। मैं पुस्तक **की** पढ़ता हूँ। / (को)। किसी **और** लड़के को बुलाओ/ (दूसरे)।

## मुहावरे

मुहावरे हिंदी भाषा के श्रृंगार की तरह हैं। मुहावरे हिंदी भाषा तथा हमारी बोलचाल की भाषा में इस तरह रच-बस गए हैं कि इनके बिना ये अधूरी लगती है। मुहावरे का अर्थ है- कोई वाक्यांश जो अपने शाब्दिक/साधारण अर्थ को छोड़कर कोई विशेष अर्थ व्यक्त करता है तो मुहावरा कहलाता है। जैसे, ईंट का जवाब पत्थर से देना- मुँहतोड़ जवाब देना, करारा जवाब देना। अब इसका अर्थ यह तो नहीं है कि कोई हमें ईंट मारे तो हम पत्थर मारें। आँख चुराना (छिपना)- इसका अर्थ छिपते हुए घूमना है, न कि किसी की आँखें चुरा लेना।

# रचनात्मक लेखन

## अनुच्छेद लेखन

अनुच्छेद अर्थात् पैराग्राफ। यह निबंध, पाठ या किसी लेखन का विशिष्ट अंश होता है। आजकल परीक्षाओं में स्वतंत्र रूप से अनुच्छेद लेखन भी करवाया जाता है। इसमें 'गागर में सागर' विधि को अपनाते हुए लेखन करना चाहिए। चुनिंदा शब्द, स्पष्ट शैली, सरल भाषा, शुद्ध वाक्य तथा स्वतंत्र और प्रवाहमयी शैली में अभिव्यक्ति होनी चाहिए।

अनुच्छेद लेखन से पहले दिए गए विषय पर अपने अर्जित ज्ञान और अनुभवी ज्ञान को मिलाकर सशक्त भाषा में चिंतन कर लेना चाहिए। तत्पश्चात् चिंतन-मनन और लेखन होना चाहिए। अनुच्छेद लेखन में क्रमबद्धता का विशेष महत्व होता है। विषय के अतिरिक्त अनावश्यक बातों का उल्लेख नहीं होना चाहिए। अनुच्छेद लेखन में मुहावरे, कहावतों, लोकोक्तियों का प्रयोग उसे सुंदर बना देता है। बिखराव नहीं होना चाहिए। शुद्धता का भी विशेष ध्यान रखना चाहिए।

## अनौपचारिक पत्र

वर्तमान युग में संचार माध्यमों में क्रांति हुई है। दूर-संचार के साधनों के कारण पत्र का महत्व कम अवश्य हुआ है, परंतु खत्म नहीं हुआ है। अनौपचारिक पत्र अपने सगे संबंधियों, रिश्तेदारों को लिखे जाते हैं। पत्र के माध्यम से हम अपने विचार, चिंतन, अनुभूति, संवेदना, पारिवारिक समाचार आदि की अभिव्यक्ति करते हैं।

प्रभावशाली पत्र-लेखन एक कला है। प्रभावी शैली उद्देश्य पूर्ति के साथ-साथ दूसरों को प्रभावित भी करती है। पत्र की विषय-वस्तु, लेखन शैली और भाषा लेखक की योग्यता पर निर्भर करती है।

**अनौपचारिक पत्र के अंग:**
- पता और दिनांक
- संबोधन
- अभिवादन
- पत्र की सामग्री / विषय-वस्तु
- पत्र की समाप्ति
- स्वनिर्देश / संबंध-शब्द
- हस्ताक्षर / नाम

पता

..............................................

..............................................

दिनांक ........................................

पूज्य/प्रिय, ........................

नमस्ते, स्नेह।

.............................................................................................

.............................................................................................

.............................................................................................

आपका पुत्र / मित्र

...............................................

## सूचना लेखन

सूचना लेखन में विशेष जानकारी दी जाती है। जैसे, खोना-पाना, परीक्षा तिथि, कार्यक्रम संबंधी बैठक, खेल प्रतियोगिता, अन्य प्रतियोगिता, कार्यालयी सूचना आदि। सूचना कम से कम व आकर्षक शब्दों में लिखी जानी चाहिए। वाक्य सरल व संक्षिप्त तथा लिखाई शुद्ध, स्पष्ट व स्वच्छ होनी चाहिए। सूचना में समय और तिथि स्पष्ट हो तथा स्थान और पते की जानकारी स्पष्ट लिखी जानी चाहिए।

प्रारूप-

शीर्षक (सूचना)

विषय ........................

सूचना का लेखन (विषय-वस्तु)

.....................................................................................................................

.....................................................................................................................

.....................................................................................................................

दिनांक ........................

सूचना देने वाले का पद, नाम, पता आदि।

## संवाद लेखन

हम प्रतिदिन अनेक लोगों से बातचीत करते हैं, उसे ही संवाद कहते हैं।

किसी विषय, समस्या, उत्सव, कार्यक्रम आदि के विषय में दो व्यक्तियों के मध्य होने वाले वार्तालाप को संवाद कहा जाता है। संवाद का साहित्यिक विधाओं (नाटक, एकांकी, उपन्यास आदि) में विशेष महत्व है।

- संवादों का रोचक होना अनिवार्य है।
- संवाद पात्रों के अनुकूल होना चाहिए।
- संवाद विषय के अनुकूल होना चाहिए।
- संवाद की भाषा सरल और संक्षिप्त होनी चाहिए।
- संवाद प्रभावी होना चाहिए।
- संवाद लेखन में विराम चिह्नों का उचित प्रयोग करना चाहिए।
- संवाद का आरंभ और अंत आकर्षक होना चाहिए।
- संवाद स्वाभाविक तथा सजीव होना चाहिए।
- संवाद संक्षिप्त तथा स्पष्ट होना चाहिए।

## विज्ञापन लेखन

'विज्ञापन' का अर्थ होता है- विशेष सूचना। 'वि' का अर्थ है- विशेष और 'ज्ञापन' का अर्थ है सूचना। विज्ञापन के माध्यम से हम अपनी किसी वस्तु या उत्पाद का प्रचार-प्रसार करते हैं। विज्ञापन से ग्राहकों को अपनी तरफ किया जा सकता है। इसे उपभोक्तावाद कहते हैं। विज्ञापन की विशेषता यह होनी चाहिए कि वह जिसके लिए हो सीधे उसके दिल में उतर जाना चाहिए। विज्ञापन में प्रमाणिकता तथ्यों एवं आंकड़ों की सहायता से प्रस्तुत की जानी चाहिए। विज्ञापन ऐसा हो कि सुनने वाले को ऐसा लगे कि यह सिर्फ उसके लिए ही है। वह ग्राहक को मज़बूर कर दे वस्तु खरीदने के लिए।

- विज्ञापन प्रसंगानुकूल होनी चाहिए। जैसे, क्रिकेट मैच के दौरान क्रिकेटर से संबंधित विज्ञापन आए तो ज्यादा प्रभावी रहता है।
- विज्ञापन से जिज्ञासा उत्पन्न होनी चाहिए।
- वस्तु क्यों खरीदें? अर्थात गुणों का बखान होना चाहिए। स्लोगन या नारा अवश्य सम्मिलित करें।
- शीर्षक आकर्षक, सरल, संक्षिप्त, प्रेरणास्पद व असरदार होना चाहिए।
- वस्तु का नाम कई बार लिया जाना चाहिए।
- चित्रों का प्रयोग व आकर्षक लिखावट हो, नयापन हो। इसे बॉक्स में लिखा जाना चाहिए।

## साहित्य

### गद्य खण्ड

हिन्दी साहित्य में गद्य में अनेक विधाएँ हैं। गद्य समृद्ध साहित्य है। कहानियाँ हमारे बचपन से हमारे साथ जुड़ी हैं। इस पुस्तक में जीवन के विभिन्न पहलुओं को छूती हुई कई कहानियाँ हैं। देश के लगभग प्रत्येक क्षेत्र की भावनाओं को समेटने का समग्र प्रयास है। गद्य की यह विशेषता होती है कि लेखक अपने मनोभावों को सहज-सरल भाषा में लिख सकता है।

### प्रेमचंद: बड़े भाई साहब

प्रस्तुत पाठ में मुंशी प्रेमचंद जी ने अपने बड़े भाई के माध्यम से उन विद्यार्थियों पर व्यंग्य किया है, जो पूरे दिन किताब हाथ में लिए रहते हैं और पढ़ने का दिखावा करते हैं, खेल को तुच्छ समझते हैं। लेखक समझाना चाहता है कि तनाव रहित दिमाग रखें, खेलने के समय खेल में और पढ़ने के समय पूरा ध्यान पढ़ाई में लगाएँ।

लेखक के भाई साहब उनसे पाँच साल बड़े थे अथक परिश्रम के बाद भी वे फेल हो जाते थे। लेखक कम पढ़कर भी पास हो जाता था। लेखक का ध्यान खेल में ज्यादा रहता था, इस कारण उन्हें बड़े भाई साहब का कोप भाजन बनना पड़ता था। बड़े भाई साहब उन्हें अंग्रेजी की जटिलता समझाते हुए बताते थे कि अंग्रेजी सीखने के लिए जी-तोड़ मेहनत करनी पड़ती है। मैं दिन-रात मेहनत करके भी फेल हो जाता हूँ। तुम तो पढ़ाई को खेल समझ रहे हो, क्यों दादा की गाढ़ी कमाई खराब कर रहे हो, घर चले जाओ।

ऐसी जली-कटी सुनकर लेखक परेशान हो जाता था परंतु गिल्ली डंडा, पतंगबाजी और क्रिकेट का मोह नहीं छोड़ पाता था। फिर जब सालाना इम्तिहान का परिणाम आया तो लेखक और भाई साहब के दरजे में अंतर कम होता चला गया। भाई साहब का आतंक कुछ कम हुआ, लेखक का आत्मविश्वास भी बढ़ता गया। भाई साहब ने मानो तलवार खींच ली और लेखक पर टूट पड़े और बोले भाईजान घमंड तो रावण का भी नहीं रहा, तुम्हारी क्या हस्ती है। इम्तिहान पास कर लेना अलग बात है, असल चीज है बुद्धि का विकास। अभिमान करने वाला दीन और दुनिया दोनों से जाता है। तुमने तो केवल एक दरजा पास किया है और सिर फिर गया। मेरे दरजे में आओगे तो अंग्रेजों का इतिहास पढ़ना पड़ेगा तो दिमाग चकराने लगेगा और ज्यामेट्री में अ ब ज की जगह अ ज ब लिख दिया तो सारे नंबर कट जाएँगे। भाई साहब की उपदेश-माला समाप्त होने का नाम नहीं ले रही थी। लेखक को ताज्जुब था कि पास होने पर ऐसा स्वागत है तो फेल होने पर क्या हाल होता।

फिर सालाना इम्तिहान हुआ और संयोग से बड़े भाई साहब फेल और लेखक पास हो गया। भाई साहब रो पड़े थे। अब वे कुछ नरम पड़ गए थे। लेखक बाजार में कनकौए लूटता फिरता था। एक दिन बड़े भाई साहब से मुठभेड़ हो गई। फिर बड़े भाई साहब ने जो कहा उसे सुनकर लेखक बड़े भाई साहब के आगे नतमस्तक हो गया। बड़े भाई साहब ने कहा चाहे तुम पढ़ाई में मुझसे आगे भी निकल जाओगे, तो भी मैं तुमसे बड़ा रहूँगा। बड़े होने का अर्थ है- जिम्मेदारी। मुझे कुछ होने पर तुम्हारे हाथ-पाँव फूल जाएंगे। परंतु दादा स्वयं इलाज करेंगे या डॉक्टर को दिखाएँगे। वे आधे पैसों में पूरा घर चलाते हैं, और आधे में हम दो रहते हैं। मेरा भी मन करता है कि खेलूँ, परंतु यदि मैं स्वयं ऐसा करूँगा तो तुम्हें सीख कैसे दे पाऊँगा। तभी एक कनकौआ लेकर भाई साहब हॉस्टल की तरफ दौड़ पड़े। लेखक के मन में आज भाई के लिए प्यार और श्रद्धा थी।

## सीताराम सेकसरिया: डायरी का एक पन्ना

सीताराम सेकसरिया ने महात्मा गांधी के साथ स्वतंत्रता आंदोलन में भाग लिया। वे गुरुदेव, महात्मा गांधी, नेताजी सुभाषचंद्र बोस के करीबी रहे। सत्याग्रह आंदोलन के दौरान वे जेल भी गए। प्रस्तुत पाठ में उन्होंने स्वतंत्रता आंदोलन के एक दिन की डायरी लिखी है। 26 जनवरी, सन् 1931 के दिन कोलकाता का नजारा अद्भुत था। दूसरा स्वतंत्रता दिवस मनाया जा रहा था। नेताजी के आह्वान पर हजारों लोग (औरतें, बच्चे, बड़े) सड़कों पर मोनुमेंट पर झंडा फहराने निकल पड़े। मोनुमेंट के नीचे सभा होने वाली थी। शाम की सभा के लिए पुलिस ने सुबह छह बजे से ही शहर को छावनी में बदल दिया।

श्रद्धानंद पार्क में प्रांतीय विद्यार्थी संघ के मंत्री अविनाश बाबू ने झंडा गाड़ा तो पुलिस ने उन्हें पकड़ लिया। तारा सुंदरी पार्क में बड़ा बाजार कांग्रेस कमेटी के युद्ध मंत्री हरिश्चंद्र सिंह झंडा फहराने गए पर वे भीतर न जा सके पुलिस की लाठियों से कइयों के सिर फट गए। लड़कियों-औरतों को गिरफ्तार कर लिया गया। मारवाड़ी बालिका विद्यालय में झंडोत्सव मनाया गया। जानकी देवी, मदालसा ने लड़कियों को इस उत्सव का महत्व समझाया।

जगह-जगह स्त्रियाँ जुलुस निकाल रही थीं। सुभाष बाबू के जुलुस का भार पूर्णोदास पर था। पूर्णोदास की गिरफ्तारी के बाद औरतों ने जुलुस की जिम्मेदारी स्वयं अपने ऊपर ले लीं। कोलकाता के माथे से ये कलंक काफी हद तक धुल गया कि यहाँ काम नहीं हो रहा है। विमल, प्रतिभा, वृजलाल गोयनका जैसे सैकड़ों कार्यकर्ता घायल हुए और आगे बढ़ते रहे। इस घटना ने अंग्रेजों की नींद उड़ा दी थी।

## लीलाधर मंडलोई: तताँरा-वामीरो कथा

लीलाधर मंडलोई की कविताओं में छत्तीसगढ़ के अंचल की मिठास और आम जन-जीवन का चित्रण है। प्रस्तुत पाठ अंडमान-निकोबार द्वीपसमूह की लोककथा पर आधारित है। प्रेम सबको जोड़ता है, परंतु एक प्रेमी के टूटे हुए दिल ने द्वीप के भी दो टुकड़े कर दिए। अंडमान द्वीपसमूह का अंतिम दक्षिणी द्वीप लिटिल अंडमान है। यह निकोबार से 96 कि.मी. दूर है। निकोबारियों को विश्वास है कि प्राचीन काल में ये दोनों द्वीप एक ही थे। एक प्रेमी के टूटे हुए दिल ने इन द्वीपों के दो टुकड़े कर दिए।

एक सुंदर से गाँव में तताँरा नामक सजीला शक्तिशाली युवक रहता था। सभी निकोबारी उससे प्रेम करते थे। वह अपनी कमर में एक लकड़ी की तलवार बाँधे रहता था। लोगों को लगता था कि वह चमत्कारी तलवार थी। एक दिन समुद्र किनारे उसे मधुर संगीत सुनाई दिया। वह वामीरो थी। दोनों एक-दूसरे के आकर्षण में बंधे घंटों एक-दूसरे को देखते रहते। आत्मीय प्रेम में खोए रहते। निकोबारी परंपरा के अनुसार कोई भी लड़की गाँव के बाहर शादी नहीं कर सकती थी, ये अपराध था। तताँरा घंटों उसका इंतजार करता, फिर मौन मिलन होता।

एक दिन तताँरा के गाँव में उत्सव था। वमीरो के गाँव के युवकों ने इस मूक प्रेम को भाँप लिया और फिर वही दीवार आ खड़ी हुई। वामीरो लपाती ग्राम की थी और तताँरा पासा का। दोनों का मिलन संभव न था। वामीरो तताँरा को रीति-रिवाज़ का डर दिखाकर समझाने का प्रयास किया गया, किंतु दोनों अपने प्रेम पर अडिग रहे।

पासा के पशु-पर्व में वामीरो तताँरा के पास आई और रोने लगी। उसका रोना सुनकर उसकी माँ भी आ पहुँची। उन दोनों को देखकर आग-बबूला हो गई। तताँरा का अपमान किया। तताँरा वामीरो का क्रंदन और अपना अपमान देखकर क्रोधित हो उठा। उसका हाथ अनायास अपनी तलवार पर जा टिका। तलवार धरती में घोंपकर अपनी तरफ खींचते हुए दूर तक पहुँच गया। जहाँ तक लकीर खिंची थी वहाँ एक दरार होने लगी मानो धरती दो टुकड़ों में बँट गई। वह दूसरी तरफ चला गया और वामीरो दूसरी तरफ दौड़ रही थी। तताँरा जमीन के टुकड़े के साथ समुद्र में डूब रहा था। दूसरी तरफ लहूलुहान तताँरा और इस तरफ वामीरो एक दूसरे को पुकार रहे थे। बाद में किसी को नहीं पता कि तताँरा और वामीरो का क्या हुआ। उनकी प्रेम कहानी तो अधूरी रह गई, परंतु मानते हैं कि अब दूसरे गाँव में भी संबंध होते हैं। दो प्रेमियों की त्यागमयी मृत्यु का यही सुखद परिणाम और परिवर्तन था।

## प्रहलाद अग्रवालः तीसरी कसम के शिल्पकार शैलेंद्र

प्रहलाद जी को बचपन से ही फ़िल्मी इतिहास पर चर्चा करने और जानने का शौक रहा है। वे फ़िल्म जगत से जुड़े लोगों पर बहुत कुछ लिख चुके हैं। प्रस्तुत पाठ फ़िल्म - तीसरी कसम के शिल्पकार शैलेंद्र जी को समर्पित है। कभी-कभी कोई फ़िल्म ऐसी आती है जो दशकों तक याद रहती है। 'तीसरी कसम' साहित्य की अति मार्मिक कृति है, जिसे सैल्यूलाइड पर पूरी सार्थकता के साथ उतारा गया है। यह फ़िल्म नहीं बल्कि सैल्यूलाइड पर लिखी गई कविता है। 'तीसरी कसम' शैलेंद्र के जीवन की पहली और अंतिम फ़िल्म है। इसे 'राष्ट्रपति स्वर्णपदक' मिला तथा बंगाल फ़िल्म जर्नलिस्ट एसोसिएशन द्वारा सर्वश्रेष्ठ फ़िल्म पुरस्कार से सम्मानित किया गया।

यह एक ऐसी फ़िल्म थी जिसे केवल कवि हृदय ही बना सकता है। इस फ़िल्म से आर्थिक लाभ की उम्मीद नहीं थी। शैलेंद्र ने राजकपूर की भावनाओं को शब्द दिए हैं और राजकपूर जी ने शैलेंद्र के शब्दों को परदे पर साकार किया। दोनों दोस्तों की दोस्ती की गवाह बनी ये फ़िल्म। राजकपूर जी ने बिना पारिश्रमिक लिए ये फ़िल्म की। 'तीसरी कसम' फ़िल्म कितनी भी महान फ़िल्म क्यों न रही हो, परंतु ये कब आई और कब चली गई पता ही नहीं चला। यह एकमात्र ऐसी फ़िल्म थी जिसने साहित्य-रचना के साथ शत-प्रतिशत न्याय किया। शैलेंद्र ने इतने बड़े स्टार को हीरामन बना दिया। हीरामन में राजकपूर कहीं खो गया था। छींट की साड़ी में लिपटी हीराबाई से जब हीरामन ने पूछा – 'मन समझती हैं आप?' तब हीराबाई जुबान से नहीं, आँखों से बोलती है। दुनिया की सारी भाषाएँ उस अभिव्यक्ति को नहीं छू सकती। अपनी मस्ती में डूबकर झूमते गाते गाड़ीवान- 'चलत मुसाफिर मोह लियो रे पिंजड़े वाली मुनिया।' टप्पर-गाड़ी में हीराबाई को जाते हुए देखकर उनके पीछे दौड़ते-गाते बच्चों का हुजूम 'लाली-लाली डोलिया में लाली रे दुलहनियाँ' नौटंकी की बाई और गाड़ीवान का अपनापन अभावों की जिंदगी जीते लोगों के सपनीले कहकहे।

शैलेंद्र-मुकेश का गीत- 'सजनवा बैरी हो गए हमार चिठिया हो तो हर कोई बाँचै भाग न बाँचै कोय....अद्वितीय हो गया है। इस फ़िल्म में राजकपूर की मासूमियत अपने चरम पर थी। इसमें राजकपूर 'हीरामन' के साथ एकाकार हो गया। इतना बड़ा शोमैन 'हीरामन' के व्यक्तित्व में ढल गया।

'तीसरी कसम' की पटकथा स्वयं इस कहानी के लेखक फणीश्वरनाथ रेणु ने तैयार की थी। कहानी की छोटी-छोटी बारीकियों पर पूरा ध्यान दिया गया। एक-एक भावना साक्षात् परदे पर उतर आई।

## अंतोन चेखवः गिरगिट

अंतोन चेखव रूसी लेखक हैं। वे विद्यार्थी काल से ही लिखने लगे थे। 19वीं सदी में रूस में शासन की दमनकारी नीति थी। ऐसे समय में मौकापरस्त लोगों को बेनकाब करती कहानियाँ लिखना साहस का काम है।

प्रस्तुत पाठ में चेखव ने एक ऐसे शासन का वर्णन किया है, जो चापलूसों और भाई-भतीजावाद के पोषक भ्रष्ट अधिकारियों के सहारे चल रहा हो। ऐसे चापलूस जो आम आदमी की अपेक्षा एक अफ़सर के कुत्ता को ज़्यादा महत्व देते हैं। दोषी होने पर भी कुत्ते को गोद में उठाकर सिपाही अफ़सर के घर पर ले जाता है और पीड़ित आम जन को डाँटता है।

बंडल थामे हुए इंस्पेक्टर ओचुमेलॉव अपना लंबा ओवरकोट पहने बाज़ार के चौराहे से जा रहा था। बाज़ार से जब्त की गई झरबेरियाँ उठाए एक सिपाही भी पीछे चल रहा था। तभी कुत्ते पर चिल्लाता ख्यूक्रिन सुनार गली में दौड़ता आया। वह इंस्पेक्टर से कुत्ते के मालिक से हरज़ाना दिलवाने की गुज़ारिश की। ओचुमेलॉव उसके मालिक को सबक सिखाने की बात करता है, क्योंकि उस कुत्ते ने ख्यूक्रिन की उँगली काट ली है। जैसे ही इंस्पेक्टर को पता चलता है कि यह कुत्ता जनरल साहब का है तो वह पलट जाता है और उलटे ख्यूक्रिन को अपराधी बना देता है। वह कहता है कि तुम्हारी उँगली में कील लगी होगी। तुमने मासूम जानवर को सिगरेट से मुँह पर दागा है।

फिर किसी ने कहा कि यह जनरल का कुत्ता नहीं है, यह तो आवारा किस्म का है। जनरल को बारजोई नस्ल पसंद नहीं है तो तुरंत पलटी मारते हुए कहता है कि यह भद्दा और मरियल-सा पिल्ला आवारा होगा। पीटर्सबर्ग में ऐसे कुत्ते की छुट्टी कर दी जाती है। जनरल साहब के तो सभी कुत्ते पोंटर हैं। महँगे और अच्छी नस्ल के हैं। इस कुत्ते को हर हाल में मज़ा चखवाया जाना जरूरी है।

तभी भीड़ से कोई कहता है कि यह कुत्ता जनरल साहब का ही है तो इंस्पेक्टर सिपाही से कहता है कि जल्दी से इस कुत्ते को जनरल साहब के पास ले जाओ और कहना कि मैंने भेजा है। यह भी कहना कि इस महँगे प्राणी को गली में आने से रोके, कोई उठा ले जाएगा। तभी जनरल का बावर्ची उधर आता है। उसने बताया कि यह जनरल का नहीं उनके भाई का है, तो ओचुमेलॉव हैरानी से पूछता है- क्या जनरल के भाई साहब बाल्दीमीर इवानिच पधार चुके हैं और मुझे मालूम तक नहीं। अभी कुछ दिन रुकेंगे? बावर्ची को कहा- इसे (कुत्ते को) ले जाओ, भाई बड़ा प्यारा पिल्ला है, और काठगोदाम से बाहर चला गया। भीड़ ख्यूक्रिन की हालत पर हँस दी कि इंसान की औकात कुत्ते से भी कम है।

इस पाठ में इंस्पेक्टर ओचुमेलॉव का पल-पल बदलता रूप दिखाया गया है। किस प्रकार वह गिरगिट की तरह रंग बदलता है।

---

## निदां फ़ाज़ली: अब कहाँ दूसरे के दुख से दुखी होने वाले

निदा फ़ाज़ली जी अपनी किस्म के इकलौते गद्यकार हैं। वे गद्य में पद्य के मनकों की शेर-ओ-शायरी पिरोकर अपनी सुंदर भाषा गढ़ते हैं। प्रस्तुत पाठ में लेखक की मानवीय मूल्यों के प्रति गहरी संवेदना उभरकर आई है। यह धरती ईश्वर ने सभी प्राणियों के लिए बनाई थी, परंतु इंसान ने अपने बुद्धिबल से सब जीवों का हक छीनकर सारी पृथ्वी को टुकड़ों में बाँट लिया है। लेखक चाहता है कि उसकी कहानियों को पढ़कर लोग दूसरों के दुख को समझें और मदद करें।

बाइबिल के सोलोमेन और कुरान के सुलेमान बहुत ही दयालु राजा थे। वे जानवरों की भाषा जानते थे। एक बार चींटियाँ उनके काफ़िले से डरकर बात कर रही थीं तो सुलेमान ने कहा- घबराओ मत! खुदा ने सुलेमान को सबका रखवाला बनाया है। चींटियों ने सुलेमान को दुआएँ दीं।

एक ऐसी कहानी का वर्णन शेख अयाज़ ने किया है। उनके पिता जी एक दिन जब कुएँ से लौटे तो एक काला च्योंटा रेंग रहा था। वह भोजन छोड़कर उसे दोबारा कुएँ पर छोड़ने गए। नूह नाम के एक पैगंबर सारी उम्र रोते रहे एक जख्मी कुत्ते के कारण। महाभारत में युधिष्ठिर का अंत तक साथ निभानेवाला भी एक प्रतीकात्मक कुत्ता ही था।

दुनिया किसी एक की नहीं थी, सब मिलजुलकर रहते थे। अब इंसानों ने दीवारे बनाकर रहने के डिब्बे बना लिए। पशु-पक्षी जानवरों के बसेरे काट दिए। समुद्र को पीछे हटने पर मजबूर कर दिया। प्रकृति की सहनशक्ति की सीमा जब समाप्त होती है, तो वह अपना विकराल रूप दिखाती है। कुछ साल पहले बंबई में देखने को मिला था। समुद्र को धकेलते हुए जब इंसान ने उसे मजबूर किया तो उसने अपनी लहरों पर दौड़ते हुए तीन जहाज़ों को तिनकों की तरह तीन दिशाओं में फेंक दिया- एक वर्ली में, दूसरा बांद्रा में और तीसरा गेट-वे-ऑफ़ इंडिया पर।

लेखक की माँ सूरज ढलने के बाद पत्ते तोड़ने से मना करती थी। मुर्गे और कबूतर को सताने से मना करती थी। एक बार माँ से कबूतर का अंडा टूट गया था, तो उन्होंने पूरे दिन रोज़ा रखा था और कई-कई बार नमाज़ अदा की थी।

इतने सालों बाद अब फिर मेरे घर में कबूतर ने घोंसला बनाया है। अब मेरी माँ नहीं, पत्नी है। उन्होंने जाली लगाकर कबूतरों का आना बंद कर दिया है। अब उदास कबूतर खिड़की के बाहर बैठे रहते हैं, क्योंकि अब न सोलोमन हैं, न नूह और न लेखक की माँ है जो इनके दुखों में सारी रात नमाज़ पढ़ें।

---

## रवींद्र केलेकर: पतझर में टूटी पत्तियाँ

### (1)   गिन्नी का सोना

रवींद्र केलेकर गांधीवादी चिंतक के रूप में हैं। इनकी रचनाओं में 'गागर में सागर' फिट बैठता है। इनकी रचनाएँ समाज के ताने-बाने से निकलकर आती हैं। प्रस्तुत पाठ में लेखक पाठक को एक सक्रिय और जागरूक बनने की प्रेरणा देता है। लेखक आदर्श और व्यावहारिकता पर चर्चा करते हुए कहता है कि गिन्नी सोने का बहुत प्रचलित रूप है। इसमें तांबा मिला होता है। यह मिलावट उसका खोट नहीं व्यावहारिक है। ताँबे से सोने में चमक और मजबूती दोनों आती है।

इसी प्रकार व्यावहारिकता को ही आदर्श बना लेने से लोग 'प्रैक्टिकल आइडियालिस्ट' बन जाते हैं। गाँधी जी सोने में ताँबा नहीं बल्कि ताँबे में सोना मिलाकर ताँबे (व्यवहार) की कीमत बढ़ा देते थे। इसलिए सोना ही आगे रहता था।

व्यवहारवादी लोग हमेशा अपने व्यवहार के प्रति सजग होते हैं। वे लाभ-हानि का हिसाब लगाकर ही कदम बढ़ाते हैं। अपने साथ-साथ दूसरों को भी ऊपर चढ़ाते हैं, यह कार्य आदर्शवादी लोगों ने किया है। समाज के पास जो भी शाश्वत जीवन मूल्य हैं, वे आदर्शवादी लोगों के दिए हुए ही हैं। व्यवहारवादी समाज को गिराते हैं, आदर्शवादी आगे बढ़ाते हैं। व्यवहारवादी अपना लाभ ढूँढ़ता है, तो आदर्शवादी समाज की उन्नति चाहता है।

## (2) झेन की देन

सारा विश्व जानता है कि दूसरे विश्व युद्ध में जापान के दो शहरों के सर्वनाश के साथ उसकी अर्थव्यवस्था की भी कमर टूट गई थी। उसके बाद जिस तरह विश्व पटल पर जापान उभरकर आया, यह एक चमत्कार ही है। यह चमत्कार हुआ वहाँ के लोगों के अथक प्रयास और देश के प्रति समर्पण से। एक महीने का काम एक दिन में ही पूरा करने लगे। जापान के लोगों के जीवन की रफ़्तार बढ़ गई। उनका जीवन दौड़ने लगा। अमेरिका से प्रतिस्पर्धा करते-करते जापान में 'मानसिक' रोगी बढ़ने लगे हैं।

इसलिए जापानी अपने दिमाग को शांत करने के लिए चा-नो-यू (टी-सेरेमनी) करते हैं। यह चाय पीने की एक विधि है। लेखक जब जापान गया तो उसका एक मित्र इसमें ले गया। छह मंजिली छत पर दफ़्ती की दीवारों वाली और तातामी (चटाई) की जमीन वाले एक सुंदर पर्णकुटी थी। मिट्टी के बरतन में रखे पानी में हाथ-पैर धोकर वे अंदर बैठ गए। 'चाजीन' ने स्वागत किया, अंगीठी सुलगाई, फिर चायदानी रखी। बरतनों को तौलिए से साफ किया। सभी क्रियाएँ लयबद्ध हो रही थीं। वहाँ इतनी शांति थी कि पानी के उबलने और सन्नाटे तक की आवाज़ सुनाई दे रही थी।

इस विधि में शांति को ध्यान में रखते हुए तीन से ज्यादा लोगों को एक साथ इजाजत नहीं होती। दो घूँट चाय की चुस्कियाँ बूँद-बूँद करके डेढ़ घंटे में पीने से दिमाग असीम शांति में पहुँच गया। पहले मन भूत-भविष्य में घूमते हुए अंत में वर्तमान की अनंतकाल की शांति में खो गया। जीना किसे कहते हैं उस दिन लेखक ने जाना। झेन परंपरा की यह बहुत बड़ी देन जापानियों के पास है।

उन्नति के चक्कर में हम मशीन बनते जा रहे हैं। अपने मन की शांति को बेचकर हमने भौतिक सुख-साधन जुटा लिए; परंतु फिर भी खुश नहीं हैं। एक पल शांति के लिए दिन-रात तड़प रहे हैं। वास्तविक सुख मन की शांति में हैं।

---

### हबीब तनवीर: कारतूस

हबीब तनवीर ने दिल्ली में पेशेवर नाट्यमंच की स्थापना की। इन्होंने लोकनाट्य के क्षेत्र में भी महत्त्वपूर्ण कार्य किया।

प्रस्तुत पाठ एक ऐसे जाँबाज़ वीर के बारे में है जिसका एकमात्र लक्ष्य अंग्रेज़ों को देश से बाहर भगाना था। वह निडर युवक मौत के मुँह में घुस गया। कंपनी की बटालियन के खेमे में घुसकर कर्नल पर ऐसा रौब जमाया कि कर्नल भी उसकी प्रशंसा किए बिना न रह सका।

सन् 1799 में गोरखपुर के जंगलों में अंग्रेज़ी फ़ौज कई महीनों से डेरा डाले हुए थी। उनका केवल एक ही लक्ष्य है 'वज़ीर अली' को पकड़ना। वज़ीर अली अवध का बेदखल नवाब है, जिसे अपनों ने ही धोखा दिया। उसके अपने रिश्तेदार ने ही अंग्रेजों के साथ मिलकर उसे अवध से बाहर भेज दिया और पेंशनभोगी बना दिया। कंपनी ने उसे तीन लाख सालाना पेंशन देकर बनारस पहुँचा दिया। कुछ महीने बाद उसे गर्वनर जनरल ने कलकत्ता तलब किया। वज़ीर अली कंपनी के वकील से पूछने गया था। वकील ने उचित उत्तर देने की अपेक्षा वज़ीर अली का अपमान किया। वज़ीर अली ने खंजर से वकील का कत्ल कर दिया और जंगलों में भाग गया। उसका इरादा नेपाल पहुँचना था ताकि वह अफ़गानिस्तान के बादशाह शाहे- ज़मा के साथ मिलकर अंग्रेज़ों से मुकाबला करे और अंग्रेज़ों को हिंदुस्तान से बाहर खदेड़ दे। अंग्रेज़ी सरकार डरी हुई थी कि यदि वज़ीर अली कामयाब हो गया तो बक्सर और प्लासी की लड़ाइयों से मिली जीत व्यर्थ चली जाएगी।

तभी कर्नल और लेफ़्टीनेंट को दूर से धूल उड़ती दिखाई दी। शायद कोई काफ़िला आ रहा था। यह सीधा खेमे की तरफ ही आ रहा था। पास आने पर पता चला कि यह तो एक ही घुड़सवार था। उसने कर्नल से अकेले में मिलने की इच्छा ज़ाहिर की। कर्नल से यहाँ खेमा डालने का कारण पूछा और वज़ीर अली को पकड़वाने के बदले कारतूस की माँग की। कर्नल ने दस कारतूस दे दिए और उसका नाम पूछा। उसने अपना नाम वज़ीर अली बताया और निडरतापूर्वक वहाँ से चला गया। लेफ़्टीनेंट ने जब कर्नल से पूछा कि कौन था तो उसने कहा एक जाँबाज़ सिपाई था।

भारत माँ के वीर लाड़लों ने देश को आज़ाद कराने के लिए जंगलों की खाक छानी अनेक कष्ट सहे। ऐसे उदाहरणों से इतिहास भरा पड़ा है।

# पूरक पाठ्यपुस्तक

### संचयन

प्रस्तुत पुस्तक में गद्य की विभिन्न विधाओं को लिया गया है। कहानी (हरिहर काका), आत्म-कथा (सपनों के-से दिन), उपन्यास (टोपी शुक्ला) के माध्यम से विधाओं की शैलीगत विशेषताओं से विद्यार्थियों को अवगत कराने का प्रयास किया गया है। साथ ही परिवार, समाज और संस्कृति के महत्त्व को समझाने का भी प्रयास है।

### मिथिलेश्वर: हरिहर काका

थक हारकर मनुष्य अपने घर आकर बड़ा शकुन महसूस करता है। घर-परिवार में हम अपनों के साथ सुख-दुख, हारी-बीमारी बाँटते हैं। संकट-खुशी में एक-दूसरे का साथ निभाते हैं। धर्म और धर्मस्थान हमारे संस्कारों-विश्वासों को जोड़ते हैं, बढ़ाते हैं। परंतु यदि यही दोनों (घर-धर्मस्थान) अपनी मूल भावना से भटककर मानव को कष्ट देने लगे तो उसको कौन सहारा देगा।

आजकल लोगों की आस्था को भड़काकर या उसका गलत फ़ायदा उठाकर धर्मस्थान और धर्मध्वजा धारक अपनी महत्वकांक्षा को पूरी करते हैं। ये स्वार्थलोलुप हो गए हैं। धर्मस्थान ताकत और धन का केंद्र बन गए हैं। बड़े-बड़े राजनेता भी अपना हित साधने के लिए इन्हें बढ़ावा देते हैं। पीड़ित-दुखी व्यक्ति का भगवान और इंसान सब पर से विश्वास उठ जाता है।

हरिहर काका का परिवार उनकी उपेक्षा करता है। अविवाहित होने के कारण भाई उनकी संपत्ति पर तो गिद्ध दृष्टि रखते हैं; परंतु उनकी उचित देखभाल नहीं करते। घर में मेहमानों के लिए तो पकवान बनते हैं; परंतु उन्हें रुखी-सूखी रोटी भी समय पर नहीं मिलती। उनके भाई भी बीमारी तक में उनका हाल नहीं पूछते। अपनी उपेक्षा से खिन्न जब हरिहर काका भाई की पत्नी को खरी-खोटी सुना रहे थे तो 'ठाकुरबारी' का पुजारी वहीं दालान में था। ठाकुरबारी का काम लोगों के अंदर भक्ति-भावना जगाना और भटके हुए लोगों को धर्म के रास्ते पर लाना है। लोग ठाकुर जी के नाम पर अनाज-पैसा निकालते हैं। ठाकुरबारी के पुजारी ने सारी बात महंत जी को बताई। महंत जी ने अपना स्वार्थ साधने के लिए हरिहर काका की आहत भावनाओं को भड़काकर उसे अपने साथ ले गए। उसे बढ़िया भोजन दिया गया और अपनी ज़मीन ठाकुरबारी को दान करने के लिए दबाव बनाया।

उधर चारों भाई भी अपने परिवार जन पर नाराज़ हुए। उन्हें भी हरिहर काका की संपत्ति अपने हाथ से फिसलती नज़र आई। दोनों तरफ संपत्ति हथियाने के लिए अनैतिक और गैरकानूनी हथकंडे अपनाए जाने लगे। इसी दौरान पता चला कि ठाकुरबारी धार्मिक संस्थान के रूप में गुंडे-निठल्ले बदमाशों का एक अड्डा बन चुकी थी। वे अपने हित के लिए हिंसक और अनैतिक कार्यों से भी परहेज नहीं करते थे। ठाकुरबारी में लठैत बदमाशों की पूरी फ़ौज थी। ठाकुरबारी की मेहरबानी से उनके भाई उसकी खूब सेवा कर रहे थे, परंतु इसी बीच महंत के गुंडों ने हरिहर का अपहरण कर लिया। हरिहर के भाइयों ने पुलिस का सहारा लिया। पुलिस ने तलाशी ली तो ठाकुरबारी

में हरिहर काका नहीं मिले। ठाकुरबारी के सब लोग भाग गए थे। तालाबंद एक कमरे में हरिहर काका बंद मिले। हरिहर काका ने बताया कि वे साधु नहीं डाकू, हत्यारे और कसाई हैं। उन्होंने सादे कागज़ पर जबरन अँगूठे के निशान ले लिए थे।

अब हरिहर काका भाइयों के साथ आ गए। दोनों तरफ खूँखार लोगों और हथियारों का जमावड़ा होने लगा था। हरिहर काका ने रिश्तेदारों के दबाव के बाद भी अपनी ज़मीन किसी के भी नाम न करने का फैसला किया। भाई धमकाते, डराते वे भी कसाई बन गए थे। हरिहर काका के भाइयों ने उन्हें मारा-पीटा और बाँधकर डाल दिया। इसके बाद हरिहर काका अलग रहने लगे। उनकी सुरक्षा के लिए पुलिस के चार जवान मिले है। भाइयों, ठाकुरबारी और नेता जी के प्रयासों का कोई प्रभाव काका पर नहीं पड़ा। वे सारे गाँव में चर्चा का केंद्र हैं। अफवाहों का बाज़ार गर्म है। संपत्ति, वारिस, अंतिम क्रिया-कर्म को लेकर अनेक बातें होती हैं, परंतु हरिहर काका तो गूँगेपन का शिकार हो गए हैं। वे किसी बात का कोई जवाब नहीं देते। आज उनके पास कहने के लिए कुछ नहीं है। उनके धन पर पुलिस वाले भोग लगा रहे हैं।

---

## गुरदयाल सिंहः सपनों के-से दिन

विद्यार्थी जीवन परविहीन सपनों का जीवन है। बिना पढ़े-लिखे प्रथम आने के सपने पटवारी, कलैक्टर, और न जाने क्या-क्या बन जाने के सपने। फिर हकीकत किताबें तो जैसे दुश्मनी पर उतर आती हैं। कितना भी पढ़ो याद ही नहीं होता। इस आयु में बहुत कुछ ऐसा होता है। जिसे भूला नहीं जा सकता । वे शरारतें, चुहलबाजियाँ, आकाक्षाएँ फिर कहाँ?

प्रस्तुत पाठ लेखक गुरदयाल सिंह की आत्मकथा का अंश है। इसमें लेखक ने बताया है कि उस समय खेलने के बदले माँ-बहन, पिता से कितनी मार खानी पड़ती थी। जगह-जगह पिटाई के निशान, चोट फिर भी अगले दिन खेलना नहीं भूलते थे। आखिर खेल में ऐसा क्या जादू है। यह लेखक ने उस समय जाना जब उसने बाल मनोविज्ञान विषय पढ़ा।

लेखक के सभी साथी लेखक जैसे परिवारों से थे। जो अक्षरज्ञान तक ही शिक्षा चाहते थे। शिक्षा के प्रति कोई विशेष रूचि या लगाव न था। आधे से ज्यादातर परिवार राजस्थान या हरियाणा से आकर मंडी में व्यापार या दुकानदारी करने आए थे। हम उनकी बोली समझ नहीं पाते थे; परंतु खेल की भाषा सब अच्छी तरह समझ जाते थे। बचपन में घास अधिक हरी लगती है। फूल-पत्ते तोड़ने का लालच नहीं छोड़ पाते थे। कलियों को तोड़ते, सूँघते और जेब में डाल लेते थे। नई कक्षा का उत्साह नई किताबें देखकर जाता रहता था। गर्मी की छुट्टियों में ननिहाल जाते थे। तालाब के पानी में नहाकर गर्म रेत में लथ-पथ होते और दौड़कर फिर तालाब में छलाँग लगा देते थे। हाथ-पैर मारकर स्वयं ही तैरना सीख लेते। भैंस के सींग या दुम पकड़कर बाहर आ जाते।

जब छुट्टियाँ खत्म होने लगती तो सब मज़ा भूलने लगते और मास्टर जी याद आने लगते। गृहकार्य का हिसाब लगाते पंद्रह दिन बचने पर रोज़ के दस सवाल हल करने की सोचते तो पाँच-सात दिन और निकल जाते। डर बढ़ने लगता, दिन घटने लगते। फिर स्वयं को ढाँढस देते कि दस का क्या पंद्रह सवाल भी किए जा सकते हैं? सोचते-सोचते छुट्टियाँ भागने लगतीं। ऐसा लगता कि दोपहर में ही सूर्य छिप जाता है। दिन बहुत छोटे लगने लगते। कितने ही सहपाठी काम करने की बजाय पिटाई को 'सस्ता सौदा' समझते। लेखक जो पिटाई से बहुत डरता था, उन बहादुरों की भाँति सोचने लगता। ऐसी सोच का नेता ओमा था।

ओमा की बातें, गालियाँ, मार-पिटाई का ढंग सब-कुछ अलग था। ठिगना शरीर, हाँडी जितना बड़ा सिर, बिल्ली के बच्चे के सिर पर मानों तरबूज रखा हो। मोटी-मोटी आँखें थीं उसकी। स्कूल में सबसे ज्यादा डर पी.टी. सर की दहकती आँखों से लगता था। साल भर कठिन अनुशासन में कठिन परिश्रम के बाद उनका 'शाबाश' शब्द किसी इनाम से कम नहीं था। लेखक हेडमास्टर की मेहरबानी से ही पढ़ पा रहा था। वे एक धनाढ्य छात्र की पुरानी पुस्तकें लेखक को उपलब्ध करवाते थे। उस समय एक रुपया भी बहुत बड़ी रकम थी। पढ़ाई में अरुचि का कारण मास्टरों की मार-पीट और विषयों का समझ में न आना था। छात्रों के साथ सहयोगात्मक रवैये की अपेक्षा शासनात्मक रवैया अपनाया जाता था। स्कूल केवल स्काउट के कारण या फ़ौजी जैसी धुली ड्रैस के कारण अच्छा लगता था। स्कूलों में फ़ौजी रंगरूटों की भर्ती के लिए अंग्रेज़ आते थे। मास्टर प्रीतम चंद स्काउट के टीचर थे, वे बहुत सख्त थे। एक बार लेखक को फ़ारसी का शब्द-रूप

याद करने के लिए कहा गया था। बार-बार याद करने पर भी जब याद नहीं कर पाया तो मास्टर जी ने मुर्गा बना दिया था। थोड़ी कमर नीची होने पर डंडा पड़ता था। इतने में हेडमास्टर शर्मा भी दफ़्तर से बाहर आए और प्रीतम जी पर बिगड़ गए थे। प्रीतम जी को मुअत्तल (सस्पेंड) कर दिया था। फिर मास्टर प्रीतम जी स्कूल नहीं आए। फिर जब भी फ़ारसी का घंटा बजता तो छाती धक्-धक् करने लगती और जब तक शर्मा जी या मास्टर नौहरिया राम जी कमरे में फ़ारसी पढ़ाने नहीं आ जाते तो चेहरे मुझाए रहते।

वे बाज़ार में किराए पर रहते थे। मुअत्तल होने के बाद भी उन्हें कोई फर्क नहीं पड़ा था, वे बड़े आराम से रहते थे। मास्टर जी बादाम भिगोकर अपने पालतू तोतों को खिलाते थे। तोतों से मीठी-मीठी बातें करना एक चमत्कार से कम न था, क्योंकि प्रीतम जी और मिठास का दूर-दूर तक कोई रिश्ता न था।

उपर्युक्त पाठ से पता चलता है कि शारीरिक दंड से बच्चों में भय का वातावरण बनता है। अत: विद्यालयों में वातावरण सहयोगपूर्ण होना चाहिए।

## राही मासूम रज़ा: टोपी शुक्ला

आज के मशीनी युग में रिश्ते-नाते स्वार्थपूर्ति के लिए ही रह गए हैं। अपनापन-प्यार खत्म होता जा रहा है। बालमन भी इस अभाव से अछूते नहीं हैं। बड़े घरों में तो हालात और भी बुरे हैं।

कहानी का पात्र टोपी को अपनापन अपने दोस्त अज़ीज़ इफ़्फ़न की दादी माँ और अपने घर की नौकरानी सीता में मिलता है। टोपी को इससे कोई फर्क नहीं पड़ता कि किसकी क्या जाति है, क्या धर्म है। कहा जाता है- प्रेम न माने जात-विजात, भूख न जाने खिचड़ी भात।

इफ़्फ़न के दादा-परदादा प्रसिद्ध मौलवी थे। उनकी आत्मा ने एक साँस भी इस देश में न ली। 'लाश' को भी करबला ले जाने की वसीयत की। इफ़्फ़न की परदादी और दादी नमाज़-रोज़े की पाबंद थीं, लेकिन भारतीय संस्कृति को मानती थी। इफ़्फ़न की दादी पूरबी थी। जीवन भर पूरबी बोलती रही। मर्दों और औरतों के फर्क को जानकर ही इफ़्फ़न को समझा जा सकता है। इफ़्फ़न की दादी जमींदार की बेटी थीं। ससुराल में मौलविन की आत्मा सदा परेशान रही। वह अपनी लाश न करबला, न नजफ़ में दफनवाना चाहती थी। वह तो अपने घर जाना चाहती थी, जो अब कराची में है। मरने से पहले इनसान शायद सबसे खूबसूरत सपने देखता है। अच्छे दिनों की याद करता है। इफ़्फ़न की दादी को बनारस के फातमैन में दफनाया गया था। इफ़्फ़न अपनी दादी से सबसे ज्यादा प्यार करता था। दादी रात भर उसे कहानियाँ सुनाती थी, कभी उसका दिल नहीं दुखाती थी।

टोपी को अपनी दादी से नफरत थी। दादी और अब्बा एक जैसी बोली बोलते थे। माँ की भाषा उसे मीठी लगती थी। जब भी वह इफ़्फ़न के घर जाता, दादी के पास ही बैठने की कोशिश करता था। इफ़्फ़न की दादी अम्मों के बारे में पूछती। उसे अच्छा लगता।

डॉक्टर भृगु नारायण शुक्ला के घर मेज़-कुर्सी पर खाना होता था। टोपी ने कहा- "अम्मी ज़रा बैगन का भुरता।" भूचाल आ गया परंपराएँ डोलने लगीं। माँ ने पूछा- अम्मी लफ़्ज़ कहाँ से सीखा। "ई हम इफ़्फ़न से सीखा है"। टोपी ने कहा उस दिन रामदुलारी ने टोपी को बहुत मारा। वह मारते-मारते थक गई। परंतु टोपी ने नहीं कहा कि वह इफ़्फ़न के घर नहीं जाएगा। टोपी के पिता को पता चला कि टोपी की दोस्ती कलेक्टर के बेटे से है तो वे कपड़े और शक्कर के परमिट ले आए। इफ़्फ़न की दादी के इंतकाल की खबर सुनकर जब वह इफ़्फ़न के घर गया तो दादी के बिना घर सूना लगा था। इफ़्फ़न की दादी और टोपी दोनों ही अपनों के बीच अनजाने थे। प्यार और सम्मान के प्यासे थे। दोनों में अटूट बंधन था। उसके बाद जब इफ़्फ़न के पिता जी का तबादल हुआ तो वह टूट गया था। दस अक्टूबर सन् पैंतालीस का टोपी के आत्म-इतिहास में बहुत महत्त्व था। उस दिन इफ़्फ़न मुरादाबाद चला गया था। अगले कलेक्टर के बच्चों से उसकी नहीं पटी और उन्होंने कुत्ते से कटवा दिया था। उसके बाद घर की नौकरानी सीता से अपनापन पाकर उसका व्यक्तित्व भी गिर गया था। वह घर में दुत्कारा जाता था। सब काम उसे ही करने पड़ते थे। वह तीन साल नौवीं में फेल होने के बाद दसवीं में पहुँचा था। इसके लिए उसे घोर अपमान झेलना पड़ा था।

प्रस्तुत कहानी बालमन के अकेलेपन का चित्रण प्रस्तुत करती है कि किस प्रकार हम अपनों के होते हुए भी अकेले हो जाते हैं। बालक हैसियत नहीं चाहते, प्यार चाहते हैं। वह प्यार उसे कहीं से भी मिलता है तो वे उसी के हो जाते हैं।

## काव्य खण्ड

काव्य की रसानुभूति, सुनकर तभी प्राप्त होती है जब काव्य सजगतापूर्वक भाषा प्रवाह, उचित, लय, ताल में पढ़ा जाए। काव्य पाठ करते समय यह ध्यान रखना चाहिए की पद्य, गद्य नहीं है। गद्य की तरह वाचन से काव्य अरुचिकर हो जाता है। विद्यार्थियों की सुविधानुसार सभी काव्य पाठों का संक्षिप्त रूप दिया जा रहा है।

## कबीर: साखी

'साखी' का अर्थ सीख भी होता है। कबीर जी समाज को देखकर तथा अनुभव करके ही बोलते थे। उनका ज्ञान साक्ष्य अनुभव का निचोड़ है।

कबीर जी कहते हैं कि हमें ऐसी वाणी बोलनी चाहिए जो मन के घमंड को खत्म कर दे। स्वयं के साथ-साथ दूसरे के मन को भी शीतल कर दे। कस्तूरी तो मृग की नाभि में होती है और वह सब जगह ढूँढता है। इसी प्रकार राम तो सबके हृदय में हैं, बंदा उसे यहाँ-वहाँ ढूँढता है। जहाँ अहंकार है वहाँ ईश्वर नहीं रहता। कबीर जी कहते हैं कि संसार अनजान है तो सुखी है, मैं जाग रहा हूँ तो दुखी हूँ। राम से बिछुड़कर आत्मा दुखी है। कोई मंत्र उसका उपचार नहीं कर पाता। कबीर जी कहते है कि निंदक आपकी कमियों को, दोषों को बिना साबुन-पानी के साफ कर देता है। सारा संसार ग्रंथ पढ़ता है परंतु कोई पंडित नहीं हुआ। यदि प्रेम का एक अक्षर पढ़ ले तो पंडित हो जाते हैं। कबीर जी कहते हैं कि हम तो मशाल हाथ में लेकर अपना ही घर (अहं) जलाने चले हैं। जो हमारे साथ हो तो वह अपना घर जलाकर ईश्वर को पा ले।

## मीरा: पद

मीरा मध्यकालीन कृष्ण भक्त कवयित्री थीं। वह श्रीकृष्ण को ही अपना आराध्य एवं सर्वस्व मानती थीं। मीरा की भक्ति में दास्य भाव था।

(1) मीरा अपने प्रभु से अपनी पीड़ा हरने की विनती करती हैं, क्योंकि उन्होंने द्रोपदी की लाज बचाई थी, नरहरि का रूप धारण कर डूबते गजराज को बचाया था और हाथी का कष्ट दूर किया था।

(2) मीरा प्रभु से कहती हैं कि हे प्रभु! मुझे अपना नौकर रख लो। मैं सुबह उठकर आपके दर्शन पाऊँगी, आपके बाग-बगीचे लगाऊँगी। वृंदावन की गलियों में गोविंद की लीला गाऊँगी। आपकी सेवा करके दर्शन प्राप्त होंगे और खर्चे के लिए (वेतन) आपका स्मरण पा लूँगी। मैं भक्ति भाव का साम्राज्य पा लूँगी। जिस मोहन ने मोर-मुकुट और पीतांबर धारण किया है, वह मुरली वाला वृंदावन में गाय चराता है। उसी साँवरियाँ के दर्शन पाने के लिए ऊँचे-ऊँचे महलों में कुसुंबी साड़ी पहनकर आधी रात में प्रभु दर्शन दो। श्री यमुना जी के किनारे प्रभु दर्शन दो, क्योंकि मेरा हृदय अधीर हो रहा है। हे प्रभु! आप ही मेरे सब कुछ हो।

## बिहारी: दोहे

बिहारी के दोहे गागर में सागर कहे जाते हैं। बिहारी के दोहे अर्थगांभीर्य और सारगर्भित हैं। बिहारी के दोहे व्यावहारिक, ज्ञानपरक और श्रृंगारपरक हैं। बिहारी श्रीकृष्ण भक्त श्रृंगारिक कवि हैं।

श्याम के साँवले शरीर पर पीतांबर इस प्रकार शोभा पाते हैं, जैसे नीलमणि पत्थर पर सूर्य का प्रकाश पड़ता हो। तपोवन के प्रचंड तापमान ने साँप-मोर और मृग-बाघ सबको एक जगह रहने पर मजबूर कर दिया है। बिहारी जी श्रीकृष्ण-गोपी लीला का वर्णन करते हुए बताते हैं कि गोपी श्रीकृष्ण की बातों का रस लेने के लिए उसकी मुरली छिपा लेती है। आँखों ही आँखों में इशारे करती है परंतु

पूछने पर मना कर देती है। यहाँ बाल-लीला प्रेम की पराकाष्ठा है। भरे भवन में आँखों ही आँखों में सब बातें हो जाती हैं। कहना-सुनना, रीझना-खीजना, मिलना, खिलखिलाना, लजाना नैनों ही नैनों में बातें होती हैं। कवि बिहारी जी रहस्यवाद की भक्ति का वर्णन करते हुए कहते हैं– ज्येष्ठ महीने की दोपहर में जिस प्रकार छाया ढूँढ़ते हैं वैसे ही आत्मा गहन वन में बैठकर शरीर रूपी भवन में घुस बैठी। कवि कहता है कि उसके हृदय की बात सब तेरे हृदय ने कह दी, जो कागज पर लिखते हुए भी लज्जा आ रही थी। बिहारी अपने कुल का वर्णन करते हुए कहते हैं कि चंद्र ब्राह्मण कुल में उत्पन्न हुए और अपनी इच्छा से ब्रज में आए। हे केशव, हे पिता मेरे सब कष्ट-क्लेश हर लो। भक्ति का दिखावा करने वाला माथे पर तिलक छापता है, माला हाथ में धारण करता है और जाप का एक काम नहीं करता, परंतु सच्चे भक्त का मन राम में रमता है।

---

## मैथिलीशरण गुप्तः मनुष्यता

गुप्त जी श्रीराम भक्त कवि हैं। ये अपने जीवनकाल में ही राष्ट्रकवि के रूप में विख्यात हो गए थे। कवि पिता के बेटे जन्म से ही काव्य प्रतिभा लेकर उत्पन्न हुए थे। कवि गुप्त जी के काव्य समग्रता लिए हुए हैं। प्रस्तुत पाठ में कवि परहित का महत्व बताते हुए कहता है कि सोचो जब तुम मरणशील हो, तब भी मृत्यु से न डरो। मृत्यु भी ऐसी हो कि सब लोग याद करें। तुम्हारी मृत्यु व्यर्थ न हो। सिर्फ अपनों के लिए ही जीना-मरना तो पशु-प्रवृति है। मनुष्य वही है जो दूसरों के लिए मरे। उदार व्यक्ति की ही कीर्ति फैलती है। पृथ्वी भी उसी के प्रति कृतार्थ होती है, और सारी सृष्टि उसी उदार को पूजती है। उसी मनुष्य में मनुष्यता है जो विश्व में अखंड भाव भर दे।

भूख से पीड़ित रतिदेव ने हाथ का भोजन दान कर दिया। दधीचि ने हड्डियाँ तथा राजा शिवी ने अपने शरीर का माँस दान कर दिया। कर्ण ने खुशी से अपना कवच दे दिया। इस मरणशील शरीर के लिए अनादि आत्मा क्यों डरे?

सहानुभूति ही मानव की 'महा पूँजी है'। स्वयं पृथ्वी भी सदा खुशी देती है। भगवान बुद्ध ने मान्यताओं का विरोध कर दया-धर्म का संदेश दिया। कवि कहता है कि उदार वही है जो परोपकारी है। वही मनुष्य है। मनुष्य को धन संपत्ति के मद में अंधे नहीं होना चाहिए। यहाँ ईश्वर के होते हुए कोई अनाथ नहीं है। दीनदयाल प्रभु सबका ध्यान रखते हैं। कवि कहता है कि देवताओं का आशीर्वाद उसी को मिलता है जो आपस में एक दूसरे का सहारा बनते हैं। परम पिता परमात्मा सबका एक है। एकमात्र मनुष्य ही के पास विवेक है। कर्म के फलों के अनुसार हम में भेद हैं, परंतु सबकी आत्मा में समानता है। उस मनुष्य का जीवन अर्थहीन है जो अपने भाई की परेशानी में काम न आए। कवि भिन्नता मिटाने और मेलमिलाप बढ़ाने के लिए प्रोत्साहित करते हुए कहता है कि अपने इच्छित मार्ग पर खुशी से विघ्न-बाधाओं को धकेलते हुए चलो। आपस में मतभेद कभी हमारे प्यार पर हावी न हों। सभी पंथ-संप्रदायों की एक ही शिक्षा है– मानवता। सभी का निचोड़ यही है कि अपनी उन्नति के साथ-साथ सबका सहारा बनता चले वही वास्तव में मनुष्य है।

---

## सुमित्रानंदन पंतः पर्वत प्रदेश में पावस

सुमित्रानंदन पंत उत्तराखंड की प्रकृति की गोद में जन्मे। वे काव्यकला के साथ ही उत्पन्न हुए थे। प्रकृति से गहरे रूप से जुड़े थे। प्रस्तुत कविता में भी कवि ने अपने आँखों देखे प्राकृतिक सौंदर्य का वर्णन किया है।

कवि कहता है कि पहाड़ों पर वर्षा ऋतु में प्रकृति पल-पल अपना रूप बदलती है। करधनी के आकार का पर्वत अपने हजारों सुमन रूपी आँखों से नीचे पानी में अपनी विशाल परछाई देख रहा है। पहाड़ की तलहटी में तालाब दर्पण का काम करता है। झरने मोती की लड़ियों से श्रृंगार कर पर्वत का गुणगान करते हैं। पेड़ पर्वत के सीने पर ऊँचे उठकर अपनी महत्वाकांक्षा बताते हैं। अनंत शांत आकाश को चिंतित हो एकटक देख रहे हैं। ऐसा लगता है कि धवल चमकीले बादल रूपी पंख लगाकर पर्वत उड़ना चाहते हों।

अंबर धरती पर जलधारा बनकर टूट पड़ा। बरसात में शाल के ऊँचे वृक्ष मानो धरती में खो गए और सरोवर से धुआँ उठने लगा। इंद्र बादलों के यान पर सवार होकर अपनी जादुई नगरी में विचरण कर रहा है। कवि ने पहाड़ों की वर्षा का मनोहारी वर्णन किया है।

## महादेवी वर्मा: मधुर-मधुर मेरे दीपक जल

महादेवी जी छायावाद की प्रसिद्ध कवयित्री हैं। उनकी कविताएँ अंतर्मन का दर्पण होती हैं। प्रस्तुत कविता में कवयित्री औरों की अपेक्षा स्वयं को समझाने का प्रयास करती हुई कहती है कि हे मेरे मन के मधुर दीपक! तुम युगों-युगों प्रतिदिन, प्रतिपल प्रियतम के पथ को प्रकाशित कर। अपार धूप का रूप ले सुगंध फैल गई है। हे कोमल मन! तू भी मोम बनकर घुल जा। इस जीवन को अपने कण-कण से असीमित प्रकाश का सागर दे। सब तुमसे ही प्रकाश की आस लगाए हैं। सारा विश्व पतंगे की भाँति पछताता है कि तुम्हारे साथ नहीं जल पाया। हे दीपक! थरथराकर जल। हे मन! आशावान होकर देख आकाश में असंख्य दीपक स्नेहहीन हैं। पानी से भरे हुए सागर का हृदय भी जल उठता है जब बादल बिजली लेकर घिर आता है। हे मेरे मन रूपी दीपक! हँस-हँसकर जल। कवयित्री अपने-आप को प्रकृति में साकार कर सचेत बनाए रखना चाहती है।

## वीरेन डंगवाल: तोप

वीरेन डंगवाल जी का जन्म टिहरी गढ़वाल में प्रकृति के सौंदर्य खजाने में हुआ। प्राध्यापक होने और पत्रकारिता से जुड़े होने के कारण वे इतिहास पर पैनी दृष्टि रखते हैं। प्रस्तुत पाठ में कवि कंपनी बाग में रखी तोप को चेतावनी मानते हैं। वे उन ताकतों को सावधान करना चाहते हैं जिनके इरादे हमारे देश के लिए नेक नहीं हैं। कंपनी बाग के दरवाज़े पर रखी गई तोप 1857 के अत्याचार की प्रतीक है। इसको साल में दो बार चमकाया जाता है। कंपनी बाग में आने वाले शैलानियों को तोप बताती है कि किसी जमाने में वह जबरदस्त थी और दुश्मनों के छक्के छुड़ा देती थी। अब तो वह बच्चों की सवारी के ही काम आती है। चिड़ियाँ उसके अंदर घुसकर यह संदेश देती हैं कि कोई तोप कितनी भी विकराल हो एक-न-एक दिन शांत हो जाती है। इसका अर्थ यह है कि अत्याचार का साम्राज्य स्थायी नहीं होता।

## कैफ़ी आज़मी: कर चले हम फ़िदा

कैफ़ी आज़मी की गिनती आज के प्रगतिवादी उर्दू शायरों की अग्रिम पंक्ति में होती है। कैफ़ी आज़मी की कविताओं में राजनीतिक जागरूकता व सामाजिक सरोकार होता है। इनकी कविताओं में कोमल भावना होती है।

प्रस्तुत पाठ 'हकीकत' फिल्म का गाना है। इसमें सैनिकों की मर्म पुकार है जिन्हें अपने किए पर नाज है और बलिदान देते समय देशवासियों से देश सेवा की अपेक्षा करते हैं। सैनिक कहते हैं कि हम अपने देश पर जान, तन सब बलिदान कर चले हैं। जब हमारी साँस रुक रही थी, नब्ज जम गई थी हिमालय की बर्फ में, फिर भी हमने कदमों को नहीं रुकने दिया। अपने सिर कटवाकर भी हमने हिमालय का सिर नहीं झुकने दिया। मरते दम तक हम सीना तानकर मौत के समने डटे रहे। कवि कहता है कि जिंदा रहने के मौसम तो बहुत हैं, परंतु देश पर मर मिटने का, कुर्बानी देने का अवसर रोज़ नहीं मिलता है। आज धरती अपने लालों के खून से रंगकर दुलहन बन गई है। हम अब देश को तुम्हारे हवाले करके इस संसार से विदा ले रहे हैं।

सैनिक जवानों से आह्वान करता है कि देश पर मर मिटने वालों की कमी न हो, कुर्बानी की राह पर नए काफ़िले आगे बढ़ते रहें। हमारे शहीद होने के बाद देश की जीत का उत्सव होगा। अब जिंदगी मौत से गले मिल रही है। हे देश के नौजवानों! अब सिर पर कफ़न बाँधकर देश पर मर मिटने के लिए तैयार हो जाओ, क्योंकि अब देश तुम्हारे हवाले है। अपने खून से सरहद पर लक्ष्मण रेखा खींच दो ताकि कोई रावण हमारी माँ का दामन न छू सके। अब तुम्हीं राम हो, तुम्हीं लक्ष्मण हो। यह देश अब तुम्हारे हवाले है अर्थात् सैनिकों ने अपना धर्म निभा दिया; परंतु देश की रक्षा का दायित्व प्रत्येक देशवासी का होता है।

## रवींद्रनाथ ठाकुर: आत्मत्राण

रवींद्रनाथ ठाकुर कई प्रतिभाओं के पुंज थे। वे नोबेल पुरस्कार पाने वाले पहले भारतीय थे। प्रस्तुत कविता में कवि मनुष्य को आत्मनिर्भर बनने का प्रोत्साहन देते हुए कहता है कि हे प्रभु! मुझे विपदाओं से बचाओ; ये मेरी प्रार्थना नहीं है, अपितु इतनी दया करना कि मैं विपदा से न डरूँ। कितना भी कष्ट हो, संताप हो, चाहे कोई साथ न हो, फिर भी मैं दुख पर विजय पा लूँ। कोई सहायता न मिलने पर भी आत्मबल कमजोर न हो। हे प्रभु! इस संसार में कितनी भी हानि क्यों न उठानी पड़े, परंतु मन न टूटे, हिम्मत न हारूँ।

हे प्रभु! अगर मैं डूब रहा हूँ तो मुझे बचा लो; ये मेरी प्रार्थना नहीं है, अपितु मुझे तैरने की शक्ति दो। दुखों के पहाड़ आने पर उसे छोटा करने की विनती मेरी नहीं है। बस उसे सहन करने की, पार पाने की शक्ति मुझे दो। सुख के दिनों में भी मैं सिर झुकाकर रहूँ, अपने आप को पहचानूँ, बस यही मेरी प्रार्थना है। हे प्रभु! दुखों की रात्रि में मेरे साथ धोखा हो, तो भी हे करुणामय! मैं आप पर संदेह न करूँ। इसका अर्थ यह है कि हमें कोई तैरना सीखा सकता है, लड़ना सीखा सकता है, परंतु तैरने-लड़ने-जीतने की कोशिश स्वयं ही करनी है। जब तक हम स्वयं अपनी सहायता नहीं करेंगे तो कोई हमारी सहायता नहीं कर सकता।

# CHAPTERWISE
# MIND MAPS
# SOCIAL SCIENCE

# UNIT I. HISTORY



▶ **Historical Timeline**

| Sl. No. | Headings | |
|---|---|---|
| 1 | **THE FRENCH REVOLUTION AND THE IDEA OF THE NATION** | |
| | 1789 | French Revolution |
| | 1790s | Setting up of Jacobin Clubs, French armies moved into Holland, Belgium, Switzerland and much of Italy. |
| | 1813 | Napoleon lost the battle of Leipzig. |
| | 1814 - 1815 | Fall of Napoleon; the Vienna Peace Settlement. |
| 2 | **THE MAKING OF NATIONALISM IN EUROPE** | |
| | 1815 | Treaty of Vienna; Autocratic conservative regimes set up. |
| | 1831 | A young man, Giuseppe Mazzini, was sent into exile after a failed revolution in Liguria. |
| | 1833 | A merchant travelling from Hamburg to Nuremberg: encountered. |
| | | different custom barriers, different weights measures and currencies. |
| | 1833 | Giuseppe Mazzini, founded Young Europe in Berne. |
| | 1834 | A customs union or Zollverein was formed at the initiative of Purssia and joined by most of the German states. |
| 3 | **THE AGE OF REVOLUTIONS** | |
| | 1821 | Sparked off a struggle for independence among the Greeks. |
| | 1824 | English poet Lord Byron organized funds. He later went to fight in the war, where he died of fever in 1824. |
| | 1830 (July) | The first upheaval took place in France. The Bourbon kings were overthrown by constitutional monarch. |
| | 1830s | Great economic hardship in Europe. |
| | 1830 - 1848 | The Age of Revolutions. |

| | 1831 | An armed rebellion against Russian rule in Polland. |
|---|---|---|
| | 1832 | The Treaty of Constantinople recognized Greece as an independent nation. |
| | 1845 | Weavers in Silesia led a revolt against contractors. |
| | 1848 | Peasants' uprising. In Europe a revolution led by the middle classes was under way. |
| | 1848 | Food shortages and widespread unemployment in Paris. |
| | 1848 | The revolution of the liberals in France. Louise Philippe forced to flee. |
| | 1848 | The autocratic monarchies of Central and Eastern Europe began to introduce changes. |
| | 18 May 1848 | The 831 elected representatives marched in a festive procession to take their place in the Frankfurt parliament which was convened in the Church of St. Paul. |
| | 21 April 1849 | Louise Otto Peters, a political activist and founder of a feminist political association, publishe the first issue of her newspaper. |
| | 1867 | The Habsburg rulers granted more autonomy to the Hungarians. |
| 4 | **THE MAKING OF GERMANY AND ITALY** | |
| | 1744-1803 | German Romantic philosopher Johann Gottfried Herder. |
| | 1785 and 1786 | The brothers Jacob and Wilhelm-Tlrimm, popularly known Grimm Brothers, were born in the German city of Hanan. |
| | 1798 | The cover of a German almanac designed by the journalist Andreas Rebmann. |
| | 1812 | The Grimm brothers published their first collection of 'Grimms' Fairy Tales'. |

| | 1848 | The German middle class tried to unite the different regions of the German confederation into a nation-state governed by an elected parliament . |
|---|---|---|
| | 1866-71 | Unification of Germany. |
| | 18 January 1871 | The Prussian king, William I, was proclaimed German Emperor in a ceremony held at Versailles. |
| **5** | **ITALY UNIFIED** | |
| | 1830s | Giuseppe Mazzini had sought to put together a coherent programme for a unitary Italian Republic. |
| | 1831 and 1848 | Failure of revolutionary uprisings. fall on Sardinia-Piedmont. |
| | 1859 | Sardinia-Piedmont succeeded in defeating the Austrian forces. |
| | 1859-1871 | Unification of Italy. |
| | 1860 | A large number of armed volunteers under the leadership of Giuseppe Garibaldi, along with regular troops, marched into South Italy and the Kingdom ofthe Two Sicilies and succeeded in winning support of local peasants to drive out the Spainish rulers. |
| | 1861 | Victor Emmanuel II was proclaimed king of united Italy. |
| | 1864-1871 | Three wars over seven years with Austria, Denmark and France ended in Prussian victory. |
| **6** | **GIUSEPPE GARIBALDI** | |
| | 1807-82 | Giuseppe Garibaldi. |
| | 1833 | He met Mazzini, joined the Young Italy movement. |
| | 1834 | Participated in a republican uprising in Piedmont. |
| | 1848 | Garibaldi had to flee to South America, where he lived in exile till 1848 . |
| | 1854 | He supported Victor Emmanuel II in his efforts to unify the Italian states. |
| | 1860 | Garibaldi led the famous Expedition of the 'Thousand to South Italy'. |
| | 1867 | Garibaldi led an army of volunteers to Rome to fight tile last obstacle to the unification of Italy. |

| | 1870 | During the war with Prussia, France withdrew its troops from Rome and the Papal states were finally joined to Italy. |
|---|---|---|
| **7** | **NATIONALISM AND IMPERIALISM** | |
| | After 1871 | The most serious source of nationalist tension in Europe was the area called the Balkans. |
| | 1905 | Slav nationalism gathers force in the Habsburg and Ottoman Empire. |
| | 1915 | First World War. |

▶ **Important Terms**

- **Absolutist :** A system of government in which there are no checks on exercise of power.

- **Conservatism :** Political philosophy that lays stress on tradition. It is the anti-thesis of a quick change or revolution.

- **Ethnic :** A common racial or tribal background with which the community is identified.

- **Ideology :** System of ideas in respect of a particular social or political idea.

- **Plebiscite :** A direct vote by all citizens by which they are required to accept or reject a proposed legislation.

- **Suffrage :** The right to vote.

- **Utopian :** An ideal society that is unlikely to exist any where.

- **Broken chains :** Being freed.

- **Crown of Oak leaves :** Heroism.

- **Female figure :** Liberty.

- **Olive branch around the sword :** Willingness to lay down arms and resort to peace.

- **Rays of the Rising Sun :** Beginning of a new dawn or era.

▶ **Points to Remember**

1. In 1848, Frederic Sorrieu, a French artist prepared a series of four prints visualising his dream of a world made up of democracy and social Republics.

- Prior to the 19th century, Europe comprised of multi-national dynastic empires.

- France was an absolute monarchy in 1789.

- These measures helped in forging among the French people a feeling of belonging to the same country. France had evolved as a Nation State.

- There were a number of monarchies within Eastern and Central Europe. Within the territories ruled by absolute monarchs, the people belonged to different ethnic groups.

- Industrialization brought about an important change in the organization of the two social groups. Apart from the aristocrats and the serfs/peasants new groups of people emerged. These were the industrial workers, the industrialists, businessmen and professionals. These groups were educated and liberal in their attitudes. Formed within the then existing two social groups-the aristocrats and the serfs, these came to be known as the Middle Classes.

2. In the early 19th C Europe were closely allied to the ideology of libaration. The term liberation is derived from the latin root liber meaning free.

- Women and those without property had to agitate for political rights all through the 19th century and even during the early years of the 20th century.

- The spirit of liberalism suffered a big jolt after the defeat of Napoleon in 1815. Once again conservatism raised its head.

- The new regimes were autocratic. Ideas of freedom and liberty could no longer be propagated through newspapers, magazines or books in these autocratic regimes.

- Giuseppe Mazzini was a doctor's son, As a child he gave promise of high intellectual ability.

- Strongly influenced by seeing a patriot fleeing from Italy after an unsuccessful insurrection, he began to think "We Italians could and therefore ought to struggle for the liberty of our country."

3. Conservative regimes set up in 1815 more autocratic. They did not tolerate criticism, and dissent and curbed activities that questioned the legitimacy of autocratic government.

- At Marseille's Mazzini spent two of his most rewarding years. He founded his patriotic movement for young men and called it Giovine Italia (Young Italy).

- Mazzini's reputation has fluctuated greatly. In his earlier years, he was an almost legendary hero in his own country, but he was later denounced by many of his compatriots.

4. The 1830s were the years of great hardships in Europe.

- In Germany the true spirit of belonging to the German nation was popularized through folk songs, folk poetry and dances.

- The year 1848 was pretty bad for the residents of Paris. Food shortages and unemployment brought out the people on roads. Louis Philippe was unable to face the people's wrath and fled from Paris.

5. There wars over seven Years- with Austria, Denmark and France- ended in Prussian victory and completed the process of unification.

- The completion of unification of Germany is an important landmark in European history. The government of Germany was a thinly veiled autocracy. There was a constitution that bound together 25 states into a federal union.

- Britain had emerged as a nation state, not through a revolution but by a long drawn process.

6. Female allegories were invented by artists in the 19th C to represent the nation.

- Nationalism in Europe had initially been associated with replacement of monarchial structures with democracy. After 1848, the conservative elements started mobilizing nationalist sentiments for promoting state power. National identities were used for achieving political domination over other states in Europe.

7. The most serious of nationalist texilen in Europe after 1871 was the area called the Balkans.

- The Act of Union 1707 resulted in the formation of the United Kingdom that covered England and Scotland.

- Ireland was forcibly incorporated into the United Kingdom in 1801.

8. European ideas of nationalism here no were replicated for people everywhere developed their our specific variety of nationalism.

## 2. The Nationalist Movement in Indo–China

▶ **Historical Timeline**

| Year | | Headings |
|---|---|---|
| 039-043 C.E. | | The *Trung* sisters fought against Chinese to save Vietnam. |
| **THIRD CENTURY C.E.** | | *Trieu Au*, organised a large army and resisted Chinese rule. |
| 1802 | | *Nguyen Anh* becomes emperor symbolizing the unification of the country under the Nguyen dynasty. |
| 1867 | | Cochinchina (the South) becomes a French colony. |
| 1868 | | Scholars revolt, Movement against spread of Christianities. |
| **CONTROL OF FRANCE OVER INDO-CHINA** | 1880 | French troops had established a firm grip over the northern region. |
| | 1887 | French took control of Tonkin and Anaam. |
| | 1887 | Creation of the Indo-China Union, including Cochinchina, Anaam, Tonkin, Cambodia and later Laos. |
| 1902 | | Rat hunt was started in 1902. |
| 1903 | | The modern part of Hanoi was struck by bubonic plague |
| 1903 | | *Phan Boi Chau* formed the revolutionary society (*Duy Tan Hoi*) with Prince Cuong De as head |
| 1905 | | The book 'The History of the Loss of Vietnam' was written by Phan Boi Chau. |
| 1905 | | Meeting of Phan Boi Chau with Chinese reformer *Liang Qichao* in Yokohama (Japan) |
| 1907 | | Tonkin Free School was started to provide western style education. |
| 1907 | | Japan got victory over Russia |
| 1907-1908 | | 300 Vietnamese students went to Japan to acquire modern education |

| Year | | Headings |
|---|---|---|
| 1908 | | Vietnamese students established a branch of the Restoration Society in Tokyo |
| 1910 | | Rail link between Yunan, China and Vietnam was completed |
| 1911 | | Monarchy in China was overthrown by a popular movement under Sun Yat-sen and a Republic was set up |
| 1913 | | *Phan Boi Chau* wrote a play based on lives of the *Trung* sisters |
| 1920 | | By the 1920s, students were forming various political parties |
| 1920s | | French business interests were pressurising the government in Vietnam to develop the infrastructure further |
| 1925 | | Only 400 students passed out of 17 million population |
| 1926 | | Vietnamese girl student was expelled from Saigon National Girls School. A major protest erupted |
| 1930 | | Great Depression |
| **LARGE EXPORTER OF RICE** | 1873 | The area under rice cultivation 2,74,000 hectares |
| | 1900 | The area under rice cultivation 11,00,000 hectares |
| | 1930 | The area under rice cultivation 22,00,000 hectares |
| | 1931 | Vietnam became third largest exporter of rice in the world |
| 1930 | | A famous novel by Nhat Linh caused a scandal, it showed courage by a nationalist woman |
| 1939 | | Hao Hao movement gained great popularity in Mekong delta area |
| 1940 | | Japan occupied Vietnam (during 2nd World War) |
| 1941 | | Huynh Phu So, founder of Hao Hao declared Mad Bronze and exiled to Laos |

| | | | |
|---|---|---|---|
| **HO CHIN MINH** | 1890-1969 | Ho Chin Minh | |
| | 1910 | Learnt baking | |
| | 1911 | Took job on a French liner | |
| | 1930 | *Ho Chin Minh* brought together competing nationalists groups to establish the Vietnamese Communist Party, later renamed the Indo-Chinese Communist Party | |
| | 1941 | After 30 years abroad, returned to Vietnam | |
| | 1943 | He took the name Ho Chi Minh (He Who Enlighten) | |
| | 1945 | Became the chairman of the Vietnam Democratic Republic | |
| | 1945 | 23-Sept., Vietminh start a general popular insurrection. Bao Dai abdicates. Ho Chi Minh declares independence in Hanoi (September 23) | |
| | 1945 | September, Vietminh recaptured Hanoi The Democratic Republic of Vietnam was formed and Ho Chi Minh became Chairman | |
| 1954 | | The French army is defeated at Dien Bien Phu | |
| 1954 | | 7 May, French tried to regain control on Vietnam; Vietminh were forced to retreat to the hills | |
| | | After 8 years of fighting, finally on 7 May 1954, the French were defeated in Dien Bien Phu | |

| | | |
|---|---|---|
| **VIETNAM WAR** | 1961 | Kennedy decides to increase US military aid to South Vietnam |
| | 1965 | US entered the war |
| | 1965 to 1975 | 17000 youth, majority of those were women, worked on Ho Chin Minh trail |
| | 1968 | Hollywood made films in support of the war |
| | 1970 | Peace talks began |
| | 1974 | Paris Peace Treaty |
| | 1974 | A peace settlement was signed in Paris in January |
| | 1975 | 30 April, NLF troops enter Saigon |
| | 1975 | 30 April, the NLF occupied the presidential palace in Saigon and unified Vietnam |
| | 1976 | The Socialist Republic of Vietnam is proclaimed |
| **DURATION OF SOME LEADERS** | 1867-1940 | *Phan Boi Chau* |
| | 1871-1926 | *Phan Boi Chau* |

▶ **Important Terms**

- **Colonization :** Political control of an underdeveloped country by a more advanced country. In international affairs this has become a term of abuse.

- **Concentration camps :** A prison where people are detained without the process of law.

- **Indentured labour :** A form of labour in which workers were taken away from their homes to work on farms in other countries. Indian were taken to countries like Mauritius as Indentured labourers. Most of them settled there.

- **Pirates :** Sea robbers.

- **Plague :** A killing disease carried by rat fleas.

- **Republic :** A form of government based on popular representation.

- **Begar :** Forced labour for which no remuneration is paid.

- **Boycott :** A form of protest leading to refusal to deal or associate with a certain group of people; also voluntary refusal to buy or use a certain product.

- **Forced recruitment :** A process by which people from the colonies were forced to join the armed forces.

- **Picket :** A demonstration by which people block the entrance to a shop, office or factory.

► **Points to Remember**

- In 1945 Vietnam gained formal independence prior to India but it took another three decades of fighting before the republic of Vietnam was formed.
- Not withstanding the fact that the colonial powers were heavily armed, the colonial possessions inspired by a strong sense of nationalism managed to fight them and regain their status as an independent nation.
- Vietnam was a colony of the French government. The French controlled the economy of this country through their military might. The French also tried to change the cultural pattern of life in Vietnam.
- European powers considered it as the white man's burden to civilize the backward people of Asia and Africa. The basic reason however was the lust for acquiring the untapped natural resources occurring in the African and Asian countries.
- The development of infra-structural facilities in otherwise backward countries of Asia and Africa was good for the colonies. It helped in the development of national economies.
- The French set up rail and port facilities to service exports of rice and the rubber plantations. However industrialization of the occupied country did not figure on their agenda.
- Schools textbooks were tailored to glorify French culture.
- French rule was praised as it had brought peace and ensured law and order within Vietnam.
- The change over in curriculum was resisted and local teachers quietly modified the texts that denigrated their traditions and culture.
- The anger against colonial power burst on many other fronts.
- The French were all out to make radical changes in the social life of the people of Vietnam.
- The anti-French uprisings got support from religious groups. One such group was led by Huynh Phu So. He founded the Hoa Hao Movement in 1939.
- He was opposed to monarchy but did not agree to a total rejection of western civilization.

- Vietnamese nationalists started looking towards their Asian neighbours for support in their struggle against French colonialism. Some 300 students from Vietnam went ot Japan in 1907. Japan had been able to resist colonization by the west and yet modernize the country.
- The great economic depression of 1930s affected the people of Vietnam in very adverse manners.
- There was wide spread unemployment leading to uprisings in the countryside, that were severely put down by the French rulers. Demonstrators were subjected to aerial bombing.
- In 1930, Ho Chi Minh brought together the various nationalist groups operating in Vietnam under a common umbrella - The Indo-Chinese Communist Party.
- Americans intervened in Vietnam in a decisive manner. They feared that communist power in Vietnam would harm US interests.
- The US media and films played an important role in both supporting as well as criticising the war. John Wayne's Green Beret's film was in support of the war whereas John Ford Coppala's Apocalypse now was critical as they tried to understand the reason of the war.
- In spite of military superiority, the US forces were unable to match the tactics and morale of the vietnamese fighters.
- The people of Vietnam displayed great courage and grit in their fight against the US forces.
- US forces were unable to crush the Vietnamese resistance.
- World opinion had turned against US policy makers. Negotiations to end the war under pressure of world opinion were held in Paris in January 1974. At the end of the negotiations, US was out but fighting continued a between National Liberation Force and the regime in Saigon. On April 30, 1975, Saigon was occupied by the NLF. Vietnam was finally unified.
- Women had performed a variety of jobs supporting armed resistance. They guarded the key points on the Ho Chi Minh trail.
- As peace returned to Vietnam, women started playing active roles in factories and agricultural cooperatives.
- Nationalism in India started taking a concrete shape with the growth of the movement for getting out of colonial control.

## 3. Nationalism in India

► **Historical Timeline**

| S.No. | Year/Date/ Month | Headings |
|---|---|---|
| 1 | 1870 | Bankim Chandra Chattopadhyay wrote Vande Matram and created the image of Bharat Mata |
| 2 | 1905 | Painting of Bharat Mata was developed by Abanindranath Tagore |
| 3 | 1909 | Gandhi wrote the famous book - Hind Swaraj |
| 4 | 1914-1918 | First World War |
| 5 | 1915 January | Mahatma Gandhi returned to India from South Africa |
| 6 | 1916 | Gandhi takes up the cause of indigo workers of Champaran |

| | | | | | | |
|---|---|---|---|---|---|---|
| 7 | 1917 | Gandhi organised a Satyagraha to support the peasants of Kheda-Gujarat | | 23 | 1921-1922 | The import of foreign cloth halved |
| 8 | 1918 | Gandhi organised a satyagraha in Ahmedabad for cotton mill workers | | 24 | 1921 | Gandhiji designed a tricolour Swaraj flag |
| 9 | 1918-1919 | Crops failed in many parts of India | | 25 | 1921 | The houses of talukdars and merchants were attacked |
| 10 | 1919 | Rowlatt Act passed by Imperial Legislative Council | | 26 | 1921 | Police fired at peasants near Raebareli |
| 11 | 1919 March | Khilafat Committee was formed | | 27 | 1921 | Non-cooperation - Khilafat Movement began |
| 12 | 1919 6-Apr | Civil Disobedience Movement started | | 28 | 1922 | Chauri Chaura incident |
| 13 | 1919 10-Apr | Police fired upon a peaceful procession in Amritsar | | 29 | 1922 | Mahatma Gandhi withdraws the Non-cooperation Movement |
| 14 | 1919 13-Apr | Jallianwala Bagh massacre | | 30 | 1924 | Alluri Sitaram Raju was captured and executed and overtime became a folklore |
| 15 | 1920-21 | Crops failed in many parts of India + Influenza, epidemic Both caused 12 to 13 million deaths | | 31 | 1926-1930 | Agricultural prices began to fall and collapsed after 1930 |
| 16 | 1920 | A militant guerilla movement spread in Gudem Hills of Andhra Pradesh | | 32 | 1927 | The Congress and the Muslim League made efforts to renegotiate an alliance |
| 17 | 1920 Summer | Mahatma Gandhi and Shaukat Ali toured extensively mobilizing support for Non-cooperation movement | | 33 | 1928 | Simon Commission arrived, protest by people - Go back Simon |
| 18 | 1920 June | Jawaharlal Nehru toured villages of Awadh (now in Uttar Pradesh) | | 34 | 1928 | Lala Lajpat Rai led people to protest against the Simon commission. He was lathicharged; due to that he died after a week |
| 19 | 1920 September | Calcutta session, Gandhi convinced other leaders to start a Non-cooperation Movement | | 35 | 1928 | M.R. Jayakar of the Hindu Mahasabha strongly opposed efforts at compromise |
| 20 | 1920 October | Oudh Kisan Sabha was set up headed by Jawaharlal Nehru, Baba Ramchandra and a few others | | 36 | 1928 | Hindustan Socialist Republic Party (HSRA) wasw founded by Bhagat Singh, Jatin, Ajoy Ghosh and others |
| 21 | 1920 November | Council elections | | 37 | 1929 | Bhagat Singh and Batukeshwar Dutta threw a bomb in the Legislative Assembly |
| 22 | 1920 December | At Nagpur Congress adopted Non-cooperation programme | | 38 | 1929 | A vague offer by Lord Irwin of 'dominion status' |
| | | | | 39 | 1929 | At Lahore, Congress demanded Purna Swaraj |
| | | | | 40 | 1930 | Sir Muhammad Iqbal reiterated the importance of separate electorates for the Muslims |

| 41 | 1930 | Celebrated as Independence Day |
| 42 | 1930 | Mahatma Gandhi wrote a letter to Viceroy Irwin stating 11 demands |
| 43 | 1930 | Started the salt march from Sabarmati Ashram with 78 of his trusted volunteers |
| 44 | 1930 | Reached Dandi and manufactured salt and started Civil Disobedience Movement |
| 45 | 1930 | Abdul Gaffar Khan was arrested in Peshawar |
| 46 | 1931 | The Civil Disobedience Movement called off pact with Irwin (Gandhi-Irwin Pact) |
| 47 | 1931 | Bhagat Singh, Rajguru and Sukhdev was hanged to death by the Government |
| 48 | 1931 | Gandhiji went to London for Round Table Conference-II |
| 49 | 1932 | Gaffar Khan and Jawaharlal Nehru were arrested, Gandhiji relaunched the Civil Disobedience Movement |

▶ **Important Terms**

- **Boycott:** A form of protest leading to refusal to deal or associate with A certain group of people; also voluntary refusal to buy or use a certain product.
- **Picket :** A demonstration by which people block the entrance to a shop, office or factory.

▶ **Points to Remember**

- Nationalism in India started taking a concrete shape with the growth of the movement for getting out of colonial control.
- During his stay in South Africa, Mahatma Gandhi had been involved in a struggle against the racial discrimination practiced by the white rulers.
- On his return to India in January 1915, Gandhiji practiced *satyagraha* against British rulers in his fight against foreign rule.
- The idea of satyagraha emphalised the power of truth and the need to search for truth.
- The two events that greatly disillusioned Mahatma Gandhi were the passing of the Rowlatt Act and the Jallianwala Bagh tragedy.

- Though the Rowlatt satyagraha was widespred movement but was confined to mostly cities and towns. Mahatma Gandhi now felt the need to launch a more broad based movement in India.
- Gandhi ji was certain that no such movement could be organised without bringers Hindus and Muslims together. He felt one way was to take up Khilafat issue.
- Gandhi ji saw this as an opportunity to brins muslims under the umbrella of a unified national movement.
- Gandhiji had lost faith in the righteousness of the British rulers. The simmering resentment found expression in the Non-cooperation Movement launched by Gandhiji.
- The Movement had the extremely enthusiastic support of the Indian people.
- The Movement could not attain Swaraj but it gave the subjugated people of India a new measure of confidence.
- Subhash Chandra Bose was the prominent leader of the radical wing within the Indian National Congress. He had the rare distinction of being selected for the ICS but resigned to join the movement for liberation from British rule.
- Subhash Chandra Bose had been elected as President of the Indian National Congress defeating the candidate sponsored by Mahatma Gandhi. The Gandhi loyalists refused to be a part of his Working committee. Subhash Bose was left with no alternative other than resigning from the Indian National Congress.
- On December 31, 1929, the Indian National Congress passed the resolution for complete independence. It was also decided that January 26 could be observed as Independence Day every year all over India
- The then existing laws did not allow individuals to make salt out of sea water. Gandhiji and his followers broke this law by making salt at the sea cost without paying any taxes.
- The Communal Award 1932 gave separate electorates to the Harijans. Mahatma Gandhi took a fast unto death to protest against this award while in jail at Poona. Ultimately it was decided that seats would be reserved for Harijans but the systems of electorate would remain unchanged.
- The exploitative policies of the British rulers had a very adverse affect on the conditions of farmers in India.
- Kisan Sabhas were formed in different parts of the country to register protests against the oppression of the landlords and the atrocities being committed by British rulers.

- In 1930 Dr. B. R. Ambedkar organized the Dalits under the banner of the Depressed Classes Association.
- Dr. Ambedkar and Gandhiji entered into a Pact at Poona in September 1932. As per terms of the agreement certain castes were listed as Scheduled castes and these were provided reservation in the provincial and Central Legislative Councils.
- A large number of Muslims did not respond to the call for Civil Disobedience Movement. In their minds they nursed apprehensions that Muslims interests would suffer in a Hindu dominated India.
- The fears were expressed by Sir Mohammad Iqbal in 1930 on behalf of the Indian Muslims. He made a demand for creation of a Muslim India within India and justified the demand for various reasons.
- Iqbal had thus provided the philosophical basis for the demand and creation of Pakistan in years to come.
- British historians had projected India as a country inhabited by people who were primitive and incapable of self governance. During the course of the National Movement, it was felt that there was need for highlighting India's glorious past. In Bengal, Rabindrnath Tagore himself began Collecting ballads, nursery rhymes, and myths and led the movement for folk revival, Natesa shastri published a four volume collection of Tamil Folk tales. The folk tales of southern India. Achievements in the field of art, architecture, culture, crafts, philosphy and science were highlighted.

## 4. The Making of Global world

► **Historical Timeline**

| Sl.No. | | Headings |
|---|---|---|
| 1 | | **THE PRE-MODERN WORLD** |
| | 3000 BCE | Active coastal trade linked the Indus Valley Civilisation with present day West Asia. |
| | 15th century | Till 15th century, several silk routes thrived linking Asia with Europe and North Africa. |
| | 1500s | The world shrank in 1500s with discovery of sea route to Asia and successful crossing of the western ocean to America. |
| | 16th century | After the discovery of America its vast lands and abundant crops and minerals began to transform trade and lives everywhere. The Portuguese and Spanish conquest and colonisation of America. |
| | 17th century | Legends spread about South America's fabled wealth. Many expeditions set off in search of EL Dorado the fabled city of gold. |
| | 1634 | John Winthorp wrote that smallpox signalled God's blessing for the colonists. |
| | 18th century | Slaves captured from Africa, were growing cotton and sugar in America |
| | 19th century | Until 19th century poverty and hunger was common in Europe. The Great Irish Potato Famine; around 1,000,000 people died of starvation in Ireland, and double the number emigrated in search of work. (e.g., USA). |

| 2 | | **THE NINETEENTH CENTURY (1815-1914)** |
|---|---|---|
| | 18th century | Population growth, expansion of urban centres and industry; increased the demand for food grains and goods in Britain. |
| | 19th century | Nearly 50 million people emigrated from Europe to America and Australia. |
| | 1890 | Global economy takes shape. |
| | 1820-1914 | Nearly 60% of the trade comprised primary produce. World trade multiplied 25 to 40 times. |
| | | **Role of Technology** |
| | 19th century | Technology (railways, steamships, the telegraph) and new inventions helped in fast growing trade. |
| | Till 1870s | Alive animals were shipped from America to Europe for meat. |
| | 1878 | Refrigerated ships enabled export of frozen meat to European countries. |
| | | **Late 19th Century Colonialism** |
| | 1885 | Carving up of Africa by big European powers in Berlin. |
| | 1890s | The US became a colonial power by taking over some colonies earlier held by Spain. |
| | | **Plague/Rinderpest** |
| | 1880s | Cattle plague or rinderpest arrived in Africa. It had a terrifying impact on people's livelihoods and the local economy |

| | | |
|---|---|---|
| | 1890s | Fast spread of cattle plague or rinderpest in Africa |
| | 1892 | Rinderpest moved west 'like forest fire' and reached Africa's Atlantic coast |
| | 1897 | Rinderpest reached the Cape (Africa's southernmost tip) |
| | 1890s | Europeans rush to Transvaal region. Transvaal gold mines contribute over 20 percent of world gold population |
| | **Labour Migration from India** | |
| | 19th century | Hundred of thousands of Indian and Chinese labourers went to work on plantations, in mines etc. |
| | 1900s | India's nationalist leaders opposed the migration of indentured labour |
| | 1921 | Abolition of migration of indentured labour |
| | **Indian Enterpreneurs Abroad** | |
| | 1860s | Indian traders and money lenders established flourishing emporia at busy ports worldwide |
| | 19th century | British manufacturers began to seek overseas markets for their cloth. By 19th century, British manufacturers flooded the Indian market |
| | 1815 | India's cotton textile exports declined to 15% (from 30% in 1800). |
| | 1870s | Cotton textile exports from India dropped to 3% |
| | 1812-1871 | Raw cotton exports from India rose from 5% to 35% |
| | 1820s | Opium shipments to China from India became India's single largest export |
| 3 | **THE INTER-WAR ECONOMY** | |
| | 1914 (August) | The First World War began |
| | 1914-1918 | Period of the First World War and war boom |
| | 1921 | End of war boom. Loss of jobs. One in every five British worker was out of work |
| | 1920s (Early) | The US economy resumed its strong growth |
| | 1920s | Important feature of the US economy was mass production |

| | | |
|---|---|---|
| | **Mass Production & USA** | |
| | 1914 | Henry Ford doubled the daily wage of workers to $5 |
| | 1920s | Mass production became a characteristic feature of US economy US economy resumed its strong growth |
| | 1920s | Fordist system of assembly line spread in the US and was widely copied in Europe US prosperity based on housing and consumer boom |
| | 1923 | The US resumed exporting capital to the rest of the world and became the largest overseas lender. Many countries financed their investments through loans from the US |
| | 1928 | US overseas loan amounted to over $1 billion |
| | 1929 | Car production in the US rose from 2 million in 1919 to more than 5 million The world was plunged into a depression |
| | **The Great Depression** | |
| | 1929 | The Great Depression began |
| | 1929-1932 | Period of the Great Depression 110,000 companies collapsed in the US during the Great Depression |
| | 1928 | In first half of 1928, US overseas loans amounted to over $1 million. A year later it was one quarter of that amount. The consumerist prosperity disappeared in a puff of dust |
| | 1920s | Many countries got their investments from the US |
| | 1933 | Over 4000 banks closed down |
| | 1935 | Modest economic recovery underway in most industrial countries |
| | **India and Great Depression** | |
| | 1928-1934 | — India's exports and imports nearly halved<br>— As international Prices crashed, weat prices in India fell by 50%. |

| | India and Great Depression | |
|---|---|---|
| | 1928-1934 | — India's exports and imports nearly halved<br>— As international Prices crashed, weat prices in India fell by 50%. |
| | 1931 | Mahatma Gandhi launched the Civil Disobedience Movement at the height of the depression |
| **4** | **REBUILDING A WORLD ECONOMY: THE POST-WAR ERA** | |
| | 1939-1944 | Second World War |
| | 1941 | July 1941, German forces attacked Russia. |
| | 1944 (July) | United Nations Monetary and Financial Conferences held at Bretton Woods, New Hampshire, USA. |
| | 1947 | The IMF and the World Bank commenced financial operations. |
| | 1950-1970 | World Trade grew annually at over 8%. |
| | 1950s | Bretton Woods institutions began to shift their attentions more towards developing countries. |
| | 1950s-1960s | Most developing countries did not benefit from the fast growth experienced by the western economies. |
| | 1950s-1960s | The worldwide spread of MNCs. (First MNCs established in 1920) US businesses expanded worldwide |
| | 1960s | US's overseas involvements weakened its finances and competitive strength |
| | 1970s | International financial system changed |
| | 1970s | The industrial world also hit by unemployment |
| | 1970s-1990s | Unemployment that hit the industrial world remained high |
| | 1970s | MNCs began to shift production operations to low-wage Asian countries. |
| | **China** | |
| | 1949 | Revolution in China |
| | 1949 | China cut off from the post-war world economy since the revolution |
| | 1990s | Many new countries (for e.g., China) brought into the field of the world economy. |

► **Important Terms**

- **Dissenter :** A person who opposes established beliefs.
- **Exchange rates :** The rates at which international currencies are exchanged in international trade.
- **Fixed exchange rates :** Exchange rates between different currencies fixed with the Concurrence of respective governments.
- **Floating exchange rate :** Exchange rates determined by the demand and supply for international currencies.
- **Indentured Labour :** A system of contract in which labourers were bound to an employer for a specific time. The workers were taken to a new country, the fare for the travel being paid by the employer.
- **Tariff :** A tax imposed on imported goods at the port of entry.

► **Points to Remember**

- Globalization is almost as old as human civilization.
- India had a bustling trade with islands in the South East Asian regions even in the ancient period.
- By the close of the 19th century, world economy had taken a global shape.
- Forest lands were cleared and turned into large scale mechanized farms. Traditional peasants from foreign countries came and started operating on these newly opened farms. There was increased traffic for ships which were now remodeled to carry much higher loads.
- Technology enabled the people of Europe to have better living conditions.
- However it had very adverse effects so far countries of Asia and Africa were concerned.
- It had very adverse effects so far countries of Asia and Africa were concerned.
- Colonialism had grown as a direct consequence of technological advancement.
- The vast resources of Africa attracted the industrialized countries of Europe. There was land and plenty of unexploited minerals.
- There was a radical change in the pattern of Indian exports during the 19th century. While the exports of manufactured products declined, there was rapid growth in exports of raw materials.
- The World War (1914-1919) had very serious consequences for both the victor and the vanquished countries.
- By the end of the war, economic power had shifted from British to United States of America.
- A combination of several factors was responsible for the economic depression starting 1929. Prices of agricultural products crashed during the post First World war era.

- As the signs of economic depression came forth, the banks in US became reluctant to advance further loans. By the year 1929 the amount of land had dwindled to just a quarter of the amount.
- US banks also cut down on loans to domestic clients.
- Many households were forced to sell out their cars and in some cases even their homes to meet both ends meet and repay the loans.
- The economic depression almost halved India's exports and imports.
- Rural indebtedness increased manifold as farmer's incomes suffered the depression.
- The Second World War broke out in the year 1939.
- At the end of the war, USA emerged as a super power, both politically and in economic terms. USSR emerged as another super power.
- The Bretton Woods Conference held in July 1944 decided to establish Inter National Monetary Fund. (Bretton Woods is in New Hampshire, USA). The Fund is intended to deal with trade deficits and surpluses that member national may have from time to time.
- The Bretton woods system was based on fixed exchange rates.
- The Agreement also led to the creation of the World Bank (International bank for Reconstruction and Development). The Bank assists in the development of the member countries by facilitating investment of capital for productive purposes.
- The later part of the 20th century marked the independence of a large number of Asian and African countries.
- The need for capital and investment now lay with the newly independent colonies.
- The developing nations decided to organize themselves into a group known as G 77, a sysem that would give them real control over their resources and better access to their products in developed industrialized countries.
- Labour costs in countries like China are much lower than in USA. A number of US manufacturers found it much more economical to get their products manufactured in China under their specifications.
- Relatively lower wages in India have attracted a number of services from USA and other European countries to be shifted to India through Call Centers.
- There have been voices of protest in USA and even Britain that their jobs were getting usurped by China and India. However, industrialialists insist that they will get their goods manufactured from places where it is economic for them.

---

### 5. The Age of Industrialisation

▶ **Historical Timeline**

| 1 | | BEFORE THE INDUSTRIAL REVOLUTION |
|---|---|---|
| | 1730s | The earliest factories in England were set up. |
| | 1760 | Britain was importing 2.5 million pounds of raw cotton to feed its cotton industry. |
| | 1787 | Import of raw cotton soared to 22 million pounds. |
| | 1781 | James Watt improved and patented the steam engine produced by Newcomen. This engine enhanced the productivity of labour manifold. They came to be used widely only later in the century. |
| | 1840s | Cotton and metals were the most dynamic industries in Britain. Cotton was the leading sector in the first phase of industrialisation. |
| | 1840s | Expansion of railways in England. |
| | 1860s | Expansion of railways, in the colonies. |

| | | |
|---|---|---|
| | 1873 | Britain exported  iron and steel worth about £ 77 million, (double the value of its cotton export). |
| 2 | HAND LABOUR AND STEAM POWER | |
| | 1764 | Spinning Jenny was devised by James Hargreaves which speeded up the spinning process and reduced labour demand. |
| | 1830s | Period of economic slump. The proportion of unemployed went up to between 35% to 75% in different regions. |
| | 1840s | Intensification of building activity provided greater opportunities of employment. |
| | 1840s | The number of workers employed in the transport industry doubled which was again doubled in the next 30 years. |
| | 1850s | Railway stations began coming up all over London. |

| 3 | | **INDUSTRIALISATION IN THE COLONIES** |
|---|---|---|
| | **3.1 The Age of Indian Textiles** | |
| | Before 1740s | Vibrant sea trade operated through pre-colonial ports-Surat on the Gujarat coast, Masulipatnam on the Coromondel coast and Hoogly in Bengal. |
| | 1740s | Decline of old ports Surat and Hoogly. The gross value of trade that passed through Surat, slumped from ₹ 16 million in the last years of the 17th century to ₹ 3 million in 1740s. |
| | 1750s | Breakdown of network of export trade, controlled by Indian merchants. |
| | 1780s | Bombay and Calcutta grew as alternate trading ports to Surat and Hoogly. |
| | **3.2 What Happened to Weavers?** | |
| | 1760s and 1770s | "East India Company consolidated power in Bengal and Carnatic. — Before that East India Company had found it difficult to ensure a regular supply of goods for export." |
| | **3.3 Manchester comes to India** | |
| | 1772 | Henry Patullo says that the demand for Indian textiles could never reduce, since no other nation produced goods of the same quality. But by beginning of the 19th century there was a long decline of textile exports from India. |
| | 1850-51 | Indian piece-goods exports account for no more than 3% of India's exports. |
| | 1850s | Most weaving regions of India narrated stories of decline and desolation. |
| | 1850 | Cotton piece-goods constituted over 31% of the value of Indian imports. |
| | 1860s | Cotton weavers faced a new problem. They could not get sufficient raw cotton of good quality. |

| 4 | **FACTORIES COME UP** | |
|---|---|---|
| | **4.1 The Early Enterpreneurs** | |
| | 18th century | The British in India began exporting opium to China and In exchange took tea from China to England. |
| | 1830s-1840s | Dwarkanath Tagore set up six joint-stock companies in Bengal. The enterprises sank in 1840s business crisis but by late 19th century he became a successful industrialists. |
| | 1850s | Jeejeebhoy was involved in the China trade and shipping. He owned a large fleet of ships, but competition from English and American shippers forced him to sell his ships. |
| | 1854 | Establishment of the first cotton mill in Bombay. |
| | 1862 | Four mills were at work with 94,000 spindles and 2,150 looms. |
| | 1855 | First jute mill established in Bengal. |
| | 1862 | Another jute mill came up in Bengal. |
| | 1860s | Elgin mill (woollen) was started in Kanpur. |
| | 1874 | First spinning and weaving mill of Madras began its production. |
| | 1917 | Seth Hukumchand, a Marwari set up the first Indian jute mill in Calcutta. |
| | **4.2 Where did the workers come from?** | |
| | 1901 | There were 584,000 workers in Indian factories. |
| | 1946 | Over 2,436,000 workers in Indian factories. |
| | 1911 | — Over 50% workers in the Bombay cotton industries came from the neighbouring district of Ratnagiri. — Mills of Kanpur got most of their textile hands from villages within the district of Kanpur." |
| | 1912 | J.N. Tata set up the first iron and steel works in India at Jamshedpur. |

| 5 | THE PECULLARITIES OF INDUSTRIAL GROWTHT | |
|---|---|---|
| | Late 19th century | Indian businessmen began setting up industries but they avoided competition with Manchester goods in the Indian market. |
| | 1905 | Swadeshi and Boycott Movement |
| | 1906 | Decline in export of Indian yarn to China. Indian industries shift from yarn to cloth production. |
| | 1900-1912 | Cotton piece-goods production doubled in India. |
| | 1914-1918 | First World War created a dramatic situation for industrial growth in India as British mills were engaged in meeting Britains war needs. Manchester imports into India declined. Indian mills had a vast Indian market plus they were called upon to meet Britains war needs. |
| **5.1 Small   Scale Industries Predominate** | | |
| | 1911 | About 67 % oflarge industries were located in Bengal and Bombay. In the rest ofIndia small-scale production continued to predominate. |
| | 1911 | Only 5% of  the total industrial labour force worked in registered factories. |
| | 1931 | "10% of the total industrial labour force worked in registered factories. Rest worked in small workshops and household units." |
| | 1900-1940 | Expansion of handicrafts and handloom production. Handloom cloth production steadily trebled during this period. |
| | 1910-1920 | Weavers began using looms with a fly shuttle. |
| | 1941 | "Over 35% of handlooms in India were fitted with fly shuttles: In regions like Travancore,Madras, Mysore and Cochin. In   Bengal the proportion was 70% to 80%." |

| 6 | MARKET FOR GOODS |
|---|---|
| | "(a)  Use of Advertisements<br>— to make products appear desirable and  necessary.<br>— to shape minds of people and create new needs.<br>— a vehicle of nationalists message of Swadeshi.<br>Example: Manchester labels carrying image of gods and goddesses and of historic figures." |
| | "(b)  Use of Calenders<br>— to popularise products.<br>**Example:** — Gripe water calender of 1928.<br>— Sunlight soap calender of 934." |

▶ **Important Terms**

- **Orient:** The countries to the east of the Mediterranean, usually referring to Asia.
- **Proto:** Indicating the first or early form of something.
- **Stapler:** A person who 'staples' or sorts wool according to its fibre.
- **Fuller:** A person who fulls-that is, gathers-cloth by pleating.
- **Carding:** The process in which fibres, such as cotton or wool, are prepared prior to spinning.

▶ **Points to Remember**

- Developments in the field of sciences have led to new technologies.
- This mode of production was different from production in factories where workers produced goods away from their homes.
- With many new inventions, production moved out from the countryside into the towns where factories were set up.
- In the Country side poor peasants and artisans began working for merchants.
- In Britain, the pace of industrialization was rather slow in the initial stages. A number of factors accounted for the slow growth. The machines were very expensive. Not many capitalists were in a position to raise the required capital for setting up factories with expensive machines.
- The industrialists were in no mood to introduce machines as long as they could hire workers at low wages.
- Having been displaced from open lands, hundreds of peasants from the countryside marched to the cities in search of gainful employment.
- Life continued to be tough and insecure for the migrants.

- The worst to suffer were the women.

- Things started turning brighter after building activities picked up in big cities. Railway stations started coming up all over London from 1850 onwards. The construction works created a big demand for manual labour.

- In the initial years of trading by European companies, Indian manufactures had good times.

- The East India Company adopted varying tactics to ensure regular supply of cotton and woollen goods from Indian weavers.

- European industrialist had specific interests in India. They established tea gardens and owned jute mills. These two items were primary expor items.

- Large scale industries in India continued to occupy only a limited space during the early years of the 20th century.

- In some areas, handicrafts registered significant increase. Handloom sector continued to Survive and expand even in the face of stiff competition from machine made cloth. Between the year 1900-1940, handloom production almost doubled in size.

- In spite of these advantages, the traditional weavers led a very hard life. By and large, the entire family was involved. in production of handloom products. In the absence of marketing facilities, the profits from the sales were largely cornered by the traders.

- The age of industries meant a major technological changes, growth of factories and making of a new industrial labour force. Hand technology and small scale production was remened

## 6. Work, Life and Leisure:

▶ **Historical Timeline**

| Sl. No. | | Headings |
|---|---|---|
| | 1880 | Durgacharan Ray wrote a novel, Debganer Martye Aagaman (The Gods Visit Earth). |
| 1 | **CHARACTERISTICS OF THE CITY** | |
| | 1750 | One out of every nine people of England and Wales lived in London. |
| | 1850s | Most western countries were largely rural. |
| | 1851 | More than three-quarters of the adults in Manchester were migrants from rural areas. |
| | 1861 | Census recorded a quarter of a million domestic servants in London. |
| | 1870s | Crime flourished in London. About 20,000 criminals were living in London. |
| | 1870 | The Compulsory Elementary Education Act was passed. |
| | 1880 | London's population multiplied fourfold. It increased from 1 million to about 4 million during 1810 to 1880. |
| | 1880s | Andrew Mearns, a clergyman wrote The Bitter Cry of Outcast London which showed why crime was more profitable than labouring in small underpaid factories. |
| | 1887 | The first social survey of low-skilled London workers in the East End of London was conducted by Charles Booth, a Liverpool shipowner. |

| | | |
|---|---|---|
| | 1902 | Beginning of factory act. These acts kept children out of industrial work. |
| | 1917 | Outbreak of the Russian Revolution. After the revolution there was widespread fear of outbreak of social disorder among London city dwellers. Worker's mass housing scheme were planned. |
| | 1914-18 | Period of the First World War. London began manufacturing motor cars and electric goods. |
| | 1919-39 | Between the two World Wars, British state accepted the responsibility for housing the working classes. |
| | **TRANSPORT IN CITY** | |
| | 1848 | Charles Dickens wrote in 'Dombey and Son', about the massive destruction in the process of construction. |
| | 10th January 1863 | The first section of the Underground (railway) in the world opened between Paddington and Farrington Street in London. |
| | 1880 | The expanded train service was carrying 40 million passengers a year |
| 2 | **SOCIAL CHANGE IN THE CITY** | |
| | 1810 | Entry was made free to the British Museum in London. |
| | 1824-25 | The numbers visiting the museum jumped from mere 15,000 to 1,27,643 in 1824-25 and to 8,25,900 in 1846. |

| | | |
|---|---|---|
| | 1870s | Women began to participate in political movements for suffrage that demanded right to vote for women, or for married women's rights to property. |
| | 1883 | Over 1 million British people spent their holidays by seaside, at Blackpool. By 1939 their numbers had gone upto 7 million. |
| **3** | **POLITICS IN THE CITY** | |
| | 1852 | Louis Napoleon III (the nephew of Napoleon Bonaparte) undertook the work of rebuilding of Paris. |
| | 1852-1870 | Baron Haussmann, the Prefect of Seine, was the chief architect of new Paris. |
| | 1860s | One in five working persons in Paris was in the building trade. |
| | 1860s | The Goncourt brothers lamented that rebuilding of Paris led to passing of an earlier way of life, and the development of an upper-class culture |
| | 1870 | One-fifth of the streets of Paris were Haussmann's creation |
| | 1886 | The winter were severe and outdoor work came to a standstill. The London poors exploded in a riot, demanding relief from the terrible conditions of poverty 10,000 strong crowd marched from Deptboard to London |
| | 1887 | In 1887, a similar riot occurred. The marchers had to be brutally suppressed by the police. It came to be known as the Bloody. Sunday of November 1887 |
| | 1889 | Thousands of London dockworkers went on 12 day strike |
| **4** | **THE CITY IN COLONIAL INDIA** | |
| | 1872-1941 | Bombay's population expanded from 6,44,405 in 1872 to 1,500,000 in 1941 |
| | 1862 | Kali Prasanna Singh wrote a satire in Bengali describing an evening scene in the Indian part of Calcutta |
| | 20th century | In early 20th century, no more than 11% of Indians were living in cities |

| | | |
|---|---|---|
| **4.1** | **Bombay: The Prime City of India** | |
| **4.2** | **Work in the City** | |
| | 1661 | Control of Bombay (group of seven islands) passed into British hands after marriage of Britain's King Charles II to the Portuguese princess. |
| | 1819 | Bombay became the capital of the Bombay Presidency after the Maratha defeat in the Anglo Maratha War. |
| | 1854 | The first cotton textile mill was setup in Bombay. |
| | 1921 | Bombay was home to 85 cotton mills with about 146,000 workers. |
| | 1881-1931 | Bombay had high migrant population. Only one-fourth of Bombay's inhabitants were born in Bombay. The rest came from outside. |
| | 1888-89 | Famine, in the dry region of Kutch, drove large number of people into Bombay |
| | 1898 | Plague epidemic in Bombay |
| | 1901 | Around 30,000 migrant people sent back to their places of origin by district authorities during years of plague. |
| | 1919-1926 | Women formed 23% of the mill workforce. |
| | 1930s | By the late 1930s, women constituted less than 10% of the total workforce. |
| **4.3** | **Housing and Neighbourhoods** | |
| | 1800s | The Bombay Fort area formed the heart of the city. It was divided between 'native' town where most Indian lived, and a European or 'white' section. |
| | 1840s | While every Londoner enjoyed an average square space of 155 square yards, Bombayite had a mere 9.5 square yards. |
| | 1872 | London had an average of 8 persons per house. The density in Bombay was as high as 20. |
| | 1850s | Mid 1850s, housing and water supply crisis became acute in Bombay. |
| | 1860s | Multi-storeyed structures called 'Chawls' were built in the 'native' parts of the town. |
| | 1865 | Arthur Crawford was appointed Bombay's first Municipal Commissioner. He tried to keep several dangerous trade out of south Bombay. |
| | 1898 | The City of Bombay Improvement Trust was established. It focussed on clearing poor homes out of the city centre. |

| | | |
|---|---|---|
| | 1918 | The Trust of schemes deprived 64,000 people of their homes. Out of these only 14,000 were rehoused. |
| | 1901 | The census reported 90% of Bombay's population lived in one room tenements (Chawls). |
| | 1918 | Rent Act was passed to keep rents reasonable. |
| **4.4** | **Land Reclamation in Bombay** | |
| | 1784 | William Hornby, the governor of Bombay, approved the building of the great sea wall. This prevented flooding of the low-lying areas of Bombay. The earliest reclamation project in Bombay began by joining the Seven Islands of Bombay into one landmass. |
| | 1864 | The Back Bay Reclamation Company won the right to reclaim the western foreshore from the tip of Malabar Hill to the end of Colaba. |
| | 1870s | Most of the private companies engaged in reclamation closed down due to the mounting cost. Still the city had expanded to about 22 sq. miles. |
| | 1914-1918 | The Bombay Port Trust, built a dry dock and used the excavated earth to create a 22 acre Ballard Estate. |
| | **Bombay as the City of Dreams: The World of Cinema and Culture** | |
| | 1896 | Harishchandra Sakharam Bhatwadekar shot a scene of a wrestling match in Bombay's Hanging Gardens. This was India's first movie. |
| | 1913 | Dadasaheb Phalke made Raja Harishchandra |
| | 1925 | Bombay became India's first film capital (a city of dreams) |
| | 1947 | Around `756 million was invested in about 50 Indian films |
| | 1987 | The film industry employed 520,000 people. |
| | 1965 | Singapore became an independent nation under the leadership of Lee Kuan Yew. Lee launched a massive housing and development programme. |
| **5** | **CITIES AND THE CHALLENGE OF THE ENVIRONMENT** | |
| | 1840 | Towns such as Derby, Leeds and Manchester in England had laws to control smoke in the city. |

| | | |
|---|---|---|
| | 1847-53 | The Smoke Abatement Acts of 1847 and 1853 were passed. These failed to clean the air. |
| | 1855 | Railway line was introduced in Calcutta which brought a dangerous new pollutant-coal from Raniganj |
| | 1863 | Calcutta became the first Indian city to get smoke nuisance legislation. |
| | 1920 | The rice mills of Tollygunge began to burn rice husk instead of coal. This was an additional cause of pollution in the city of Calcutta. |

▶    **Important Terms**

- **Metropolis :** A large, densely populated city of a country or state, often the capital of the region.

- **Urbanisation :** The process of development of a city or town.

- **Philanthropists :** Someone who works for social upliftment i.e., welfare of mankind.

- **Reclamation :** It is the reclaiming of marshy or submerged areas for settlement, cultivation and other use.

- **Tenement :** Run down and often overcrowded apartment house, especially in a poor section of a large city.

- **Temperance Movement :** A largely middle-class-led social reform movement which emerged in Britain and America from the nineteenth century onwards. It identified alcoholism as the cause of the ruin of families and society, and aimed at reducing the consumption of alcoholic drinks, particularly amongst the working classes.

▶    **Points to Remember**

- Industrialization gave a new shape to the cities. London and Mumbai.

- London had grown into a metropolitan city as early as the year 1750. Gradually its population increased from 675,000 in 1750 to 4 million in 1880.

- The city of London was a powerful magnet for migrandt papulations even though it did not have large factories The Migration of people from the countryside to London and similar cities created the problem of housing the immigrants.

- Poor living conditions in industrial cities were very unfavourable to the industrial workers during the 19th century.

- Public opinion gradually built up for providing  better housing facilities rather than just clearing the slums.

- London, with the above stated consideration  in mind, was decongested through a variety  of measures. The city had solved the problem  through plans to build large blocks of houses for the immigrant population. Local authorities built around a million houses during the period  1919-1939(the period between the two World Wars). Suburban housing and fast transport facilities made a significant change in social and domestic life.

- The london underground railway to an extent solved the housing crilis by carrying large number of people to and from the cits. the underground railway in the world.

- Paris is considered as the hub of fashion all over the world.

- The new Paris was designed with wide streets, open spaces and broad avenues. In this process around 350,000 persons had to be displaced from the centre of the proposed new city.

- Unlike London, Mumbai did not grow into a big city even upto the early years of the twentieth century.

- In the year 1819, Mumbai became the capital of Mumbai Presidency. Traders, bankers, artisans flocked to Mumbai as trade in cotton and opium expanded within the city.

- Mumbai was important both as a port and as the terminus of two railway systems.

- By the mid 1850s, available civic amenities had grown short of the requirements of the residents of the city.

- Finding a house even in a chawl was a great problem if the person belonged to the lower caste. These people had to live in shelters built out of bamboo and leaves or at best corrugated iron sheets.

- Housing in Mumbai has some peculiar limitations. Land availability is strictly limited. Land is now being reclaimed from the sea to provide for more housing projects.

- Since there are jobs for all grades of people, migration to Mumbai seems a never ending process.

- Today Singapore is a city that has high degree of civic comforts. However the citizens have to follow very strict codes that in some cases appear to be infringing on individual freedoms.

- The challenge before the governments is how to balance of employment opportunities with concern for keeping the healthy environment today and even for the generations to come.

## 7. Print, Culture and the Modern World

Opened on January 10 between paddington and Farrington streat in london.

▶ **Historical Timeline**

| Sl.No. | Headings | |
|---|---|---|
| 1 | **THE FIRST PRINTED BOOKS** | |
| | AD 594 onwards | Books in China were printed by rubbing paper. |
| | AD 768-770 | Hand-printing technology was introduced into Japan from China by the Buddhist missionaries. |
| | AD 868 | The oldest Japanese book. The Diamond Sutra was printed. |
| | 17th century | Urban culture bloomed in China, the use of print diversified. |
| 2 | **PRINT COMES TO EUROPE** | |
| | 1295 | Marco Polo, a great explorer, on his return to Italy, brought the knowledge of producing books with woodblocks to Europe. |
| | 1430s | Johann Gutenberg developed the first-known printing press. |
| | 1448 | Gutenberg perfected the system of casting the metal types for the letters of the alphabet. |
| | 15th century | Woodblocks were widely used in Europe. |
| | 1450 and 1550 | Printing presses were setup in most countries of Europe. |
| 3 | **THE PRINT REVOLUTION AND ITS IMPACT** | |
| | 1508 | Erasmus' a Latin scholar and Catholic reformer, criticised the excesses of Catholicism but kept his distance from Martin Luther. He wrote 'Adages'. |
| | 1517 | The religious reformer Martin Luther wrote 'Ninety Five Theses' criticizing many of the practices and rituals of the Roman Catholic Church. |

|  |  |  |
|---|---|---|
|  | 16th century | Menocchio, a miller in Italy reinterpreted the message of the Bible. |
|  | 1558 | An 'Index of Prohibited Books' was formulated by the Roman Church to control publishers and booksellers. |
| **4** | **THE READING MANIA** | |
|  | 1780s | There was an outpouring of literature, in France that mocked the royalty and criticised their morality. |
|  | 1791 | James Lackington, a London publisher, wrote in his diary about the tremendous increase in the sale of books. |
|  | 17th and 18th century | Literacy rates went up in most parts of the Europe. — By the end of the century, in some parts of Europe the literacy rates were as high as 60 to 80%. |
|  | 18th century | — The periodical press developed from the early 18th century |
| **5** | **THE NINETEENTH CENTURY** | |
|  | 18th century | By late 18th century, press came to be made out of metal. |
|  | 19th century | Primary education become compulsory. |
|  | 1812 | Grimm Brothers (Germany) stories based on traditional folk tales gathered from peasants were published in a collection. |
|  | 1832 to 1835 | Penny Magazine that aimed primarily at the working class was published in England by the "Society for the Diffusion of useful knowledge." |
|  | 1857 | In France, a children's press, devoted to literature for children alone, was setup. |
|  | 19th century | Series of innovations. |

|  |  |  |
|---|---|---|
|  | 19th century | Lending libraries in England grew. |
|  | 19th century | Working days of workers shortened. |
|  | 19th century | —Series of innovations in printing technology. — By the mid-19th century, Richard M. Hoe of New York had perfected the power driven cylindrical press. —In the late 19th century the offset press was developed. It could print up to 6 colours at a time. |
|  | 20th century | In the beginning of the 20th century, electrically operated presses accelerated printing operations. |
|  | 1920s | In England, popular works were sold in cheap series, called the 'Shilling Series'. |
|  | 1930s | Cheap Paperback editions. |
| **6** | **INDIA AND THE WORLD OF PRINT** | |
|  | 1579 | Catholic priests printed the first Tamil Book in Cochin. |
|  | 1674 | About 50 books had been printed by Jesuit priests in Konkani and in Kanara languages. |
|  | 1710 | Dutch Protestant missionaries had printed 32 Tamil texts. Many of them were translations of older works. |
|  | 1713 | The first Malayalam book was published. |
|  | 1780 | James Augustus Hickey began to edit the *Bengal Gazette*, a weekly magazine. |
|  | 18th century | By the end of 18th century, a number of newspapers and journals appeared in print. |
| **7** | **RELIGIOUS REFORM AND PUBLIC DEBATES** | |
|  | 19th century | Intense debates around religious issues in early 19th century. |
|  | 19th century | A number of Muslim sects and seminaries appeared. |

| | | |
|---|---|---|
| | 1810 | The first printed edition of '*Ramcharitmanas*' of Tulsidas, a sixteenth century text, came out from Calcutta. |
| | 1821 | Rammohan Roy published the '*Sambad Kaumudi*'. |
| | 1822 | — Two Persian newspapers were published, '*Jam-i-Jahan Nama*' and '*Shamsul Akbar*'. <br> — Gujarati newspaper, *Bombay Samachar* was published. |
| | 1867 | The *Deoband* Seminary was founded. It published thousands of '*fatwas*' telling muslim readers how to conduct themselves in their everyday lives. |
| | 1880s | The Naval Kishore Press at Lucknow and the Shri Venkateshwar Press in Bombay published numerous religious texts in vernaculars. |
| **8** | **NEW FORMS OF PUBLICATION** | |
| | 1860s | Many Bengali women writers like Kailashbashini Debi wrote books highlighting the experiences of women. |
| | 1870s | — Caricapture and cartoons were published in journals and newspapers. <br> — Hindi printing began seriously. |
| **8.1** | **Women and Print** | |
| | 1876 | Rashsundari Debi wrote her autobiography Amar Jiban in Bengali. |
| | 1880's | Tarabai Shinde and Pandita Ramabai wrote about the miserable lives of upper-caste Hindu women, especially widows. |
| | Late 19th century | — Issues of castes discrimination began to be written in printed tracts and essays. <br> — A new visual culture was taking place. <br> — Mid 19th century women's schools were setup. <br> — In Calcutta-the Battala was famous centre for famous centre for printing of books. <br> — A lot of these books were illustrated with colour photographs. |
| | 1926 | Begum Rokeya Sakhawat Hossein, an educationists and literary figure strongly condemned men for withholding education from women. |
| | Early 20th century | — Public libraries were setup. <br> — Folk literature was widely printed. <br> — Ram Chadda published the fast selling *Isri Dharam Vichar* (स्त्री घर्म विचार) to teach women how to be obedient wives. |
| | 20th century | In early 20th century journals written for and sometimes edited by women, became popular. |
| **8.2** | **Print and the Poor People** | |
| | 19th century | Very cheap small books were brought to markets in Madras town. |
| | 1871 | Jyotiba Phule, wrote about the injustices of the caste system in Gulamgiri. |
| | 1930s | Bangalore cotton millworkers setup libraries to educate themselves. |
| | 1938 | Kashibaba, a Kanpur millworker, wrote and published 'Chhote Aur Bade Ka Sawal' (छोटे और बड़े का सवाल). The work showed the link between caste and class exploitation. |
| | 1920 | The rice mills of Tollygunge began to burn rice husk instead of coal. This was an additional cause of pollution in the city of Calcutta. |
| | 1935 to 1955 | The poems of Kanpur millworker, who wrote under the name *Sudarshan Chakr*, were brought together and published in a collection called 'Sacchi Kavitayan'. (सच्ची कविताएँ). |
| | 20th century | B. R. Ambedkar in a Maharashtra and E.V. Ramaswamy Naicker in Madras (Periyar), wrote powerfully on caste and untouchability. |
| **9** | **PRINT AND CENSORSHIP** | |
| | 1798 (Before) | The colonial state under the East India Company was not too concerned with censorship. |

| | 1820s | The Calcutta Supreme Court passed certain regulations to control press freedom. |
|---|---|---|
| | 1835 | Governor-General Bentinck revised press laws because of petitions by editors of English and vernacular newspapers. |
| | 1857 | After the revolt of 1857, the attitude of the English to freedom of the press changed. |
| | 1877 | The Statesman was founded. |
| | 1878 | The Vernacular Press Act was passed. It was modeled on the Irish Press Laws. |
| | 1907 | Punjab revolutionaries were deported, Bal Gangadhar Tilak wrote with great sympathy about them in his 'Kesari'. |
| | 1908 | Bal Gangadhar Tilak imprisoned. This provoked widespread protests all over India. |

▶ **Important Terms**

- **Ballad:** A historical account or folk tale in verse usually sung or recited.

- **Calligraphy :** The art of beautiful and stylised writing.

- **Compositor :** The person who composes the text for printing.

- **Galley :** Metal frame in which types are laid and the text composed.

- **Vellum :** A parchment made from the skin of animals.

- **Platen :** In letterpress printing, platen is a board which is pressed onto the back of the paper to get the impression from the type. At one time it used to be a wooden board; later it was made of steel.

- **Sedition:** It means an action speech or writing that is seen as apposing the gvernment.

▶ **Points to Remember**

- Much before the era of print or the invention of the Printing Press, writing of books was a purely manual affair.

- China is credited with the invention of paper.

- Ancient Indian scriptures were written on palm leaves (*Bhoj patra*).

- By the 19th century, mechanical printing presses made their appearance in China.

- Buddhist missionaries from china introduced hand printing technology into Japan.

- Hand printing was substituted by machine printing to meet the demands of the schools.

- The printed books in fact closely resembled the written manuscripts in appearance and layout.

- The art of producing books from wood blocks travelled from China to Europe courtesy the Explorer Marco Polo. From Italy, the Chinese technology spread to other countries of Europe.

- The invention of the printing press radically changed the process of production of books. The first ever printing press was invented in 1430s by Johannes Gutenberg at Strasbourg.

- Germany took the lead in revolutionizing printing all over Europe. Printers travelled to different European countries to setup printing press.

- The second half of the 15th C saw 20 million copies of printed books of looded the markets in Europe.

- Access to books created a new culture of reading. Earlier it was limted to the elites, now books reach to wider section of people.

- New forms of popular literature appeared in print There were almanacs or ritual calendars a long with ballads and folk tales.

- Many historians argued that print culture created the conditions within which french Revolution took place.

- The 19th C saw a mass literacy in Europe brought large number of new readers among. Children, women and workers.

- Despite repressive measures clamped by colonial goverment nationalist newspapers grew in numbers in all parts of India.

## 8. Novels, Society and History

▶ **Historical Timeline**

| SI. No. | | Headings |
|---|---|---|
| **1** | | **THE RISE OF THE NOVEL** |
| | 17th Century | "Novels began to be written from the 17th Century in England and France." |
| **1.1** | **The Publishing Market** | |
| | 1740 | With the introduction of circulating libraries. it became easier for people to get books. |
| | 1749 | Henry Fielding's Tom Jones was issued in six volumes. It was priced at three shillings each. |
| | 1828-1910 | "Leo Tolstoy a famous Russian novelist wrote extensively on rural life and peasantry." |
| | 1836 | Charles Dickens's Pickwick Papers was serialized. |
| **1.2** | **The World of the Novel** | |
| | 1838 | Charles Dickens's Oliver Twist was published. |
| | 1854 | Hard Times by Charles Dickens was published. It describes Coke Town, a fictitious industrial town and the terrible effects of industrialisation on people's lives and characters. |
| | 1885 | Emile zola's 'Germinal' was published. It was on the life of a young miner in France and the harsh conditions of miners lives. |
| **1.3** | **Community and Society** | |
| | 1840-1928 | Thomas Hardy |
| | 1886 | Thomas Hardy's novel Mayor of Casterbridge was published. He wrote about fading traditional rural communities of England. |
| **1.4** | **The New Woman** | |
| | 18th Century | Involvement of women |
| | 1775-1817 | Jane Austen; 'Pride and Prejudice' |
| | 1816-1855 | Charlotte Bronte |
| | | Charlotte Bronte's Jane Eyre was published in 184 7. |
| | 1819-1880 | George Eliot (pen-name of Marry Ann Evans) |
| | | George Eliot, published 'Silly Novels by lady novelists' in 1856. |

| 1.5 | **Novels for the Young** | |
|---|---|---|
| | 1832-1902 | G.A. Henty wrote historical adventure novels. |
| | 1872 | What Katy Did a series written by Sarah Chauncey Woolsey. |
| | 1883 | - G.A. Henty's Under Drake's Flag . |
| | | - In Under Drake's Flag two young Elizabethan adventurers face their approaching death. |
| | 1883 | R.L. Stevenson's Treasure Island was published. |
| | 1884 | Ramona (a romantic novel) was written by Helen Hunt Jackson. |
| | 1894 | Rudyard Kipling's 'Jungle Book' became a great hit among youngsters. |
| **1.6** | **Colonialism and After** | |
| | 1719 | Daniel Defoe's 'Robinson Crusoe' was published . The hero was an adventurer and slave trader. |
| | 1857-1924 | "Joseph Conrad wrote novels that showed the darker side of colonial occupation." |
| **2** | | **THE NOVEL COMES TO INDIA** |
| | 7th Century (and before ) | ( 1) Banabhatta's Kadambari' wri tten in Sanskrit<br>(2) *Panchatantra*<br>These are examples of stories in prose. |
| | | 'Dastan' prose tales of adventure and heroism in Persian and Urdu. |
| | 1857 | Yamuna Paryatan (Marathi), by Baba Padmanji, was the earliest novel in Marathi. It spoke about plight of widows. |
| | 1861 | Muktamala (Marathi) by Lakshman Moreshwar Halbe. |
| | 1868 | "(i) Naro Sadashiv Risbud wrote the Marathi novel Manjughosha . (ii) He used a highly ornamental style." |
| **2.1** | **The Novel in South India** | |
| | 1847-1899 | O' Chandu Menon midway gave up hi s attempt to translate English novel 'Henrietta Temple' by Benjamin Disraeli into Malayalam. |

| | | |
|---|---|---|
| | 1848-1919 | "Kandukuri Viresalingam began translating Oliver Goldsmith's Vicar of Wakefield into Telugu. He later cancelled his plan." |
| | 1889 | "The first modern novel Irdulekha by Chandu Menon in Malayalam was published." |
| | 1878 | Later Kandukuri Viresalingam wrote a Telugu novel called 'Rajasekhara Caritamu'. |
| | 1899 | "Indirabai' by Gulavadi Venkata Rao, written by upper caste members about upper caste characters." |
| **2.2** | **The Novel in Hindi** | |
| | 1882 | Srinivas Das's novel Pariksha-Guru (The Master Examiner) was the first modern novel in Hindi. It reflects on the inner and outer world of th e newly emerging middle classes. |
| | 1888 | Devak i Nandan Khat ri wrote his best seller 'Charuirakanta'. |
| | 1916 | Premchand's novel Sevasadan (The Abode of Service ) was published. |
| **2.3** | **Novels in Bengal** | |
| | 1838 - 1894 | Bankim Chandra Chattopadhyay would host 'Jatra in the courtyard. |
| | 1865 | Bankim Chandra Chattopadhyay pu blished his first novel 'Durgeshrumdini' ( 5~ ., ., F", ';I). |
| | 1876-1938 | Sarat Chandra Chattopadhyay was the most popular novelist in Bengal. He was known for short stories in simple language. |
| | **Novels in Assam** | |
| | | First novels were written by missionaries. |
| | | Two of them were translations of Bengali novels 'Phulmoni' and 'Karuna', |
| | 1888 | Assamese students in Kolkata formed the 'Asamya Bhasar Unnatisadhan'. They brought out a journal called ',Jonaki', |
| | 1900 | Rajanikanta Bardoloi wrote the first historical novel in Assam called Manomati. |
| | **Novel in Oriya** | |
| | | Saudamini' first Oriya novel. |
| | 1877-78 | "Ramashankar Ray, a dramatist, began seria lisiog the firs t Oriya novel 'Saudamini'. " |

| | | |
|---|---|---|
| | | Novel in Oriya |
| | | Saudamini' first Oriya novel. |
| | 1877-78 | "Ramashankar Ray, a dramatist, began serialising the first Oriya novel 'Saudamini'." |
| | 1843-1918 | Fakir Mohan Senapati was a major novelist of Orissa. |
| | 1902 | Fakir Mohan Senapati (from Orissa ) published his novel Chaa Mana Atta Guntha . It dealt with the possession of land. |
| **3** | | **NOVELS IN THE COLONIAL WORLD** |
| **3.1** | **Uses of the Novel** | |
| | 1899 | Kannada novel Indirabai was written by Gulavadi Venkata Rao. It carried a clear message of social reform . |
| | 1951 | "— Tamil novel Ponniyin Selvan, written by R. Krishnamurthy. most popular novelist, under pen name Kalki. It was serialised in the magazine Kalki. - Tamil magazines Anandavikatan and Kalki." |
| **3.3** | **Pleasures of Reading** | |
| | 1929 | Kan nada magazine Kathanjali started publication. It regularly published short stories . |
| **4** | | **WOMEN AND THE NOVEL** |
| | 1852 | Hannah Mullens , a christain missionar y authored 'Karuna o Phulmonir Bibaran'. It was reputedly the first novel in Bengali . |
| | 1880-1932 | Rokeya Hossein, a reformer. after she was widowed, started a girl's school in Calcutta . |
| | 1905 | Rokeya Hossein wrote a satiric fantasy in English called Sultana's Dream. It showed a topsy -turvy world in which women take the place of men. Her other novel 'Padmarag' showed need for women to reform their condition by their own actions. |
| | 1927 | A Tamil essay 'Why women should not read novels', was publi shed. |

| 4.1 | | Caste Practices, Lower-Castes and Minorities |
|---|---|---|
| | 1889 | Indulekha' by O, Chandu Menon. |
| | | - Apart from being a love story, the novel was about how younger generation of English-educated Nayar men began arguing against Nambuthiri alliances with Nayar woman. |
| | 1892 | Potheri Kunjambu, a 'lower-caste' writer from north Kerala, wrote a novel called Saraswativijayam attacking caste oppression . |
| | 1908-94 | Vaikkom Muhammad Basheer, an early Muslim writer, gained wide recognision as a novelist in Malayalam . His novels made space for experiences of communities who were ignored in literary scenes. |
| | 1848-1906 | Raja Ravi Verma was one of the foremost oil painters of his time. |
| | 1920s | Novels that depicted the lives of peasants and low castes emerged in Bengal. |
| | 1956 | "Advaita Malla Burman's (1914-1951) Titash Ekti Nadir Naam was an epic on Mallas , a community of fisherfolk, who liveoff fishing in river Titash." |
| 5 | | THE NATION AND ITS HiSTORY |
| | 1857 | Bhudeb Mukhopadhyay's (1827-94) Anguriya Binimoy, the first historical novel written in Bengal. |
| | 1882 | Anandmath' written by Bankim Chandra Chattopadhyay. The novel was about a secret Hindu militia that fights Muslims to establish a Hindu kingdom. |
| | 1956 | The novel Chemmeen (Shrimp ), about fishing community, was written by Thakazhi Sivasankara Pillai (1912 - 1999). It was made into a film chemmcn, directed by Ramu Kariat in 1965. |
| 5.1 | | The Novel and Nation Making |
| | 1861-1941 | Rabindranath Tagore developed Bengali novels after Bankim Chandra Chattopadhyay's death . |

| | 1916 | Ghare Baire written by Rabindranath Tagore. |
|---|---|---|
| | 1919 | The novel Ghare Baire was translated as The Home and the World. |
| | 1930 | 'Chomana Dudi' a Kannada novel written by Sivarama Karanth. |
| | 1880-1936 | Premchand |
| | 1936 | Godan (The Gift of Cow) became Premchand's best known work. Others were 'Ranghbhoomi' (The Arena) and 'Seyasadan' (The Abode of Service). |

▶ **Important Terms**

- **Gentlemanly Classes:** People who claimed noble birth and high social position. The standard setters for proper behaviour.

- **Epistolary:** Written in the form of a series of letters .

- **Serialised:** A format in which the story is published in instalments, each part in a new issue of a journal.

- **Vernacular:** The normal, spoken form of a language rather than the formal , literary form.

- **Satire:** A form of representation through writing, drawing, painting etc. that provides a criticism of society in a manner that is witty and clever.

- **"Kissa-goi":** Art of story telling.

▶ **Points to Remember**

- A novel is different from a short story or even a long story in many ways. While a story focuses on a single event in the life of an individual or a group, a novel is made up of multi ple characters and multiple events involving them.

- The novels written during the early years of industrialization in England are about men being reduced to machines devoid of all human emotions and living just to satisfy the greed of the factory owners.

- The language of the novel was not the classical English. The local dialects are frequently used to give the novel a realistic touch. The characters appeared real as they spoke in a language that is actually spoken by them in real life.

- The early European novels glamorized colonization. Much later authors like Joseph Conard (1857-1924) wrote novels that put forth before the readers the evil side of colonial rule.

- Many other novels in 19th century India dealt with other themes like love stories based on historical events.

- In Bengal novels were read by the elite sections of the society in the privacy of their homes. This was in contrast to poetry recital sessions that were held as public entertainments.

- Novels were not just a portrayal of society as it really existed at that time. Novelists had their own vision of how society ought to be and they views through the characters in their novels.

- In the early years of the 20th century, host of women novelists appeared on the literary scene. Many novels had love as the main theme.

- The works of Bankim Chandra are classic in as much as the themes covered by him are of eternal value. His works have a literary merit while the characters portrayed in his novels are both real as well as ideal. Bankim Chandra remains the tallest among Bengali novelist

long after his death in 1894.

- Munshi Prem Chand (1880-1936) is hailed as the greatest novelist in Hindi literature.

- The central theme of most of his works was the life in villages as it then existed.

- Prem Chand presented life as it then existed in the countryside. His works have a social purpose. They are intended to awaken the reader to the harsh realities of life as it existed . There are no imaginary or fanciful characters. His characters are real and living .

- He was in the nature of a social reformer. His works do not just entertain. They raise the reader to higher planes where he is expected to do something about the social evils and reigning poverty.

- The developments in print technologies allowed the novel to break out of its small cirle of readers and started new ways of reading.

- Novels produce a sense of sharing and promote an understanding of various people different values and varied communities.

# UNIT-II. GEOGRAPHY

## 1. Resources and Development

▶ **Important Terms**

- **Natural Resources:** Natural endowments in the form of land, water, vegetation and mineral are termed as natural resources.
- **Human made Resources:** Resources created by humans such as engineering, technology, machines, buildings, monuments, painting, social institutions etc., are called human-made or human or cultural resources.
- **Resource Planning:** Technique or skill of proper utilisation of resources is termed as resource planning.
- **Growing Season:** The period of the year in which crops are sown, grown and harvested, is known as growing season.
- **Gully Erosion:** The spectacular type of soil erosion in which , gullies occur in the soil surface, rendering it useless for cultivation, is known as gully erosion.

▶ **Points to Remember**

- Resources include both natural and human resources.
- Processing of natural resources opens up wide employment opportunities for the people.

**Clasification of Resources**

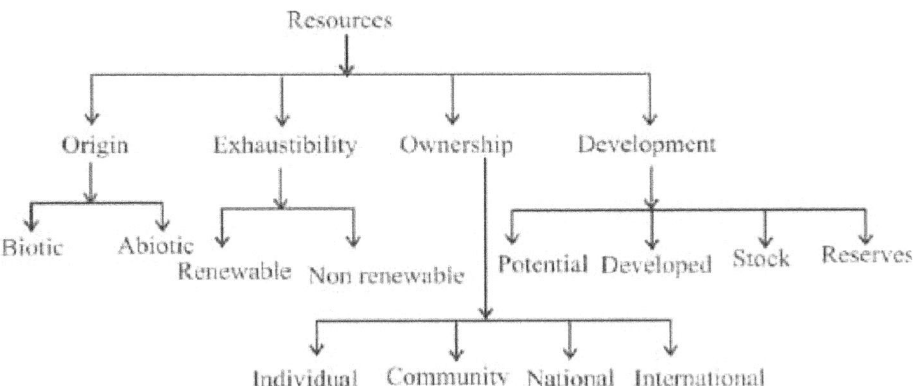


- Resources like coal are exhaustible while energy source like wind power is inexhaustible.
- While some resources are living organisms, other are abiotic or non-living. Biotic resources can in most cases be regenerated. Abiotic resources need to be used with great caution.
- Factors like cost of extraction, transport and level of available technology influence exploitation of natural recourses.
- Resources occur in the lithosphere, Hydrosphere and even the Atmosphere.
- Unexploited resources are referred to as potential resource.
- Resources that are surveyed and their quality and quantity have been determined for utilisation are developed resources.
- Stock are the minerals in the environment which have the potential to satisfy human needs but human being do not have the appropriate technology to access these.
- Soil as resource is most natural renewable natural resource. On the basis of the factors responsible for soil formation, colour, thickness, texture, age, chemical and physical properties. The soils of India can be divided in different types such as alluvial soil, black soil, red and yellow soils arid soils, laterite soils and forest soils.

- Available resource need to be used in accordance with a predetermined plan. Planning avoids duplication of efforts, leaving enough for the coming generations and avoiding environmental pollution while exploiting the natural resources.

- Humans resources are equally important. Highly skilled manpower is by itself a valuable resources. In India there is much that remains to be done in developing skilled manpower. Universal literacy, expansion of facilities for technical education and linking industries to schools can go a long way in achieving this goal.

## 3. Water Resources

▶ **Important Terms**

- **Floods:** Inundation of large areas beyond the bank of rivers is termed as floods.
- **Hydrological Cycle:** Movement of water through lithosphere, atmosphere and hydrosphere is known as hydrological cycle.
- **Precipitation:** Falling of moisture after condensation in the form of droplets, rain, snow and hailstones is called as precipitation.
- **Scarcity of Water:** Shortage of water to meet the basic requirements of the people is called scarcity of water.
- **Ground Water:** The portion of water which percolates into the ground and gets stored into the aquifers is referred to as the ground water.

▶ **Points to Remember**

- Availability of water is basic to the existence and survival of life.
- Potable water becomes available through rain, snow melting and flowing through rivers, and underground water reserves.

- Water is needed for irrigation. Multipurpose Projects provide electricity besides water for irrigation. Canals, Tube wells and tanks are popular modes of irrigation.
- Multi-Purpose projects provide electricity and are inexhaustible source of energy. They are helpful in flood control and ensure a more dependable water supply for irrigation canals.
- Irrigated areas are very unevenly distributed. While at some places excessive flood irrigation has made some soils saline, some other regions remain perpetually short of water.
- Water scarcity is being caused by neglect of traditional water sources and excess demands with modernization of agriculture.
- There is therefore urgent need for water management and conservation. Rainwater harvesting can help in raising the level of ground water. Tamil Nadu being the first state in India which made roof top rainwater harvesting structure compulsory to all the houses in the state. There is need for strict enforcement of measures that would check wastage of water and pollution of water sources.

## 4. Agriculture

▶ **Important Terms**

- **Commercial farming:** The key feature of this type of farming is the use of modern input and HYV seeds.
- **Intensive subsistence agriculture:** This type of farming is practised in the tropical regions having high density of population and output is high.
- **Subsistence agriculture:** This is a type of farming where the farmer grows crops for their present and future consumption.
- **Shifting Agriculture:** In this system, land is used for a few years until fertility level drops then the farmer moves on to a new plot of land.
- **Plantation farming:** A single crop is grown on a large area. E.g. – tea, coffee, banana etc.

- **Paddy crops:** Aus, Aman and Boro are paddy crops and commonly cultivated in Assam, West Bengal and Orissa.
- **HYV:** It is high yielding varieties of seeds.
- **Green Revolution:** Crop production is excessively increased due to the implementation of modern inputs.
- **White Revolution:** It is the programme under which production of milk increased.
- **Horticulture:** Growing fruits, vegetables and flowers on a small piece of land.
- **Genetic Engineering:** It is a powerful technique to invent new hybrid variety of seed. It is associated with 'Gene Revolution'.
- **Sericulture:** Rearing of silk worms for the production of silk fibre is sericulture.

▶ **Points to Remember**

- Agriculture is the primary activity of Indian economy. About 70% of the total population of the country is dependent on agriculture for their livelihood.
- Agriculture provides raw materials for many industries besides foodgrains.
- Various types of farming in India →
1. Primitive Subsistence Farming
2. Intensive Subsistence Farming
3. Commercial Farming
4. Plantation Farming
- Cropping Season →

   There are mainly three types of cropping seasons –

(i) **Rabi –**

   (A) Rabi Crops are sown in winter and harvested in the month of April to June.

   (B) Wheat, barley, peas and mustard are the examples of Rabi crops.

(ii) **Kharif –**

   (A) The crops which are sown in the rainy season and harvested at the end of monsoon season.

   (B) Paddy, Maize, Soyabean, Groundnut and Cotton are the major Kharif crops.

(iii) **Zaid Crops –**

   (A) It is grown between Rabi and Kharif crops.

   (B) Watermelon, muskmelon and cucumber are main zaid crops.

- Major crops →

   **Rice–**

   - India is the second largest producer of rice in the world.
   - It is a kharif crop.
   - It requires temperature between 20° and 35° and well distributed rainfall about 100 cm for growing.
   - The major rice producing states are U.P., West Bengal, Bihar, Tamil Nadu and Andhra Pradesh.

   **Wheat–**

   - Wheat is the main crop in north and north western parts of the country.
   - It is a Rabi crop.
   - Wheat requires moderate rainfall.
   - Punjab, Uttar Pradesh and Rajasthan are the major wheat producing states.

**Maize–**

- It is a Kharif crop.
- It grows in alluvial soil
- It requires temperature between 21° to 27°C.
- Maize is grown as a foodgrain and livestock feed.

**Millets–**

- Millets refer to ragi, jowar and bajra.
- It is grown in tropical region.
- Despite being named as coarse gain, it contains nutrients.
- In India, millets are grown in Rajasthan, Maharashtra, Gujarat, U.P. and Haryana.

**Pulses–**

- India is the largest producer and consumer of pulses in the world.
- It requires less moisture.
- It is basically a dry crop which survives even in dry climate.
- They are grown in Punjab, U.P., M.P., Rajasthan, Maharashtra and Karnataka.
- Tur, Urad, Moong, Masur, Peas and grains are the varieties of pulses.
- Food crop other than Grains –

**Sugarcane–**

- It is a tropical as well as a subtropical crop.
- India is considered the original homeland of sugarcane after Brazil.
- It is main source of sugar, gur, khandsari and molasses.
- U.P., Maharashtra, Karnataka, Tamil Nadu, Andhra Pradesh, Bihar, Punjab and Haryana are the sugarcane producing states of India.

**Oilseeds–**

- Oilseeds comprise seeds of plants which produce oil.
- Groundnuts, Mustard, Sunflower, Soyabean, Olive and coconut are the major oilseeds.
- Sesamum is a Kharif crop in north and rabi crop in south.

**Tea–**

- India is the largest producer of tea after China.
- It is an example of plantation farming.
- It is grown mainly on hilly slopes and requires cheap and skilled labour.

- Warm and moist climate, heavy rainfall and wide land areas are required for the growth of tea.
- Assam, Darjeeling and Jalpaiguri of West Bengal, Tamil Nadu, Kerala, Uttarakhand, Andhra Pradesh are major tea producing states.

**Coffee–**
- India produces 40% of the world's coffee production.
- Karnataka, Kerala and Tamil Nadu are the major coffee producing states.

**Horticulture crops–**
- India is the largest producer of fruits and vegetables in the world.
- India produces 13% of the world's vegetables.
- Apple, mango, banana, grapes, oranges, apricot, walnuts are world famous.

**Non Food Crops –**

**Rubber–**
- Rubber is an equatorial crop but also grown in tropical and subtropical areas.
- It is an industrial raw material, tyres, footwear, belts, latex foam, dipped goods and many other things are made up of rubber.
- India ranks 5th among the world's rubber producers.

**Fibre crops–**
- Cotton, jute, hemp and natural silk are major fibre crops.

**(A) Cotton –**
- Cotton is obtained from the plant.
- Cotton can be grown in drier areas with the help of irrigation.
- Black soil is suitable for growing cotton.
- The largest producers of cotton are Gujarat, Maharashtra, Haryana, Tamil Nadu, Punjab and Karnataka.

**(B) Jute –**
- It is called golden fibre.
- It grows on well drained fertile soil and areas with high temperature.
- West Bengal, Bihar, Assam, Orissa and Meghalaya are the chief jute producing states.

**Technological and Institutional Reforms**
- India is an agriculture based country.
- More than 60% of India's population are dependent on it.
- Despite the introduction of modern techniques most of the farmers still depend upon monsoon.
- Some reforms are necessary to increase the productivity.
- Land reforms were introduced after the independence.

**Food Security-**
- In order to ensure availability of food to all sections of society our government has developed a national food security system. It consists of two components (i) buffer stock and (ii) public distribution system.

## 5. Minerals and Energy Resources

▶ **Important Terms**
- **Offshore drilling:** Drilling mineral from the bottom of the sea.
- **Extraction:** Withdrawing resources from the nature.
- **Quarry:** Large surface mine for the excavation of stones.
- **Shaft mines:** Deep and tunnelled mines.
- **Photovoltaic:** Cell to generate solar energy.
- **Leaching:** Process of washing out clay from the soil.
- **Mulching:** To provide protective cover over the soil.

▶ **Points to Remember**
- Minerals are non-renewable resources but they are recyclable.

**Mineral resources –** Many things that we use in our day to day life are made up of minerals. It is a natural resource which also constitutes rocks.
- Earth's crust is made up of minerals in the form of rocks.
- Minerals are classified into two parts.
  - (a) Metallic            (b) Non-metallic
- Metallic has been further divided into three parts :
  - (a) Ferrous – It contains iron. Example – Iron Ore, Nickel, Manganese, Cobalt.
  - (b) Non-ferrous – Lead, Copper, Tin and Bauxite are non-ferrous minerals. They contain metals.
  - (c) Precious – Precious metals like Gold, Platinum and Diamond are precious minerals.
  - (d) Non-metallic minerals – Sandstone, Marble, Granite, Salt, Potash are non-metallic minerals.

**Energy Resources –** Resources through which energy is generated are known as Energy resources–

It has two types–
- (i) Conventional source of energy – Example – Coal, Natural gas and Petroleum. It is naturally found.
- (ii) Unconventional source of energy – Energy is generated from natural source like Sun, Wind and Tide.
- It can be generated from fuel minerals in the form of coal, petroleum, natural gas and uranium.
  1. Firewood, cowdung cake, coal, petroleum are conventional sources of energy.

2.   Solar, wind, Tidal, geothermal, biogas and atomic energy are non-conventional sources of energy.

**Coal–**
- The fossil fuel is found in sedimentary rocks.
- Anthracite, bituminous, lignite and peat are few varieties of coal.
- Coal contains carbon.
- India is the world's largest coal producing country – nearly 500 mines of coal are available in India.

**Natural gas–**
- It shares 20% of total energy consumption.
- It is colourless inflammable hydrocarbon.
- It is found in Mumbai High and the Gulf of Cambay.

**Petroleum –**
- Petrol, diesel, kerosene and aviation fuel are the products of petroleum.
- It is a crude oil.
- It is a mixture of petroleum, natural gas and bitumen.
- Petroleum producing states –
  (a)  Mumbai High – 63%
  (b)  Assam – 16%
  (c)  Gujarat – 18%

**Electricity –**
- Electricity is generated by running water which drives hydro turbines and generates hydro electricity. Electricity is also generated by coal, petroleum and natural gas. It is called thermal power. There are 310 thermal power plants in India.

  **Nuclear or Atomic Energy–**
  - Uranium and Thorium type of minerals are required for generating atomic energy.
  - Jharkhand, Rajasthan and Kerela are Uranium and Thorium producing states.

  **Solar Energy –**
  - Sunlight is a source of energy.
  - Solar energy can be obtained by the solar cells which are also called photovoltaic cells.

- It is costly method.
- Many photovoltaic cells can generate thousands of kilowatts of electricity.

**Wind Power–**
- Wind produces 1.6% of the country's electricity.
- It is a renewable energy.
- Tamil Nadu and Gujarat have largest number of windmills.

**Biogas–**
- Shrubs, farm waste, animal and human waste are used to generate biogas.
- It improves the quality of organic fertilizers.
- It is very popular in rural areas.

**Geothermal Power–**
- Hot springs and volcanic gases also generate electricity.
- Geothermal power plants are located in Parvati Valley near Manikaran in Himachal Pradesh and Puga valley in Ladakh.
- It is produced by the heat of interior parts of the earth.

**Tidal Energy–**
- During high tides electricity can be generated through a turbine.
- It is a potential resource.
- It can be reproduced. So it is a renewable resource.
- First tidal power project is commencing in West Bengal.
- Gulf of Kutch, Gulf of Cambay, the Ganga delta and eastern coast have been surveyed as potential sites.
- Conservation of Resources–
- Land, Soil, Mineral and energy resources are the backbone of Indian economy.
- They are also very essential for the mankind.
- They should be utilized in proper manner.
- Many of these resources are not renewable.
- Resource planning should be done so that maximum can be obtained from the scarce resources.
- Gandhiji's view on conservation–
  "There is enough for everyone's need and not for everybody's greed".

## 6. Manufacturing Industries

▶  **Important Terms**
- **Cottage industry:** Industry in which artisans work on wood, tusk, cane, brass, gold, silver and stone in their home.
- **Integrated steel plant:** It is very large and handles everything in one complex, from accumulating raw material to steel making, rolling and shipping etc.
- **Synthetic fibre:** Human made fibre.
- **Teritary sector:** Economic activity that provides services to other sectors in the form of banking, education, distribution and transportation.
- **Village industry:** Industry in which the finished products are consumed in local areas.

▶  **Points to Remember**
- Manufacturing means production of goods on large scale and conversion of raw materials into valuable products. Example – aluminium from bauxite, sugar from sugarcane, textile from cotton etc. It is an organised human efforts.

- The economic strength of a country is measured by the development of manufacturing industries.

**Importance of Manufacturing**

(a) Manufacturing industries help in modernising agriculture and reduce the heavy dependence of people on income generated by agriculture. They provide jobs to the people in secondary and tertiary sectors.

(b) Industrial development helps in reducing unemployment and poverty from the country.

(c) Export of manufactured goods brings foreign exchange.

**Industrial Location**

**Industrial locations are influenced by**

(a) Availability of raw material

(b) Capital

(c) Labour

(d) Power supply

(e) Accessibility to market

**Classification of Industries**

**Manufacturing industries are classified as follows**

A. On the basis of source of raw materials used

    (a) Agro based – It depends on agriculture like cotton, textile, sugar, tea etc.

    (b) Mineral based – It needs minerals for the manufacturing of goods. Example – Iron and Steel, Cement, Machine tools etc.

B. On the basis of their main role

    (a) Basic or key industries– They supply products to manufacture other goods. Example – Iron and Steel Industry, Aluminium smelting industry etc.

    (b) Consumer industries – They produce goods for direct use of customers. Example– Toothpaste, Sewing machines, Paper industries etc.

C. On the basis of Capital investment

    (a) Small scale industries – They refer to industries in which the maximum investment is one crore rupees.

    (b) Large scale industries – Investment is more than one crore rupees.

D. On the basis of ownership

    (a) Public sector – Which is owned and operated by government agencies. Example– BSNL, SAIL, BHEL etc.

    (b) Private sector – It is owned and operated by individual or a group of individuals. Example – TISCO, Dabur Industries etc.

    (c) Joint sector industries – They are run jointly by the public and private sectors. Example – Bharat Aluminium Company, oil India Ltd.

    (d) Co-operative sector industries– These are owned and managed equally by a group of people like producers, suppliers and workers for their benefit. For example sugar industry in Maharashtra.

E. On the basis of the weight of raw material & finished goods

    (a) Heavy industries – They use heavy raw materials. **Example** – Iron & Steel Co., Automobiles.

    (b) Light industries – They use light raw materials and produce light goods. Example – Electrical industries.

**Agro-Based Industries**

**(1) Textile Industry**

- It contributes 4% in GDP.

- It contributes to industrial development, employment generation and foreign exchange earnings.

**Cotton textiles**

- It is the most important industry in terms of employment and production of export goods. Tamil Nadu, Maharashtra and Gujarat have many textile units.

- India exports yarns to Japan, U.S.A., U.K., Nepal, Russia, France, Sri Lanka and other African countries.

**Jute Textile**– India manufactures the largest quantity of jute goods in the world. West Bengal, Andhra Pradesh, Bihar, U.P. and M.P. are its producing states.

**Silk Textile**– Karnataka leads in silk textiles followed by Assam.

**Woollen Textiles** – The distribution of the woollen industry is affected by market rather than raw materials.

**(2) Sugar Industry**

- India stands second as a world producer of sugar.

- India stands first in gur and khandsari.

- There are 460 sugar mills in the country.

- The largest number of sugar industry is located in Uttar Pradesh followed by Maharashtra

- Seasonal nature of the industry, old and inefficient methods of production and transport delay affect the production.

**(3) Mineral Based Industries–**

Industries that use minerals and metals as raw materials are called mineral based industries.

**(i) Iron and Steel Industry–**

- It is the basic industry.

- Production and consumption of steel is regarded as the index of country's development.
- It is a heavy industry because its raw material and finished goods are heavy and bulky.
- India produces 32.8 million tons of steel but only 32 kg of per capita steel is consumed.
- India ranks 9th in the world's crude steel producers.
- TISCO, Bhilai, Bokaro, Durgapur, Rourkela, Burnpur are India's famous steel plants.

**(ii) Aluminium Smelting–**

- It is the second most important metallurgical industry in India.
- It is light, resistant to corrosion, malleable, good conductor of heat and strong when mixed with other metals.
- India produces 600 million tonnes of aluminium.
- Chhattisgarh, Maharashtra, W.B., Orissa, Kerala, U.P., have aluminium smelting plants.

**(iii) Chemical Industry–**

- Chemical industry of India is the fast growing industry.
- Its share is 3% of the GDP.
- It has 3rd rank in Asia and 12th rank in the world.
- Inorganic chemicals consist of sulphuric acid, synthetic fibres, plastics, adhesive, soap etc.
- Organic chemicals include petrochemical, synthetic, rubber, plastics, pharmaceuticals plants.

**(iv) Fertilizer Industry–**

- India is the third largest producer of nitrogeneous fertilizers.
- There are 10 public sector undertakings and one co-operative sector undertaking is located at Hazira in Gujarat.
- Gujarat, Tamil Nadu, Uttar Pradesh, Punjab, Kerala are fertiliser producing states.

**(v) Cement Industry–**

- Cement is used for construction work.
- It requires bulky and heavy raw materials like limestone, Silica, alumina and gypsum.
- The first cement plant was established in Chennai in 1904.
- There are 128 large plants and 332 mini plants in country.

**(vi) Automobile Industry–**

- It provides various types of vehicles like trucks, buses, cars, two wheelers, three wheelers and multi-utility vehicles.
- There are 15 manufacturers of passenger cars and multi-utility vehicles, 9 of commercial vehicles and 14 of the two and three wheelers.
- Delhi, Mumbai, Chennai, Kolkata, Indore, Jamshedpur and Bangalore are major centres.

**(vii) Information Technology and Electronics Industry–**

Bangalore is famous as the electronic capital of India.

18 software technology parks provide single window service and high data communication facility to software experts.

- This industry earns major foreign exchange.
- The success of IT industry depends on the growth of hardware and software.

**Industrial Pollution and Environmental Degradation**

Industries contribute in the economic development of the country. But at same time there are many bad effects of it like increase in water, air and noise pollution and land degradation.

**(a) Air Pollution**

It is caused by the presence of high proportion of undesirable gases like sulphur dioxide and carbon monoxide. It adversely affects the health of the mankind as well as the environment. Toxic gas leakage can be very hazardous. Example– Bhopal Gas Tragedy.

**(b) Water Pollution**

- Industries pollute the water by discharging large quantities of chemical wastes and garbage in it.
- This water sometimes become poisonous.

**(c) Thermal Pollution**

It occurs when hot water from factories and thermal plants drained into river.

Wastes from nuclear power plants can cause cancer, birth defects and miscarriages.

**(d) Noise Pollution**

- It can cause hearing impairment, increased heart rate and blood pressure.
- Unwanted sound irritates and  is a source of stress.

**Steps to Control Environmental Degradation**

1. Reuse and recycle water in two or more successive stages.

2. Harvesting of rainwater.

3. Treating hot water and effluents. It can be done in three phases–

    (a) Primary treatment by mechanical means like grinding, flocculation and sedimentation.

    (b) Secondary treatment by biological process.

    (c) Teritary treatment by biological, chemical and physical processes.

4. Machinery should be redesigned to increase energy efficiency.

5. Generators should be fitted with silencers.

The challenge of sustainable development needs integration of economic development with environmental concerns.

## 7. Lifelines of National Economy

▶ **Important Terms**

- **Harbour:** The place where there is a provision of loading and unloading the ships.

- **Hinterland:** It is the area which is served by a port by exporting and importing goods and commodities.

- **Locomotives:** All types of railway engine.

- Gauge: Width between the two rails of the railway lines.

- **Expressway National Highways:** Roads with 4 to 6 lanes for fast traffic requirements.

▶ **Points to Remember**

- Efficient means of transport are prerequisite for fast development of the country.

- The movement of goods and services from their supply locations to demand place requires good transport.

- Land, water and air are three important domains of our earth.

- Transport, communication and trade are complementary to each other. The trades from local to international levels have added to the vitality of country's economy.

- Modes of transport are divided into three parts:
  1. Land    2. Water    3. Air

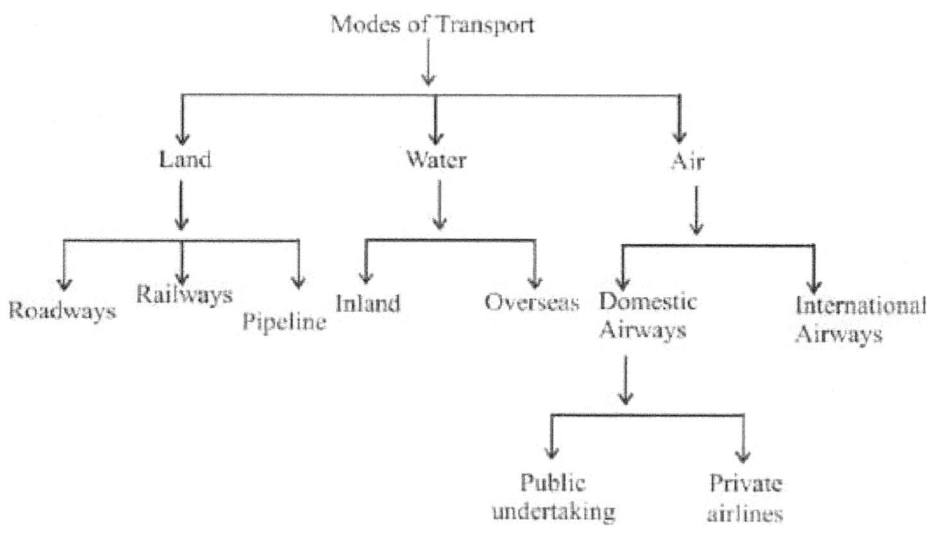


- **Advantages of Transport :**

1. Men and material are quickly transported from one place to another.

2. It helps is supplying the raw material to the industries.

3. Immediate relief can be provided in times of war, natural calamity, etc.

4. It has made travelling convenient.

5. The developed means of transport have brought the people of the world closer to one another.

6. The world has been converted into a large village with the help of efficient and fast moving means of transport.

- Land transport →
  Roadways :

- India has one of the largest road networks in the world aggregating to about 2.3 million km. at present.
- Road transport is more important than railways because
  (a) Construction cost of roads is much lower than railways.
  (b) Roads can traverse comparatively more dissected.
  (c) It is affordable for many people.
  (d) It provides door to door service.
  (e) It is used as a feeder to other mode of transport.
- Indian roads are classified in the following six classes –
1. Golden Quadrilateral Super Highways -
- It links Delhi – Kolkata – Chennai – Mumbai and Delhi by six lane Super Highways.
- The North-South corridor links Srinagar and Kanyakumari.
- The East - West corridor connects Silchar to Porbandar.
- These projects are being implemented by National Highway Authority of India.
2. National Highways –
- National highways are primary road systems and are maintained by CPWD in state and union territories.
- The historical Shershah Suri Marg is called National Highway No. 1 between Delhi and Amritsar.
  National Highway 2 → Delhi – Kolkata
  NH3 → Agra – Mumbai
  NH4 → Varanasi – Kanyakumari.
  NH 8 → Delhi – Mumbai.
3. State Highways –
  (i) Roads linking a state capital with different district headquarters are known as state highways.
  (ii) It is maintained by PWD.
4. District roads –
- It connects the district headquarters with other place of district.
- It is maintained by Zilla parishad.
5. Other roads –
- Rural roads – It links rural areas and villages with towns.
- *Pradhan Mantri Grameen Sadak* Yojna is a scheme which has provision to link every village in the country with major town.
6. Border roads –
- It is a Government of India undertaking which constructs and maintains road in the border areas of the country.
- It is established in 1960 for northern and north-eastern border areas.
- Roads can be classified on the basis of the type of materials used to construct it like –
  (a) Metalled road        (b) Unmetalled road

- Road density –
- The length of 100 sq. km. of area is known as road density.
- Our road network is inadequate in respect of the volume of traffic.

Railways :
- Trains are the most important means of transport.
- It accounts nearly three-fourth of the passenger traffic and four – fifth of the foreign traffic in India.
- First train was started between Bombay and Thane of a distance of 34 km in 1953.
- The Indian railway have a network of 7,031 stations spread over a route length of 63, 221 km.
- The Indian railways is divided into 16 zones and headquarters.
- It operates in 4 different gauges –
- Broad gauge – 1,676 in meters
- Meter gauge – 1000 meters.
- Narrow gauge – 0.762 & 0.610 meters
- Light gauge
- It is the important source of icome to enhance national economy than other means of transport.

**Pipelines :**
- Pipeline transport network is a new arrival on the transportation map.
- Earlier it was used as a transporter of water to cities and industries.
- Now-a-days, it is used for transporting crude oil, petroleum products and natural gas from natural gas fields to refineries.
- Barauni, Mathura, Panipat are famous for pipelines.
- Three important network of pipeline transportation are –
  (a) From oilfield in the upper Assam to Kanpur via Guwahati, Barauni and Allahabad.
  (b) From Salaya (Gujarat) to Jalandhar (Panjab) via Kishan Garh, Mathura, Delhi and Sonipat.
  (c) From Hazira in Gujrat to Jagdishpur in U.P. via Vijaypur (M.P).

**Waterways :**
- India has inland navigation waterways of 14,500 km in length.
- It is the cheapest mode of transport.
- These are considered as the National waterways by the Government.
  (i) The Ganga river between Allahabad and Haldia (1620 km) – N.W. –1
  (ii) The Brahmaputra river between Sadiya and Dhurbi (891 km) – N.W. – 2
  (iii) The west coast canal in Kerala (Kottapuram – Kollam Udyogmandal and Champakara Canals – 205 km.) – NW. 3.
  (iv) 95% of trade is done by sea.

**Major Sea Parts**

- With a coastline of 7, 51, 6.6 km., India has 12 major and 181 medium and minor ports.
- It handles 95% of foreign trade.
- Kandla in Kutch was the first port.
- Mumbai is the biggest port with a well-sheltered harbour.
- Mormugao port (Goa) is the iron one exporting port of the country.
- Kochi is the extreme south-western port.
- Tuticorin (Tamil Nadu) is south eastern port.
- Kolkata is an inland reverine port.

**Airways**

- It is the fastest and most comfortable mode of transport.
- The air transport was nationalised in 1953.
- Domestic and international are two types of airways.
- Air India provides international air services.
- Pawan Hans Helicopters Ltd. provides helicopter services to ONGC to the inaccessible and difficult terrains or north-eastern states.
- It is a costly means of transport.

**Communication**

- Essential to development, communication services in India comprise of the post, telephone, television, press etc.
- The Indian postal network is the largest in the world.
- The first class mail includes cards and envelops and the second class mails include book packets, periodicals etc.

- Six mail channels have been introduced recently – Rajdhani Channel, mber of newspapers and periodicals annually. Newspapers are published in about 100 languages.

- **International trade** :
- The exchange of goods among people, states and countries is called trade.
- Trade between two countries is called international trade through sea, air and land routes.
- It is considered as the economic barometer of the country.
- Exports and imports are the components of trade.
- Ores and minerals, agriculture and allied products, gems and jewellery, engineering goods are some export commodities.
- Petroleum, precious stones, coke, inorganic materials are imported items.

**Tourism as a Trade :**

- Tourism in India contributed ₹ 21,828 crore of foreign exchange in 2004.
- Over 2.6 million foreign tourists visit India every year.
- More then 15 million people are engaged in the tourism industry.
- Rajasthan, Goa, Jammu and Kashmir and temple towns of South India are important tourist places.
- Tourism promotes national integration provides support to local handicrafts and cultural pursuits.

# UNIT-III. POLITICAL SCIENCE

## 1. Power Sharing

▶ **Important Terms**

- **Power Sharing**: Power sharing is necessary to ensure the stability of political order in a democracy. It is desirable to reduce the possibility of conflict between social groups. It ensures stability of government and unity of the nation.

- **Majoritarianism**: It means, a belief that the majority community should be able to rule a country in its own way. They can disregard the views and wishes of the minority. It exists in Sri Lanka where Sinhala people (74%) constitute the majority and Tamils (about 18%) constitute the minority.

- **Community Government**: A form of government which is elected by the people belonging to one language community. This type of government exists in Belgium where Dutch, French and German speaking people, no matter where they live in the country, elect their government.

- **Coalition Government**: When no single party is able to get an absolute majority in the legislature, two or more parties join to form the government. Such a government is known as coalition government. Before May 2014, UP government in India, with S. Manmohan Singh as Prime Minister, was a coalition government.

- **Civil War**: A war like conflict between two opposite groups in a country (between Sinhala and Tamils in Sri Lanka) is known as civil war.

- **Organ of the State/government**: It means the various component of the government that helps in running of the country, e.g., Legislature, executive and judiciary.

- **Executive**: A body of persons having authority to initiate major policies, making decisions and implement them on the basis of the Constitution and laws of the country.

- **Judiciary**: An institution empowered to administer justice and provide a mechanism for the resolution of legal disputes. All the courts in the country are collectively referred to as judiciary.

- **Legislature**:An assembly of people's representatives with the power to enact laws for a country. In addition to enacting laws, legislatures have authority to raise taxes and adopt the budget and other money bills.

▶ **Points to Remember**

Intelligent sharing of power among legislature, executive and judiciary is very important for the design of democracy. The vertical division of power among different levels of government is one of the major forms of power sharing in modern democracies. This form is commonly referred to as Federalism.

**Forms of Power Sharing**

- Power is shared among different organs of government, such as the legislature, executive and judiciary. This is called horizontal distribution of power because it allows different organs of government, placed at the same level to exercise different powers. It results in checks and balance of power.

- Power can be shared among governments at different levels, a general government for the entire country called Federal government and governments at the provincial or regional level. In India, we refer to it as the Central or Union government. The governments at the provincial or regional level are called State governments. The constitution clearly lays down the powers of different levels of government.

- Power may also be shared among different social groups, such as the religious and linguistic groups. For example, 'Community government' in Belgium. In some countries there are constitutional and legal arrangements, where by socially weaker sections and women are represented in the legislatures and administration.

- Power sharing arrangements can also be seen in the way political parties, pressure groups and movements control or influence those in power. Power is shared among different political parties that represent different ideologies and social groups.

- In a democracy, we find interest groups such as those of traders, businessmen, industrialists, farmers and industrial workers. They have a share in governmental power, through participation in governmental committees or bringing influence on the decision making process.

**Accommodation in Belgium**

- Belgium is a small country in Europe. It has borders with Netherlands, France and Germany and a population of little over one crore. The ethnic composition of this small country is very complex.

- Of the country's total population, 59 percent lives in the Flemish region and speaks Dutch language. Another 40 percent people lives in the Wallonia region and speaks French. Remaining 1 percent of the Belgians speak German.

- In the capital city Brussels, 80 percent people speak French, while 20 percent are Dutch speaking.

- The minority French speaking community was relatively powerful. This was resented by the Dutch speaking community who got the

- benefit of economic development and education much later, which led to tension between them during the 1950s and 1960s.
- Brussels presented a special problem - the Dutch speaking people constituted a majority in the country but minority in the capital.
- The Belgian leaders recognized the existence of regional differences and cultural diversities so they amended their constitution four times between 1970 and 1993.
- Constitution prescribes that the number of Dutch and French speaking ministers shall be equal in the central government. No single community can take decisions unilaterally.
- Many powers of the central government have been given to state governments of the two regions of the country. The state governments are not subordinate to the central government. Brussels has a separate government in which both the communities have equal representation.
- Apart from the A 'community government' is elected by the people belonging to one language community; Dutch, French and German speaking in this case, in which the government has the power regarding cultural, educational and language related issues.
- This Belgian model has worked well so far and helped to avoid civic strife between the two major communities and a possible division of the country on linguistic lines.

**Majoritarianism in Sri Lanka**

- Sri Lanka is an island nation, just a few kilometers off the southern coast of Tamil Nadu. It has about 2 crore people.
- Sri Lanka has a diverse population. The major social groups are the Sinhala speakers (74 percent), and the Tamil speakers (18 percent).
- Among Tamils, there are two sub groups. Tamil natives of the country are called 'Sri Lankan Tamils' (13 percent). The rest, whose forefathers came from India as plantation workers during colonial period are called 'Indian Tamils'.
- Most of the Sinhala speaking people are Buddhist, while most of the Tamils are Hindus or Muslims. There are about 7 percent Christians, who are both Tamil and Sinhala.
- Sri Lanka emerged as an independent country in 1948. The democratically elected government adopted a series of majoritarian measures to establish Sinhala supremacy.

- In 1956, an Act was passed to recognize Sinhala as the only official language, disregarding Tamil. Sinhala applicants were favoured for university positions and government jobs. A new constitution stipulated that the state shall protect and foster Buddhism.
- Sri Lankan Tamils felt that move of the major political parties led by the Buddhist Sinhala leaders, were sensitive to their language and culture.
- They felt that the constitution and government policies denied them equal political rights, discriminated against them in getting jobs and other opportunities and ignored their interests.
- As a result, the relations between the Sinhala and Tamil communities strained over time.
- Sri Lankan Tamils launched parties and struggles for the recognition of Tamil as an official language, for regional autonomy and equality of opportunity in securing education and jobs.
- By 1980s, several political organizations were formed demanding an independent Tamil Eelam (state) in northern and eastern parts of Sri Lanka.
- The distrust between the two communities turned into a Civil War. As a result, thousands of people of both the communities have been killed. Many families were forced to leave the country as refugees and many more lost their livelihood.
- Sri Lanka has an excellent record of economic development, education and health. But the Civil War has caused a terrible setback to the social, cultural and economic life of the country.
- Thus in Belgium, the leaders have realized that the unity of the country is possible by mutually acceptable arrangements for sharing power, whereas in Sri Lanka, it shows that a majority community wants to force its dominance and refuses to share power by undermining the unity of the country.
- Thus governments at different levels should agree to some rules of power sharing. They should also trust that each would abide by its part of the agreement.

## 2. Federalism

▶ **Important Terms**

- **Federalism**: It is a system of government in which the power is divided between a central authority and various constituent units of the country.
- **Unitary system**: Under the unitary system, there is either only one level of government or two levels. The second level of state government act as a subordinate to the central government.
- **Jurisdiction**: The area over which someone has legal authority. The area may be defined in terms of geographical boundaries or in terms of certain kinds of subjects.
- **Coming together federations**: This federation include the USA, Switzerland and Australia. In this category of federations, all the constituent states usually have equal power and are strong vis-a-vis the federal government.
- **Holding together federations**: A large country decides to divide its power between the constituent states and the national government. India, Spain, U.A.E. and Belgium are examples of this kind of 'holding together' federations.
- **Union List**: Includes subjects of national importance such as defence of the country, foreign affairs, banking, communications and currency. The Union Government alone can make laws relating to the subjects mentioned in the Union List.

- **State List**: It contains subjects of State and local importance such as police, trade, commerce, agriculture and irrigation. The State Governments alone can make laws relating to the subjects mentioned in the State List.
- **Concurrent List**: It includes subject of common interest to both the Union Government as well as the State Governments, such as education, forest, trade unions, marriage, adoption and succession. Both the Union as well as the State Governments can make laws on the subjects mentioned in this list.
- **Residuary' subjects**: Subjects, which do not fall under any list. These are new areas, which came up after the constitution was made. Here only Union government has the power to legislate. For example, cyber law, genome science, computer.
- **Linguistic States**: The state, which is formed, on the basis of language, for example, Punjab, Haryana, Gujarat etc.

▶ **Points to Remember**

- Federalism is a system of government in which the power is divided between a central authority and various constituents, units of the country. Usually, a federation has two levels of government.
- One is the government for the entire country that is usually responsible for a few subjects of common national interest. The others are governments at the level of provinces or states that look after much of the day to day administering of their state. Both these levels of governments enjoy their power independent of the other.
- Different tiers of government govern the same citizens, but each tier has its own jurisdiction in specific matters of legislation, taxation and administration.
- The jurisdictions of the respective levels of government are specified in the constitution. So, the existence and authority of each tier of government is constitutionally guaranteed.
- The fundamental provisions of the constitution cannot be unilaterally changed by one level of government; such changes require the consent of both the levels of government.
- Courts have the power to interpret the constitution and the powers of different levels of government. The highest court acts as an inspire, if disputes arise between different levels of government in the exercise of their respective powers.
- There are two kinds of routes through which federations have been formed. This first is coming federations and the other holding together federations.
- Sources of revenue for each level of government are clearly specified to ensure its financial autonomy.
- The federal system thus has dual objectives - to safeguard and promote unity of the country, while at the same time accommodate regional diversity.

**Practise of Federalism**

- The real success of Federalism in India can be attributed to the nature of democrative politics in our country. This ensured that the spirit of federalism, respect for diversity and desire for living together became a shared ideal in our country.
- **Linguistic States :** The creation of linguistic states was the first and a major test for democratic politics in our country. Some states were created not on the basis of language but to recognize differences based on culture, ethnicity or geography. This include states like Nagaland, Uttarakhand and Jharkhand. The formation of linguistic states has made the country more united and administration easier.
- **Language Policy :** Second test for Indian federation is the language policy. Besides Hindi, there are 21 other languages recognised as scheduled languages by the constitution. A candidate, in an examination conducted for the central government positions, may opt to take the examinations in any of these languages.
- **Centre-State Relations :** Restructuring the centre-state relations is one more way in which federalism has been strengthened in practice. After 1990, regional political parties came up in many states of the country. This was also the beginning of the era of coalition governments at the centre. Since no single party got a clear majority in the Lok Sabha, the major national parties had to enter into an alliance with many parties, including several regional parties, to form a government at the centre. This led to a new culture of power sharing and respect for the autonomy of state governments. Thus federal power sharing is more effective today.

**Indian Federation**

- Indian Union is based on the principles of Federalism. The constitution originally provided for a two-tier system of governments - the Union government and the State government. Later, a third tier of Federalism was added in the form of Panchayats and Municipalities. The constitution clearly provided a three fold distribution of legislative powers between the Union government and the State governments.
- **Union List :** It includes subjects of national importance such as defence, foreign affairs, banking, communication and currency. They are included in this list because we need a uniform policy on these matters throughout the country. The Union government alone can make laws relating to the subjects mentioned in the union List.
- **State List :** It contains subject of state and local importance such as police, trade, commerce, agriculture and irrigation. The state governments can make laws relating to the subjects mentioned in the state list.
- **Concurrent List :** It includes subjects of common interest to both the union and the state governments, such as education, forest, trade unions, marriage, adoption and succession. Both the union and the state governments can make laws on these subjects. If their laws conflict with each other, the law made by the union government will prevail.

**Decentralisation in India**

- The need for decentralisation was recognised in our constitution. Several attempts to decentralise power to the level of village and towns. There was been very little decentralisation in real sence.
- A major step was taken towards decentralisation in 1992. It is constitutionally compulsory to hold regular elections to local government bodies.
- Constitutional status for local government has helped to deepen democracy in our country.

## 3. Democracy and Diversity

▶ **Important Terms**

- **Civil Rights Movement**: In the USA (1954-1968) refers to a set of events and reform movements aimed at abolishing legal racial discrimination against African-Americans. Led by Martin Lurther King Jr., this movement practiced non-violent methods of civil disobedience against racially discriminatory laws and practices.

- **African-American/Afro-American**: Black American or Black is the terms used to refer mainly to the descendants of Africans who were brought into America as slaves between the 17th century and early 19th century.

- **The Black Power movement**: This movement emerged in 1966 and lasted till 1975, which was a more millitant anti-racist movement, advocating even violence if necessary to end racism in the US.

- **Homogenous society**: A society that has similar kinds of people, especially where there are no significant ethnic differences.

- **Migrant**: It means anybody who shift from one region or country to another region within a country or to another country generally for work or other economic activities.

▶ **Points to Remember**

- Apart from language and regions, people also identify themselves with gender, caste, tribe, physical appearance, religion etc. In 1968, Olympics were held at Mexico city in which gold and bronze medals were won by the African-Americans named Tommie Smith and John Carlos and the silver was bagged by the white Australian in 200 m race. In the ceremony, Tommie Smith and John Carlos stood on the dias with clenched fists, upraised and heads bowed while the American national anthem was played.

- They received their medals wearing black socks and no shoes to represent Black Poverty. This they did so to draw the international attention to racial discrimination in the United States. The black-gloved and raised clenched fists were meant to symbolise Black Power. The silver medalist, white Australian athlete, Peter Norman, wore human rights badge on his shirt to show his support to the two Americans.

- **The consequences of their action**
  The International Olympics Association held Carlos and Smith guilty of violating the Olympic spirit by making a political statement. Their medals were taken back. But their action did succeed in getting international attention for the Civil Rights Movement in the US.

- **Social differences** are mostly based on accident of birth. At the same time, some differences are based on our choices.

- Every social difference does not lead to social divisions. Social differences divide similar people from one another but they also unite different people. People belonging to different social groups share differences and similarities cutting across the boundaries of their groups. e.g.

  — It is common for people belonging to the same religion to feel that they do not belong to the same community because their caste or society is different. It is also possible for the people from different religions to have same caste and feel close to each other.

  — Rich and poor persons from the same family often do not have close relations with each other for they feel they are very different.

  — Thus, it can be said that we all have more than one identity and can belong to more than one group.

- **Overlapping differences**

  — It happens when some social difference overlaps with other difference.

  — Situations of this kind produce social divisions, when one kind of social difference becomes more important than the other and people start feeling that they belong to different communities.

  — Overlapping differences create possibilities of deep social divisions and tensions.

- **Cross-cutting differences**

  — If social differences cross-cut one another, it is difficult to pit group of people against the other.

  — It means those groups that share a common interest on the issue are likely to be on different sides on a different issue.

  — Cross-cut social differences are easier to accommodate.

- **Three determinants.** There are three factors which are crucial in deciding the outcome of politics of social divisions:

  — The outcome depends on how people perceive their identities. If they perceive their identities in singular and exclusive terms, it becomes difficult to accommodate. It is much easier, if people see that their identities are multiple and are complementary with the national identity.

— The outcome of politics in social divisions depends how the political leaders raise the demands of any community. It is easier to accommodate demands that are within the constitutional framework and are not at the cost of another community.

— The outcome of politics in social divisions also depends upon how the government responds to such demands of various social groups. Example – in Belgium and Sri Lanka. If the rulers are willing to share power and accommodate the reasonable demands of minority community, social divisions become less threatening for the country. If the reasonable demands of a community are suppressed by the government, then it leads to social divisions, which in turn threaten the integrity of the country.

In a democracy political expression of social divisions is very normal and can be healthy.

## 4. Gender, Religion & Caste

▶ **Important Terms**

- **Sexual division of labour:** A system in which all work inside the home is either done by the women of the family, or organised by them through the domestic helpers.

- **Feminist:** A woman or a man who believes in equal rights and opportunities for women and men.

- **Patriarchy:** A male dominated society. This concept is used to refer to a system that values men more and gives them power over women.

- **Family Laws:** The laws that deal with family related matters such as marriage, divorce, adoption, inheritance etc. In India, different family laws apply to followers of different religion.

- **Urbanisation:** Shift of population from rural areas to urban areas.

- **Occupational mobility:** Shift from one occupation to another, usually when a new generation takes up occupations other than those practised by their ancestors.

- **Caste hierarchy:** A ladder like formation in which all the caste groups are placed from the 'highest' to the 'lowest' castes.

▶ **Points to Remember**

- The existence of social diversity does not threaten democracy. Political expression of social differences is possible and sometimes, quite desirable in a democratic system. In India, there are three kinds of social differences that can take the form of social divisions and inequalities. These are social differences based on gender, religion and caste.

**Gender and Politics**

- Gender division is a form of hierarchical social division seen everywhere, but is rarely recognised in the study of politics.

- The gender division tends to be understood as natural and unchangeable. However, it is not based on Biology but on social expectations and stereotypes.

- Boys and girls are brought up to believe that the main responsibility of women is housework and bringing up children. This is reflected in a sexual division of labour in most families.

- Women do all sorts of household work and men do all the work outside the home. It is not that men cannot do housework, when these jobs are paid for, men are ready to take up these works.

- Similarly, it is not that women do not work outside their home. They work in offices and factories. In fact, the majority of women do some sort of paid work, in addition to domestic work. But their work is not valued and does not get recognition.

- Gradually, the gender issue was raised in politics. Women in different parts of the world organised and agitated for equal rights, voting rights, enhancing their political and legal status, improving their educational and career opportunities.

- More radical women's movements aimed at equality in personal and family life as well. These movements are called feminist movements.

- Ours is still a male dominated, patriarchal society. Women face disadvantage, discrimination and oppression in various ways. The literacy rate among women is only 54 percent compared with 76 percent among men.

- Similarly, a smaller proportion of girl students go for higher studies because parents prefer to spend their resources for their boys' education, rather than spending equally on their sons and daughters.

- The proportion of women among the highly paid and valued jobs is still very small. The Equal Wages Act provides that equal wages should be paid to equal work, However, women are paid less than men, even when both do exactly the same work.

- In many parts of India, people prefer to have sons and find ways to have the girl child aborted before she is born Such sex-selective abortion lead to a decline in the child sex-ratio. According to the Census of 2001, in India the sex-ratio is 927 on an average.

- There are reports of various kinds of harassment, exploitation and violence against women. Urban areas have particularly become unsafe for women. They are not safe from beating, harassment and other forms of domestic violence even in their homes.

**Women's Political Representation**

- In India, the proportion of women in legislature has been very low, the percentage of elected women members in Lok-Sabha has never reached even 10 per cent of its total strength. Their share in the state assemblies is less than 5 per cent.

- One way to solve this problem is to make it legally binding to have a fair proportion of women in the elected bodies. Panchayati Raj is successful in this case. One-third of seats in local government bodies – in Panchayats and Municipalities – are now reserved for women.

- Women's organisations and activists have been demanding a similar reservation of at least one-third of seats in the Lok Sabha and State Assemblies for women. A bill with this proposal is pending before the Parliament and has not been passed.

**Religion, Communalism and Politics**

- The division based on religious difference is not as universal as gender, but religious diversity is fairly widespread in the world today. Many countries, including India, have in their population, followers of different religions, which are often expressed in the field of politics.

- Gandhiji used to say that religion can never be separated from politics as he believed that politics must be guided by ethics drawn from religion.

- Most of the victims of communial riots in our country are people from religious minorities, who have demanded that the government take special steps to protect them.

- Women's movement have demanded that the government should change the family laws to make them more equitable.

- All these instances involve a relationship between religion and politics.

- People should be able to express in politics their needs, interests and demands as a member of a religious community.

- Those who hold political power should sometimes be able to regulate the practice of religion so as to prevent discrimination and oppression. These political acts are not wrong as long as they treat every religion equally.

**Communalism**

- The problem begins when religion is seen as the basis of the nation, expressed in politics in exclusive and partisan terms, when one religion and its followers are pitted against another.

- This happens when beliefs of one religion are presented as superior to those of other religions, when the demands of one religious group are formed in opposition to another and when state power is used to establish domination of one religious group over the rest.

- This manner of using religion in politics is communal politics, which is based on the idea that religion is the principal basis of social community.

- Communalism can take various forms in politics and in everyday beliefs. These routinely involve religious prejudices, stereotypes of religious communities and belief in the superiority of one's religion over the other religions.

- A communal mind often leads to a quest for political dominance of one's own religious community.

- Political mobilisation on religious lines is another frequent form of communalism. This involves the use of sacred symbols, religious leaders emotional appeal and plain fear in order to bring the followers of one religion together in the political arena.

- Its most ugly form is communal violence, riots and massacre. India and Pakistan suffered some of the worst communal riots at the time of the partition.

**Secular State**

- Communalism was and continues to be one of the major challenges to democracy in our country. This is why the makers of our constitution chose the model of a secular state.

- There is no official religion of the Indian state; our constitution does not give a special status to any religion.

- The constitution provides to all individuals and communities freedom to profess, practice and propagate any religion, or not to follow any.

- The constitution prohibits discrimination on grounds of religion but at the same time allows the state to intervene in the matter of religion, in order to ensure equality within religious communities.

- Secularism is not just an ideology of some parties or persons. It constitutes one of the foundations of our country. This is why communalism needs to be combated.

- A secular constitution like ours, is necessary but not sufficient to combat communalism. Communal prejudices and propaganda need to be countered in everyday life and religion based mobilisation needs to be countered in the arena of politics.

### Caste and Politics

- Casteism is rooted in the belief that caste is the sole basis of social community. People belonging to the same caste belong to a natural social community and have the same interest, which they do not share with anyone from another caste.
- Caste can take various forms in politics. When parties choose candidates in elections, they keep in mind the caste composition of the electorate and nominate candidates from different castes so as to muster necessary support to win elections.
- When governments are formed, political parties usually take care that representatives of different castes and tribes find a place in it.
- Political parties and candidates in elections make appeal to caste sentiment to muster support.
- Universal Adult Franchise and the principle of 'one person one vote', compelled political leaders to gear up to the task of mobilising and securing political support.
- No parliamentary constituency in the country has a clear majority of one single caste. So, every candidate and party needs to win the confidence of more than one caste and community to win elections.
- No party wins the votes of all the voters of a caste or community. When people say that a caste is a "vote bank" of one party, it usually means that a large proportion of the voters from the caste vote for that party.

- Many political parties may put up candidates from the same caste. Some voters have more than one candidate from their caste.
- The ruling party and the sitting M.P. or M.L.A. frequently lose elections in our country, which could not have happened, if all castes and communities were frozen in their political preferences.
- People's assessment of the performance of the government and the popularity rating of the leaders matter and are often decisive in elections.

### Politics and Caste

- Politics too influences the caste system and caste identities by bringing them into the political arena. Thus, it is not politics that gets caste ridden, it is the caste that gets politicised. This takes several forms–
- Each caste group tries to become bigger by incorporating neighbouring castes or sub-castes within it, which were earlier excluded from it.
- Various caste groups are required to enter into a coalition with other castes or communities and thus, enter into a dialogue and negotiation.
- New kinds of caste groups have come up in the political arena like 'backward' and 'forward' caste groups. In some cases, many disadvantaged communities have got the space to demand their share of power. In this sense, caste politics has helped people from Dalits and OBC castes to gain better access to decision making.

---

## 5. Popular Struggles and Movements

**Note :** Chapter 5 is to be done as a project worl and will not be evaluated in theory.

---

## 6. Political Parties

▶ **Important Terms**

- **Affidavit:** A signed document submitted to an officer, where a person makes a sworn statement regarding his or her personal information.
- **Defection:** Changing party allegiance from party on which a person got elected (to a legislative body) to a different party.
- **Partisan:** A person who is strongly committed to a party, group or faction. Partisanship is marked by a tendency to take a side and inability to take a balanced view on an issue.

▶ **Points to Remember**

- A Political party is an organized group of persons who have common view on the social and economic problem and their solution. They try to capture power i.e ., government by constitutional means i.e, through elections.
- Ruling party is the party that forms the government and runs the administration.

- The political party or a group of parties that are a part of the legislature but not a part of the government.
- It is an independent multi-member body (at present 3 members) which is constituted for the superintendence, direction and conduct of election in the country.
- A political system when a country has more than two political parties who contest election together for sharing power.
- There are some country wide parties which have their units in various states, all these units by and large follow the same policies programmes and strategy that is decided at the national level National parties include Indian National Congress, Bhartiya Janta Party Communist Party of India.
- The party which originates in a particular state or a region and works for it and its people is called regional political Party.
- Functions of political parties are (i) contest election making laws, put forward different policies and programmes provide access to government machinery, form the government and shape public opinion.

- Some efforst and suggestions were made to reform political parties.
  - (i) The constitution has been amended to prevent elected MPs and MLA's from changing parties.
  - (ii) As per order passed by Supreme Court it has become compulsory for the condidate contesting elections to file an affidavit giving details of his property and criminal cases pending against him/her.
  - (iii) The election commission has passed an making it neccessary for political parties to hold their organisational elections and file their income tax returns.
- It is difficult to reform policies, if ordinary citizen do not take part in it and criticise it from outside.

## 7. Outcome of Democracy

▶ **Important Terms**

- **Democracy**: It is a form of government in which the power of governance resides in the hands of the people. They exercise their power directly or through the representatives elected by them.
- **Dictatorship**: It is a form of government in which the power of the government is in the hands of one person or party and no opposition to the dictator is tolerated.
- **Outcomes means**: Result – successes or failures of democracy. Democracy – political and economic equality, social justice and dignity of the individual.
- **Rule of law**: It means that everyone is equal in the eyes of law, no one is above law and any one who violates law will get the same punishment irrespective of his official or financial status.
- **Transparency**: It means that a citizen can know about the process of decision-making and can examine it also.

▶ **Points to Remember**

- Democracy is considered as the better form of government in comparison or any other alternative. Democracy produces an accountable, responsive and legitimate form of government.
- Two conditions are essential for a democracy to achieve harmonious society. These are
  - (i) majority and minority opinion are not permanent. Democracy is not simply rule by majority opinion.
  - (ii) Rule by majority does not become rule by majority community in terms of religion or race or linguistic groups.
- Legitimate government is a government which is chosen legally.
- A government in which people have the right to know the decisions taken by the government and also have the right and means to examine the process of decision-making.
- Democracy stands much superior to any other form of government in promoting dignity and freedom of the individual. It strengthened the claims of disadvantaged and discriminated castes. Democracy transforms people from the status of a subject into that of a citizen. These is transparency in democracy. The Right to information Act (2005) ensures all its citizens the rigt to seak all the information with regard to thefunctions of the government departments.

## 8. Challengers to Democracy

▶ **Important Terms**

- **Challengers to Democracy:** Problems that come in the way of working of democracy in a country.
- **Poverty:** A situation in which a person does not have basic necessities of life like food, clothing, sanitation, security, clean drinking water etc.
- **Regionalism:** A felling or situation when the people living in a particular region of the country awaken to their separate existences due to social, economic or cultural reasons, the leaning towards their region.
- **Regional Imbalance:** means that some regions are economically advanced and some are economically backward and poor.
- **Democratic Reforms (Political Reforms):** Suggestions or proposals about overcoming various challenger to democracy are called 'Democratic Reforms' or 'Political Reforms'.

▶ **Points to Remember**

- In a democracy different types of countries faces different kinds of problems.
- The chanllange faced by democracy are:
  - (i) **Foundational challenge:** It relates to making the transition to democracy and then instituting a democratic government.
  - (ii) **Challange of expansion:** This challange involves applying the basic principle of democratic government across all regions, different social groups and varied institutions.
  - (iii) **Challange of deepening of democracy:** It involves strengthening of institutions and practices of democracy.
- The legal constitutional changes by themselves cannot overcome challenge to democracy. The democratic reforms needs to be carried out chifly by political activists, parties movements and politically conscious citizens.
- Any proposal for political reform should think not only about what is a good solution but also about who will implement it and how.
- The measures that rely on democractic movements citizens organisations and the media are likely to get success.

# UNIT IV. ECONOMICS

## 1. Development

▶ **Important Terms**

- **Development**: Growth of economy along with the improvement in the quality of life of the people like health, education etc.
- **Social Development**: Growth of different section of the society in a country.
- **Health**: State of complete physical, mental and social soundness.
- **Education**: Awareness of the society regarding the laws of the land.
- **Sex Ratio**: Percentage of females population per thousand males in a country.

▶ **Points to Remember**

- The rate at which children in a country die within an age of 0-1 year known as infant mortality rate.
- Net attendance ratio total number of children of age group 6-10 attending school as a percentage of total number in the same age group known as net attendance rate.
- Level of under-nourished adults in an economy are known as body mass index.
- Resources created by man like, roads, bridge, plant and machinery etc are man-made resources.
- The resources provided by the nature like, crude oil, land, mountains, sunlight, etc are natural resources:
- The proportion of literate population in the 7 and above age group is called literacy rate:
- Period of 12 months starting from 1st april and ending on 31st march of the next year is accounting period.
- The official enumeration of population along with certain economic and social statistics in a given territory and carried out on a specific day is census.

## 2. Sectors of the Indian Economy

▶ **Important Terms**

- **Primary Sector**: Primary sector is the sector which involves agricultural activities, mining, forestry, poultry, etc.
- **Secondary Sector**: It is the sector which is engaged in manufacturing of goods from raw material provided by the primary sector.
- **Industry**: It is a combination of firms engaged in similar activity like textile industry, banking industry, insurance industry, auto industry, etc.
- **Public Investment**: The money invested by the government in construction of roads, bridges, dams, schools, colleges, law and order etc.
- **Employment**: It is a situation where the able-bodied persons willing to work and are engaged in some productive activity to earn the income.
- **Unemployment**: It is a situation where the able-bodied persons willing to work but are not able to get work. They are not engaged in any productive activity.

▶ **Points to Remember**

- Tertiary sector is a service sector which helps both primary and secondary sectors. It includes transportation, banking, financing, insurance, etc.
- National sample survey organisation is an organisation which conducts surveys on employment and unemployment in an economy.
- Disguised unemployment is a type of hidden unemployment where people seem to be working but they do not contribute to the actual production.
- Gross domestic product the value of goods and services produced in an economy in a financial year.
- Organised sector it covers those enterprises where the terms of employment are regular and they have assured work.
- Unorganised sector is a small and scattered units which are outside the control of the government come under the unorganised sector.
- Public sector are those enterprises in which government owns majority of the shareholding of the company/enterprise.
- Private sector are the enterprises where the ownership of assets is in the hands of private individual/companies.
- Small scale industry are the group of small units which is engaged in productive activities for generation of employment.

- Large scale industry are the group of companies which employ large number of labour, use superior technology and need high investment.

- Cottage industry is an industry which require low investment and does not employ labour but uses the services of the family member to produce the article of local use.

- **Mahatma Gandhi National Rural Employment Act 2005:** Under NREGA all those who are able to and are in need of, work have been guaranteed 100 days of employment in a year by the government. If the government fails in its duty to give employment it will give unemployment allowances to the people.

- Tertiary sector has become important in India because in any country several services like hospitals, banks, transport, educational institutions courts. etc are required. the developtment leads of agriculture and industry leads to the development of services e.g. transport trade etc. In the past decades new services like information technology have become important and essential.

---

## 3. Money and Credit

▶ **Important Terms**

- **Money**: It means anything chosen by common consent as a medium of exchange.

- **Credit**: It refers to the activity of borrowing and lending money between two parties.

- **Financial System**: A system which deals with the management of public money collected from tax.

- **Banking**: The activity of deposit, withdrawal of money and other related monetary activities.

- **Credit Money**: The money whose money value is greater than the commodity value of the material from which the money is made is known as credit money.

- **Standard Money**: The legal money, in which the government discharges its obligations is known as standard money.

▶ **Points to Remember**

- Bank is an institution which accepts deposits from public for the purpose of lending and investment.

- Indian monetary system is the system of managing demand and supply of money by the reserve bank of india is known as indian monetary system.

- Reserve bank of india is the central bank of india which controls the monetary policy of the economy. It was established as shareholder bank.

- Automated teller machines is a free standing self-service terminal performing 60% of tellers job quickly and at lesser cost.

- Crossing of the cheque is drawing two parallel lines on the left side on top of a cheque is called crossing of the cheque.

- Cash reserve ratio is minimum cash which a commercial bank needs to keep with itself as per the regulation of rbi.

- Formal institutions are the institutions which are regulated by rules and regulations laid down by the government/rbi.

- Informal institutions are self managed and they are out of the reach of rbi regulations due to their unorganised structure and way of working.

- Local moneylenders are informal institutions who lend money on the basis of nearness of the local population.

---

## 4. Globalisation and the Indian Economy

▶ **Important Terms**

- **Globalisation**: It means opening up the economy to facilitate its integration with the world economy.

- **Liberalisation**: It refers to liberal and easy policy for carrying business or profession within or outside the country and it also seeks to make licensing policy easy.

- **Privatisation**: Privatisation means removing strict control over private sector and making them free to take necessary decisions.

- **Outsourcing**: It is the process of giving some internal functions of the business to some outside vendor, who will take care of that particular process to help the overall business objective.

- **Foreign Trade**: It is a process of buying and selling goods and services from one country to another.

▶ **Points to Remember**

- Economic reform is the process of liberalisation, globalisation and privatisation of the industrial sector of the economy to bring competitiveness and market driven functioning of the economy.

- A multinational company is a company that owns or controls production in more than one nation.

- A BPO is an organisation which works on different processes of different companies to help them in reducing cost of operation and providing standard and high quality service delivery.

- An international financial institution established to extend financial assistance to member-nations for development purpose. Known as World Bank.

- Wto stands for world trade organisation. The aim of this organisation is to conduct the international trade among member countries.

- Mixed economy is a system in which private and public sector work together.

- Information technology sector provides hardware, software and other related services to companies based within or outside the country.

## 5. Consumer Rights

▶ **Important Terms**

- **Adulteration**: It is the practice of mixing bad substances in a good substance which is sold in the market.

- **Agmark**: It is implemented under the "Agricultural Produce Act 1937". It was amended in the year 1986 and it covers products like Honey, species, etc.

- **Market Place**: It is a place where buyers and sellers come together to exchange goods and services.

- **COPRA**: Consumer Protection Act, 1986.

- **Consumer**: The person who uses goods and services for his self-consumption.

- **Customer**: The person who buys goods and avails services from the market is called customer.

- **Consumer Awareness**: Consumer's consciousness towards their rights and the social and legal obligations of the business and the government towards consumers is known as consumer's awareness.

▶ **Points to Remember**

- Consumer protection means protection of consumers against wrong practices of sellers in the market.

- The rights which help the consumer in protecting himself from being exploited are known as consumer rights.

- World consumer day is observed every year on 15th march of every year.

- Right to information act 2005 is the act gives rights to the citizen of the country to have information about the government departments, their policies, practices and procedures.

- Ralph nadar was the father of the consumer movement.

- Maximum retail price (mrp) is a maximum retail price printed on packaged goods. The seller cannot charge a price more than mrp.

- Public distribution system is also known as ration shop. The aim of pds is to prevent hoarding, black marketing etc.

- Consumer courts are the courts dealing in consumers cases only.

- The enactment of COPRA has led to the setting up of separate departments of consumar affairs in central and state governments. Due to the enactment of COPRA consumer awareness is spreading but slowly.